THE LAND OF THE GREAT IMAGE

THE LAND OF THE GREAT IMAGE

BEING EXPERIENCES OF FRIAR MANRIQUE IN ARAKAN

MAURICE COLLIS

GYAN

Published by

GYAN

Gyan Publishing House
5, Ansari Road
Daryaganj, New Delhi-110002
Phone: 011-47034999, 9811692060
E-mail: books@gyanbooks.com

Distribution Network
gyanbooks.com
India, USA, Canada, UK, Australia, France

ISBN : 978-81-212-3683-6 (PB)
First Published, London, 1945

2nd Impression 2020

Printed at: Gyan Press, Delhi.

The Land of the Great Image
Author: Maurice Collis

Preface

In a previous book of mine, *The Great Within*, the political theory at the back of Confucianism was shown to be connected with the vision of a world state. Here is disclosed an analogous Buddhistic theory, which is as curiously related to the Christian *Civitas Dei* as is the Confucian. No direct exegesis of this is given, but it will be found to emerge from the episodes constructed round Friar Manrique's adventures, to which it gives both coherence and meaning.

MAURICE COLLIS

Maidenhead

Contents

Contents

Illustrations

PLANS

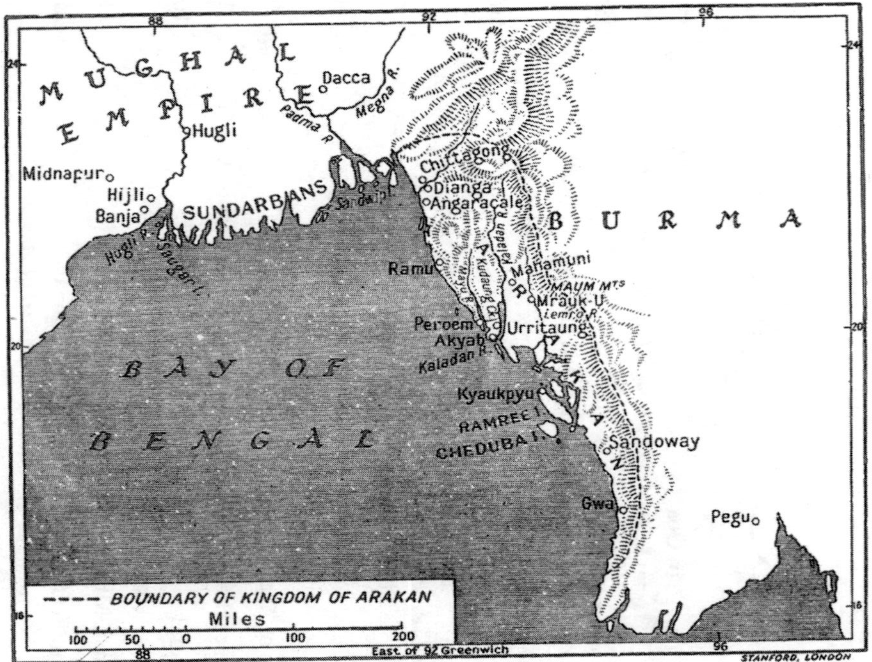

SKETCH MAP ILLUSTRATING FRIAR MANRIQUE'S TRAVELS IN ARAKAN

I

Introductory

The narrative which follows is concerned with a part of the travels made by the Augustinian friar, Sebastião Manrique. This Portuguese worthy was born at Oporto some time between 1590 and 1600. When a boy—though at what age precisely is unknown—he was attached to the Augustinian Order and later sent out to Goa, the capital of Portuguese Asia, as the eastern dominions of Portugal were called. In that strange and beautiful Indian city he remained for many years, first as a novice and then as a friar, resident at the monastery of his Order, a splendid baroque building, or rather group of buildings, which included besides the monastery proper, a chapel, a college, and a novitiate.

In 1628, when he was between thirty and forty years of age, he was transferred to Bengal, where at Hugli, near the present Calcutta, the Portuguese had a settlement and the Augustinians another monastery. Bengal is adjacent to Arakan, a country which is now part of Burma, but then was an independent kingdom inhabited by a Mongolian race closely resembling the Burmese. To this kingdom Manrique was obliged to go the following year and his experiences there, as related in his *Travels*, disclose a world which will be found quite novel. These *Travels* he did not compose until after his return to Europe in 1643. They are written, not in his native Portuguese, but in a Spanish which often is obscure and meretricious, a 'castellano desastroso', as Vela, the historian of the Augustinian Order, phrases it.

Manrique travelled to many other places besides Arakan, but it is with his visit to that Court that we shall be chiefly concerned. His style in this part is generally less tiresome. It seems to lift, his narrative to take life. No other seventeenth-century writer has left us so detailed and intimate a description of an oriental king nor raised so many questions of interest. Neither the Jesuits at the

Court of Akbar, nor at the Court of King Narai of Siam, nor those of the Society whose learning gained them access to the Ming and Ch'ing Courts of China, have narrated so rounded and astonishing a story.

My resolution to write of him dates from the year 1924, when I had the opportunity of exploring the places he visited in Arakan. His *Travels* had not then been published in book form, but Father Hosten, a Jesuit scholar resident in Bengal, had translated a portion of them, and Mr. San Shwe Bu, an old friend of mine, who lived at Akyab, the chief town of modern Arakan, placed this part at my disposal, together with much interesting information, which he had extracted from Arakanese sources. At the time I put together some short papers and published them in the *Burma Research Journal* of that year.

In 1927 the whole of Manrique's *Travels* was edited for the Hakluyt Society by the late Lt.-Colonel Luard and by Father Hosten. The volumes issued by that Society are largely reserved for its members and few come into the hands of the general public. It is probable that the number of people who know more than the name of Sebastião Manrique is small.

My object here is to introduce him with the assistance of what special knowledge I possess, and so to tell his story that its rare flavour is brought out, its queerness relished and its implications understood, and not only his story but that of the extraordinary king he met. To accomplish this I shall have to take the reader first to Goa. When he has wandered round its sights, he will possess the requisite background to assess what follows.

II

Portuguese Asia

Portuguese Asia was not a purely mercantile venture like the British settlements in India. The Portuguese who discovered the sea-route to Asia, who established fortresses from the Persian Gulf to the Straits of Malacca and beyond, who built Goa and introduced the Inquisition there, were a totally different class of people from the directors, the shareholders, and the employees of the East India Company. They were romantics, crusaders, conquistadors, as well as traders, while the members of the East India Company, coming on the scene a century later, were modern business men whose whole aim was dividends.

Taking a broad view, the Portuguese irruption into Asia was the culmination of the long struggle against the Moors at home. From the tenth to the fifteenth century the Iberian peninsula was the scene of three thousand seven hundred battles, so it is computed, between its Christian tribes and the Arabian Emirs. In the course of those unending wars the Portuguese and the Spaniards emerged as nations. It was as late as 1492 that Granada, the last emirate, fell.

So lengthy a struggle, far from leaving the Iberians exhausted, seems to have invigorated them. When the Mohammedan power was overthrown in the Peninsula, instead of settling down and developing their country, they found themselves so overflowing with energy that they set sail across the oceans, to discover the Americas and the African sea-route to the East. Mr. Arnold Toynbee has noticed this paradox in his *Study of History*. Arguing from conceptions which he calls 'Challenge and Response' and 'The Stimulus of Pressures', he declares that their tremendous voyages, their further battles all over South America and Asia, their vast ambitions, the fanatical courage with which they prosecuted their designs, were the natural response to the stimulus which victory at home had given to their minds. And he sums up their place in history thus, referring, of course, to both Portuguese and Spaniards: 'These Iberian pioneers of Western Christendom performed an unparalleled service for the civilization which they represented. They expanded the horizon, and thereby potentially the domain, of our Western Society from an obscure corner of the Old World until it came to embrace all the habitable lands and navigable seas on the surface of the planet. It is owing to this Iberian energy and enterprise that Western Christendom has grown, like the grain of mustard seed in the parable, until it has become "the Great Society"; a tree in which all the nations of the world have come and lodged. This latter-day Westernized World is the peculiar achievement of Western Christendom's Iberian pioneers.'

Portuguese Asia was the seed from which grew the British Dominion in Asia. Portuguese ascendancy lasted a century and a quarter, say, from 1500 to 1625. After a period when the Dutch, the British, and the French fought each other for first place, the British attained it after Plassey. Their dominion in turn is now passing away, possibly to be absorbed into a world dominion of a Western type.

That the Portuguese conceived of their drive eastward as a continuation of the crusade against the Moors is very clear from the opening paragraph of Faria y Sousa's *Portuguese Asia*, published in 1666: 'Like an Impetuous Torrent did the Mohametans spread themselves over the Lesser Asia, after the Catholic arms had expelled them our Provinces,' he writes, referring to the taking of Constantinople by the Turks in 1453 and to their threatened invasion of Austria. 'The Christian Princes, busied in destroying each other, looked on their Progress, without attempting to put any stop to this Current; when the Kings of Portugal, as the first who had shaken off themselves the Burthen of these Barbarians, and the first who passed over to crush them in Africk (obeying the Decrees of Heaven which required it) undertook to be the first to stop their proceedings in Asia.'

In Asia all trade to Europe was under the control of the Moslem Sultans through whose kingdoms it passed. Europe's imports from India, China, and the Islands came overland from the Persian Gulf and paid toll. The Turks, and Islam in general, would be harder hit by breaking that monopoly than they would be by a defeat in the field. That was the practical idea behind the Portu-

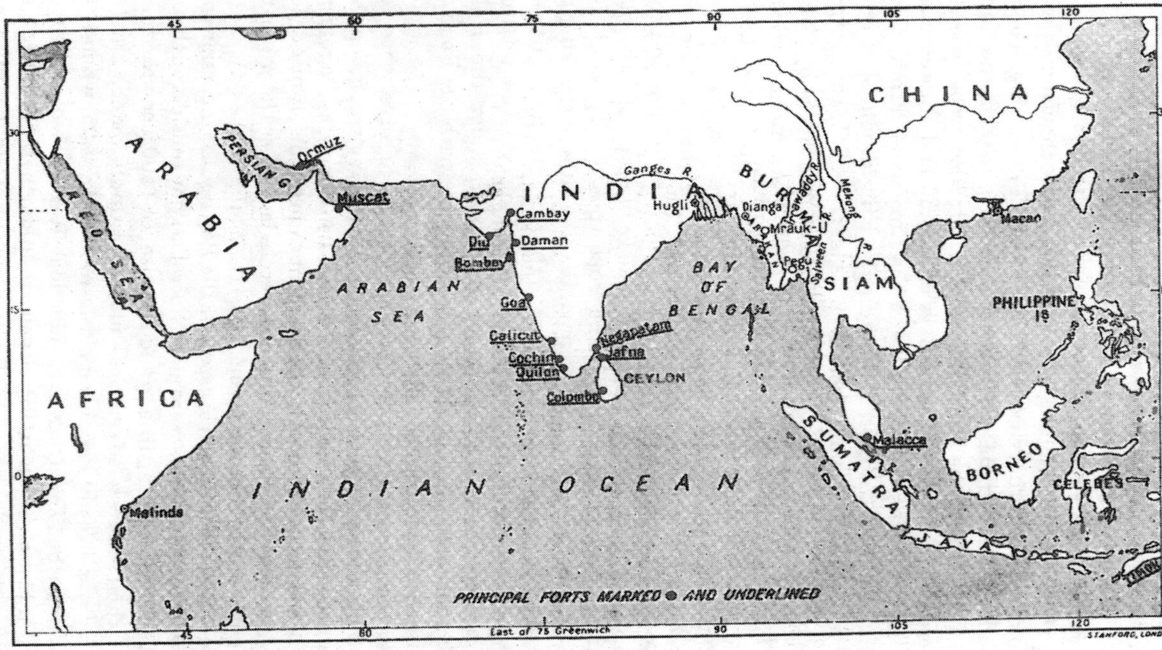

PLAN OF THE PORTUGUESE POSSESSIONS IN ASIA ABOUT A.D. 1630

guese attempt to find a sea-route to India and the Far East. And, of course, while the loss of the monopoly of the eastern trade would damage Turkish finances, its transfer to Portugal would enormously increase the resources of that kingdom. Though the Portuguese drive east took the form of a struggle for a trade route, the crusading element was so marked that the Church was able to bless what otherwise would have been filibustering. To get the trade, the Portuguese would not only have to open the Cape route, but also fight the Mohammedans, who carried goods by sea to the Persian Gulf. But since the days of Roland and Roncesvalles Islam had been the mortal enemy of the Christian Church. That now sufficed for a *casus belli*. Accordingly, King Emanuel of Portugal was able to procure from Pope Alexander VI, the Borgia whose brutal face as depicted by Pinturicchio and carved by Caravaggio is so familiar to us, a Bull, dated 1494, granting him title to all the lands which might be discovered east of a line drawn north and south at a distance of 370 miles from the coast of Europe. Eight years later, after Vasco da Gama had returned from his voyage to India, the same Pope allowed the King to style himself 'Lord of the Navigation, Conquest and Commerce of Ethiopia, Arabia, Persia, and India'. For the Pope thus to dispose of the world—for at the same time he gave the like title to the King of Spain in respect of all territories west of the aforementioned line—was in accordance with the theory of the Papacy as an institution, not only uniting all Europe spiritually under the Holy Father, but which potentially was a world state with the Pope as its Priest-Emperor.

This conception makes it clear that the Portuguese were regarded by the Holy See as its emissaries. Their king was given the Bull and the title because it would be his duty to bring all Paganism to the steps of St. Peter's. It is important to bear this in mind, for it explains why Goa was as much the ecclesiastical as the mercantile capital of Portuguese Asia.

The romantic or chivalric aspect of the Portuguese incursion was very notable. The leaders were all aristocrats. They considered themselves knights fighting in a grand emprise. In 1500, the year from which their eastern adventures may be roundly dated, knight-errantry was already somewhat old-fashioned. In 1605, when Cervantes published *Don Quixote* to ridicule it, it was tiresomely out of date. But just as Spain and Portugal are to-day behind the rest of Europe, so were they also in the sixteenth century. Chivalry remained a factor in their policy after it had disappeared from France and England. The most striking example of its persistence is the battle of Alcazar which took place as late as 1578, when the Portuguese were at the height of their power in Asia. This battle was fought by Dom Sebastião, King of Portugal, against Abd al-Melik, Sultan of Morocco. The king, who was a mixture of Don Quixote, Byron, and a pre-Raphaelite hero, led the whole of his nobility on an expedition to Morocco for no reason of state but because he saw himself a Christian knight in the tradition of St. Louis. He was dreadfully defeated. A member of nearly every noble family in Portugal perished on the field. The list of dead and prisoners reads like the index of the Almanac de Gotha. Dom Sebastião himself fell in the thick of the fray. His body was never recovered for burial.

Alcazar could not have happened had the Portuguese aristocrats not conceived of themselves as paladins. The characters in *Orlando Furioso*, published by Ariosto in 1516, were not unlike them. This romantic epic corresponded to a Renaissance tapestry, but in Oporto might well have seemed a transcript from contemporary life. Its hero, Roland, who had been dead seven hundred years, behaved as did the mad knights who were to follow Dom Sebastião. Its opening verse would have sounded like a trumpet for the men who sailed in 1497 against the Moors of Asia:

Le donne, i cavalier, l'arme, gli amori,
Le cortesie, l'audace imprese io canto,
Che furo al tempe che passaro i Mori
D'Africa il mare, e in Francia nocquer tanto,
Sequendo l'ire e i giovenil furori
D'Agramante lor re, che si diè vanto
Di vendicar la morte di Troiano
Sopra re Carlo imperator romano.

This analogy between the *Orlando Furioso* and the state of mind of the Portuguese who sailed to Asia is not fanciful, for their exploits were celebrated by Camoens in his epic *Os Lusiadas*, written in 1556, in a style not unlike that in which Ariosto describes the exploits of Roland. Take this verse from Canto X, where the poet hails Albuquerque's capture of Goa from the Mohammedans in 1510:

Que gloriosas palmas tecer vejo,
Com que victoria a fronte lhe coroa,
Quando sem sombra vãa de medo, ou pejo,
Toma a ilha illustrissima de Goa!
Despois, obedecendo au duro ensejo
A deixa, e occasião espera boa,
Com que a torne a tomar; que esforço, e arte,
Vencerão a fortuna, e o proprio Marte

The palms of Goa offer their leaves to bind Albuquerque's victorious forehead. Like a lion or a bull he charges the Moors and puts them to flight.

At this point one can profitably recall the story of Vasco da Gama's first visit to India, as related by Faria y Sousa, for it illustrates what has been said and gives the atmosphere.[1] The Navigator's fleet consisted of three small ships, and 160 men. Before he started, King Emanuel delivered to him a banner embroidered with the cross of the Military Order of Christ, upon which the paladin, 'a Gentleman of sufficient Quality, Ability, and Spirit for such a difficult Enterprise', took an oath of fidelity. He weighed on 8 July 1497, and making his way round the Cape, which previous navigators had already mapped, sailed north into uncharted seas. At Melinde, north of Zanzibar, on the African coast, he was able to engage an Indian pilot and with his assistance crossed the Arabian Sea, 'that great Gulph of 700 Leagues', and on 20 May 1498 let go his anchors in Calicut road.

Calicut, which lies towards the bottom of the west coast of India, was the capital of an independent Hindu kingdom. The Mohammedans or, as we now say, the Moslems, who during the previous five hundred years had been striking ever deeper into India, had not yet conquered as far south. But since their merchants controlled the maritime trade between Indian ports and the Persian Gulf, their ships were in Calicut harbour and their warehouses on shore. The ports further north, including Goa, three hundred miles away, were in their possession and though Calicut still had its Hindu rulers, Moslem influence was very strong. Da Gama, who had learnt these facts from his Indian pilot, knew that his only chance of opening trade was to negotiate with a Hindu prince. To treat with the Moslems would be impossible, for they would never willingly accept an interloper nor, indeed, had he

[1] Early accounts of da Gama's visit to Calicut differ much in detail, but Faria y Sousa's is the most entertaining.

contemplated approaching them. But there was no reason why a Christian should not negotiate with a Hindu. Such were lost souls, no doubt, but they were not enemies of Christianity. Moreover, it was rumoured that there lived Christians among the pagans. St. Thomas, the Apostle himself, was held to have travelled to India and the descendants of his converts still survived, it was said, in the south of the continent. These men might rally to him and facilitate his task.

Accordingly he sent a civil message to the King of Calicut. In return a personage, described by Faria y Sousa as the mayor, came aboard to conduct him into the city. Soon he was being carried through the streets in a palanquin, the populace, black and naked, beholding with pleased astonishment his breeches and doublet, his ample cloak, and the coif on his head. Presently the party reached a large building, at the gate of which the Dom was invited to descend. He complied gracefully and, looking up at the wall, perceived five bells. In front of the gateway was a brass pillar with a cock on the top or what looked like a cock. He entered the porch. Four men now came forward to receive him, dressed only in cotton skirts, a cord of three threads strung across one shoulder. These Brahmins—he did not know they were Brahmins nor, indeed, had ever heard of such people—sprinkled him with water and smeared sandal on his forehead.

These ceremonies, to which he willingly lent himself, set him wondering. The building, he had already perceived, was connected with religion. Could it be a church, one of those founded by the Apostle Thomas? It seemed possible this was so, for why otherwise should they have carried him directly to it? And had they not sprinkled him with holy water at the gate?

Pleased at the thought, he gladly let them conduct him into a quadrangle. A devout expression on his haughty face, he began to scan the frescoes with which the walls were decorated. They perplexed him somewhat, for, if this were a church, was it not surprising to see represented beasts, prancing and fanciful, and monsters that seemed to bay or playfully mouth? Yet, on reflection, it was only to be expected that during the many centuries since the time of the saint some peculiarities, even errors, might have crept into the faith. If so, it would be his duty on return to inform his master and on the next voyage friars could be sent out, when, if these frescoes were heretical, they could be destroyed.

The party proceeded leisurely on its way. In the centre of the courtyard was 'a round Chappel of good Structure with Brass Gates'. The Brahmins led him in. Coming from the bright sunshine it seemed so dark inside that some moments elapsed before the hero perceived the statue of a woman. The moment he did so, his doubts disappeared, if, indeed, he still doubted. Turning to the Brahmins he inquired eagerly how they called the figure. 'With a joyful reverence they answered Mary, Mary, Mary' (or so it seemed to him) and prostrated themselves before it. Not to be outdone in joy and reverence, he fell on his knees and worshipped—the goddess Parvati, perhaps.

But the Portuguese became much more sophisticated at a later date. Though it does not appear they ever precisely understood that the Christians who undoubtedly existed in southern India derived, not from any supposed visit of St. Thomas but from the Church founded by Nestorius, Patriarch of Constantinople, after the Council of Ephesus in A.D. 431, there came a time when, easily distinguishing a Hindu temple from a Nestorian church, they destroyed all of the former which stood on the territory of Goa, while the Inquisition arrested many adherents of the latter faith, tried them for heresy, and burnt them at the stake.

When Dom Vasco withdrew from the temple, he did so with some difficulty, for a large crowd had collected, excited, no doubt, by the rumour that a strange visitor from oversea had been adoring their goddess. One is drawn to inquire why he had been invited to enter and can only suppose that, if he found it natural for them to take him immediately on landing to a church, his conductors for their part believed that after his voyage he would be glad to give thanks to any god or goddess, known to him or unknown, for was not every deity a manifestation of Brahma and was not Brahma the Truth which all persons adored? Be that as it may, the occasion was curious and symbolical. The Dom represented the first appearance of that Western civilization which was destined within two hundred years to overthrow India in the political field; the goddess that body of belief which neither the violence nor the persuasion of the Western Church could shake, nay, which on its philosophical side made more converts in Europe than the other in India. Da Gama's prostration had therefore an ironic fitness. It has its place in the high comedy of history.

On entering his palanquin again, he was carried to audience with the king. In the throne-room of the palace he found him on a dais, seated upon his bed of state, and dressed in white cotton robes embroidered with foliage and roses of gold thread. On his head was a crown in the form of a mitre, set with pearls, and he wore gold anklets inlaid with rubies. Beside him 'a Grave Person held a Gold Plate with some leaves of Betele, an Herb comfortable to the stomach'. A Court Brahmin of venerable appearance took the visitor by the hand and presented him to His Majesty. Da Gama swept the ground with his hat as he bowed, a salutation which the king returned with a friendly look but an inclination so scanty 'that the motion of his head could scarcely be perceived'. Da Gama was then invited to seat himself on the steps of the dais.

The conversation which ensued was of short duration. The Navigator presented a letter with which King Emanuel had provided him against just such an occasion, wherein a request was made for trade between the two countries. His Indian Majesty replied that on consultation with his ministers he would return answer, a promise which he kept, for in the course of a week permission was given to lade a cargo.

As might have been expected, the Moslem merchants of the city were disturbed when they heard of what had transpired. It had been known for some years that the Portuguese were making attempts to establish a rival trade route via the Cape. The cargo which Da Gama's three small ships could take was of little moment, but if he got it, more ships would be sent. They formed a deputation and waited on the mayor.

This worthy was in their pay, as were also the ministers, who, it appears, had advised the king against the Portuguese. Accordingly, he listened with attention when they made their protest, and when they hinted that it might be impossible for them to continue their contributions to his private purse, were their profits diminished by the encroachments of foreigners, he hastened to the palace and told the king that the Portuguese were fugitives, their letter forged, and their intentions piratical.

It does not seem that His Majesty was much surprised by this news. Perhaps, he had been expecting a protest from the Moslems. Possibly, he had already schemed to use the intruding foreigners to extort a present from the established traders. But he summoned his ministers and, since they supported the mayor's allegations, he consented to send for da Gama.

When the hero arrived, the king had repeated to him, with more frankness and civility than was usual on such occasions, the gist of the charges which had been made against him, and himself added that were the Dom, in fact, a banished nobleman or some fugitive from justice, he would be well advised to confess it. when honourable asylum would be offered to him at Calicut.

To all this the paladin listened 'with a great deal of firmness in his Countenance'. When it was time for him to reply, he unfolded the banner upon which was emblazoned the Cross of Christ and, telling the king that it was a sacred object by virtue of which he had come safely ten thousand leagues through storms and every danger of the sea, he swore upon it that he was not as alleged. During his discourse, which was long and interspersed, it is said, with learned quotations—though how it was interpreted Faria y Sousa does not explain—the king kept his eyes fixed on him, 'hoping', surmises our authority 'by exteriour signs to discover the truth of his assertions, and drew a conclusion from the security of his Looks, the elegancy of his Words and the gravity of his Person, that there could be no deceit couched under such fair appearances'.

It would be otiose to speculate whether the king, in fact, drew any such conclusion, but it is probable that he was impressed by the banner, for the East was, and is to this day, full of magical banners, and as the navigator had unquestionably survived a formidable voyage, what was more likely than that he owed his preservation to the power of a holy thing? But we must conclude that his real reason for favouring him—for favour him he did—was, as we have seen, to force the Moslems to pay higher for their monopoly. In the event, permission was renewed for the Portuguese to ship a small cargo.

But Moslem influence in Calicut was evidently stronger than the king supposed. The Dom left the presence, but while he was passing through the town on his way to the wharf, he was suddenly arrested by the mayor's orders, along with his staff, numbering twelve persons. When brought before that functionary he was abruptly informed that he and his ships must leave Calicut at once, without cargoes and without compensation for such goods as had been already landed. Da Gama was obliged to consent to this and seven of his men were detained as hostages, to be released only on the eve of his departure.

Back on board, he called a council of officers. It was resolved that, as the king was clearly unaware of his subordinate's action, efforts be made to get into touch with him. But these failed, for the mayor was on the watch. The question, then, was what to do.

Calicut roadstead was full of Moslem ships. The Portuguese were exposed to a surprise attack, as they rode at anchor, unable to manœuvre. There was no alternative, they must leave at once. But could they depend on the return of the hostages? They had already been so flagrantly deceived. It was decided to provide against such a turn.

An armed party was sent in boats along the shore and twenty fishermen were seized. When these were brought on board, 'immediately da Gama let fly his sails, making shew of departing'. The seizure had been observed in the city and the relatives of the fishermen rushed to the mayor. A commotion was threatened, to avoid which and the news of it reaching the king, the mayor hurriedly sent the seven hostages to the wharf. When they were safe on board, da Gama liberated the fishermen, all but a few whom he desired to show to King Emanuel. Then weighing immediately, he stood out to sea. By this time, however, Moslem indignation had boiled over and sixty small vessels tried to cut him off. The affair was decided by gunnery and seamanship, in both of which the Portuguese were greatly superior.

This first voyage was a reconnaissance. On reaching Portugal the next spring (1499), da Gama advised the king that provided a sufficiently strong force were sent, the Moslems could be driven off the sea and the trade diverted from the Persian Gulf to the Cape route. Emanuel accepted this advice and in the following years put it into operation. A series of expeditions were dispatched. Fortresses were built on the Asiatic coast after suitable sites had been selected and seized. From Ormuz at the mouth of the Persian Gulf and Aden at the entrance to the Red Sea these fortresses continued all down the west coast of India to Ceylon and across to Malacca, which commanded the Straits and the route to China. That was what Portuguese Asia consisted of, an immense string of fortresses, which were also roadsteads and trade emporiums. In the centre of this line was Goa, the largest fortress and the seat of the Viceroy of the Indies. All this was accomplished within a generation. Before the middle of the sixteenth century the Portuguese were complete masters of the seaborne trade between East and West. They became enormously rich. As the century wore on and their monopoly continued—for no other European nation had as yet appeared to challenge them and no Indian land power or combination of powers was strong enough to dislodge them from their fortresses—they continued to enlarge and beautify Goa.

III

Golden Goa

When Albuquerque took Goa in 1510, the city was the most important trade emporium on the west coast of India. The inhabitants were chiefly Hindus, but it belonged to the state of Bijapur, one of those Mohammedan kingdoms into which India was divided before the Mughal dynasty united the continent. The first irruption of the Mughals was in 1519, but Bijapur and the other kingdoms of the south were not incorporated into their dominion until after 1595, when Akbar began his conquest of that region.

From 1510 until 1595 the Portuguese at Goa had to protect themselves from counter-attack by Bijapur, alone or in combination with other Moslem states. Their fortifications, their cannon, and their naval supremacy sufficed to beat off such assaults. By the time of Akbar, when, perhaps, the forces of the new empire might have driven them into the sea, they had become a settled institution with their representatives at the Imperial Court, clever Jesuits who were able to persuade the Great Mughal that it was worth his while to leave them unmolested. The eventual ruin of Portuguese Asia was not due to any Moslem pressure, but to lack of support from at home in face of Dutch attacks. It should be borne in mind that in 1580, after the battle of Alcazar, Philip II possessed himself of Portugal, which remained a part of the Spanish dominion until 1640. The Netherlands, also, were in that dominion and when, before 1600, the Dutch threw off the Spanish rule, their attack upon Portuguese Asia followed.

Sebastião Manrique while quite young was sent to Goa some time between 1604 and 1614. His stay coincided with the last years of Portuguese prosperity. Though approaching its eclipse, Goa was still unshadowed. Lavishly provided with churches, public buildings, great squares, and markets, full of merchandise and slaves, the harbour of ships, it was the most sumptuous city which Europeans have ever built in Asia.

1

THE JESUIT HOSPITAL

So many visitors have left records that it is possible to reconstruct Goanese society in some detail. To get the feel of the place, we can hardly do better than listen to François Pyrard while he describes his experiences there in 1608. He was a talkative and observant Frenchman of the seaman class, a *brave homme*, as will be seen, honest and careful. Leaving France in 1601 on board a ship fitted out by the merchants of St. Malo, he was cast away on the Maldives, then an island monarchy, and did not reach Calicut till 1607. Moving south to Cochin, like Calicut a Portuguese fortress, he was arrested because he had no papers and was thrown into prison. From thence, his health much impaired by the dreadful dungeon in which he was confined, they sent him in chains by ship to Goa.

Landing on the wharf near the Viceroy's palace, he expected to be lodged in the main gaol, the Sala das Bragas, and was surprised when out of pity the police took him to the Royal Hospital, a palatial institution controlled by the Jesuits. The Society was the most cultivated and modern element in Goa, and the hospital was administered by them in so admirable a fashion, that many declared it superior even to the Hospital of the Holy Ghost in Rome or the Infirmary of the Knights at Malta, the two leading hospitals of Europe at that time. Poor Pyrard, after his rough experiences, thought it a paradise. He was carried up 'a lofty and magnificent staircase' to a bed 'beautifully shaped and lacquered with red varnish', upon which was a mattress and silk coverlet, sheets of fine cotton, pillows of white calico, luxuries unknown in Europe among his class. A barber immediately shaved him, he was given pyjamas, a cap, and slippers, and provided with a bedside table on which was a fan, drinking water, a clean towel, and a handkerchief. Under the bed he noted a chamber-pot, an article which appeared to him the most satisfactory piece of furniture in the place after his experiences in Cochin gaol, where he had been herded with two hundred others in one room without any sanitary arrangements whatever. Supper brought further pleasant surprises. Each patient was served with a complete fowl, and the plates, bowls, and dishes were of Chinese porcelain, that is, of Ming porcelain, then such a rarity in Europe that Lord Treasurer Burghley thought 'a porringer of white purselyn garnished with gold' a very choice new-year present to give Queen Elizabeth.

When Pyrard felt better, he asked the head Jesuit physician for leave to go, saying that he longed to explore the great city of which he had heard so much. He seemed to think that the charge against him had been withdrawn, but the Jesuit knew better and out of kindness advised him to be in no hurry. Not taking his meaning, Pyrard agreed reluctantly to stay on, and when quite recovered pressed for his discharge. This time it was granted and he descended the grand staircase in the highest spirits. The Father had given him a new suit of clothes, a piece of silver, and his benediction. He had had a good breakfast, though, as he says, he 'little required it for the haste he was in to be off'. So it was a cruel shock when he was accosted by a sergeant at the bottom of the stairs and a warrant was flourished in his face. 'His partisans' —they were giant negro slaves imported from Africa—'seized me and bore me off in rough sort', he writes.

However, things did not go too badly. In his new clean suit and with the silver piece he won the heart of the gaoler's wife at the Sala das Bragas, for it was there that they took him. Instead of flinging him into the common dungeon where galley-slaves were confined, they put him, thanks to the lady, into a fairly decent room, a wonderful piece of luck, for the dungeon was 'le lieu le plus ord et sale qui soit au monde comme ie croy', as he notes in his old-fashioned French.

There existed in Goa a prisoners' welfare society, at the head of which was a Jesuit. This Father came to see him, heard his story, considered that he had been unjustly arrested, since a shipwrecked mariner can have no papers, and approached Dom Fr. Aleixo de Menezes, the Archbishop and Primate, who was acting as Governor of the Indies, pending the arrival of a new Viceroy. This Augustinian friar, known in ecclesiastical history as the zealot who handed over many Nestorian Christians to the Inquisition, had lately, in his capacity as Governor, successfully beaten off a Dutch attack on Goa and was in no mood to have any truck with suspicious foreigners. To the Jesuit's solicitations he replied with heat that his protégé deserved to hang. Had it not been that the Father persevered, such might have been the fate of the Frenchman. It seems that what turned the scale was his offer to enlist in the army of India.

2

LIFE OF A SOLDIER

For two years Pyrard served the Portuguese as a private soldier and has left an account of the way his companions lived. Most of the soldiers were recruited in Portugal. The prospects were good and, as a rule, volunteers came forward, but if they did not, they were pressed, even boys of ten years old being taken, for there was a great shortage of man-power in Portugal which had too small a population to meet the vast demands of its empire. Many of the soldiers were ex-convicts, released for the purpose, and all belonged to the lowest class, but as soon as they landed in India they became gentlemen. 'Dès qu'ils sont là,' writes Mocquet, a traveller who arrived in Goa the same year as did Pyrard, 'pour vils et abjets qu'ils soient, ils s'estiment tous fidalques et nobles, changeant leurs noms obscurs à des noms plus illustres.' The real nobility winked at this practice. If Indians could be induced to believe that all Portuguese were aristocrats, or, at least, that all Portuguese in India were gentlemen of quality, so much the better. In this connection Mocquet cites the story of the swineherd, Fernando. On arrival at Goa this rustic followed the current practice and called himself Dom Fernando. One day, riding through the streets, well mounted and magnificently dressed, he met the son of his old master in Portugal. 'Good heavens! Fernando, is that you?' exclaimed the young gentleman. Fernando was put out, he tried to ride past, though it was an effort to pretend not to know his master's son. When the other rallied him: 'Come, come, Fernando, no need to pretend with me!' he could keep it up no longer and sheepishly dismounted. 'But don't tell anyone here,' he begged, as he knelt and paid the customary respects.

The common soldier was able to make this fine appearance for several reasons. His principal occupation was that of marine on board the warships which protected the convoys from the Dutch and the pirates, but during the monsoon from May to October he lived in Goa as a private person. As there were no barracks, he rented a house along with a dozen comrades. Clubbing together they bought three or four good suits and engaged a few slaves to wait and cook. At home they would sit about in loose shirts and pyjama trousers, playing the guitar or gossiping with those who passed, but when they went out, which they did in rotation, the grand suits were put on. 'You would say they were lords,' says Pyrard, 'with an income of 10,000 livres, such is their bravery, with their slaves behind them and a man carrying over them a big parasol. There are places where these slaves are to be hired and one can be got for half a day for a copper.'

As they masqueraded in this fashion, they copied to the best of their ability the elaborate manners of their betters. Linschoten, who was at Goa in 1583, has some phrases which show the flourish they aimed at. 'They step very softly and slowly forwards, with a great pride and vaine-glorieus majestie,' writes the bluff Dutchman of the way real fidalgos promenaded. When two met, while they were still some paces apart they began 'to stoope with their bodies, and to thrust forth their foot to salute each other, with their Hats in their hands, almost touching the ground.' Yet, behind this screen of manners they were watching each other narrowly, ready to take offence at the most trifling lapse in punctilio, such as a less number of bows returned, or the giving of a sober for an extravagant compliment. When such an insult was observed, the wronged man would allow no sign of resentment to escape him, but retiring with a smile would assemble his friends and presently lie in wait for the offender, set on him, and beat him with sandbags or bamboos. There were some even more fatal, who would order their slaves to deal a stab in the back.

Such behaviour having passed into the tradition of our melodrama, it is hard to believe that real people ever conducted themselves so.

Cheap though living was in Goa, the common soldier could hardly have managed on his pay alone to turn himself out so well. But he had another source of income. By 1600 the city was full of half-caste women. For a century the Government had been encouraging mixed marriages and there had also been the freest intercourse with female slaves. It is in the nature of Eurasian women to desire a man of pure European blood. The Portuguese soldiers were, therefore, in great demand. To get a soldier such a woman was prepared to house him, feed him, pay for his clothes, see to his washing, and provide him with pocket-money. No marriage usually took place, though the Government recognized the relationship to the extent of giving the children the right to inherit from both parents.

But Pyrard notes that, if a soldier left the house which he shared with his comrades and went to live with a Eurasian mistress, it was not as delightful as it sounded. The girls were temperamental and uncontrolled. They were more jealous and less amenable than either Portuguese or Indian women. Their whole life was to keep the man they had got. But he was surrounded by temptations to infidelity, as there were far more girls than white soldiers. If he yielded to the solicitations of another, or if, tired of his mistress, he sought to terminate the connection, he was in imminent peril. Unless he used the greatest cunning and dissimulation in quitting her, says Pyrard, she would infallibly poison him. What poison they used, Pyrard never precisely discovered. But he describes its effects, which were so curious that, had we not also Linschoten's testimony in addition, it would be hard to believe him. The action of the poison could be delayed by varying the dose. After taking it the victim might go a month, even six months, and be none the worse. Then one day he suddenly fell dead.

A soldier, were he good-looking or had he made a name for himself in fights with the Dutch, might also find women of the upper class eager for his acquaintance. In this class there were more women of mixed blood than of pure European descent. Dressed in a gauze blouse, a flowered skirt, and loose slippers, they idled indoors through the day, listening to the gossip brought in by their slaves, chewing betel or sucking sweetmeats. Even those of pure Portuguese extraction preferred rice to bread and ate curry without a spoon. It was to enliven this existence that they sought the attentions of handsome soldiers. 'They use all the slights and practices they can devise,' says Linschoten, 'by sending out their slaves and baudes by night, and at extraordinary times, over Walls, Hedges, and Ditches, how narrowly soever they are kept and looked unto.' For they were very narrowly kept in a seclusion hardly different from Indian purdah.

To introduce a gallant into the house would have been risky or impossible, had they not known how to use datura, a narcotic weed of the nightshade family, called in Europe stramonium. Administered in quantity it is a poison, but in small doses its narcotic properties merely weaken the will and confuse the intelligence. The husbands of these women, if a soldier-lover were coming to the house, used to be given sufficient of it to render them insensible, not wholly stupefied and sleeping, but rather tranced, and, so, ignorant of what happened even before their eyes, and when its effects had worn off, of the fact that they had been drugged. Pyrard has a passage describing such a scene. After stating that the datura is put in drink or soup, he says: 'An hour afterwards the husbands become giddy and insensible, singing, laughing, and performing a thousand antics (*singeries*), for they have lost all consciousness and judgement. Then do the wives make use of their time, admitting whom they will, and taking their pleasure in the presence of their husbands, who are aware of nothing.'

Anyone acquainted with the less reputable corners of the East will know that Pyrard was accurately describing what he had seen. Datura is still used by certain oriental women in ways not dissimilar. There are many cases known of modern Englishmen who have been reduced to poor tame creatures on being dosed with this drug by their native mistresses.

3

A GREAT LADY GOES TO MASS

In one of his most evocative passages Pyrard describes a woman of this upper class as she appeared at the Mass, practically her only distraction away from home. The scene is a medley of the Occident and the Orient, of the Latin and the Indian, of the Catholic and the Pagan. It is a feast-day, a special occasion, and the lady is 'superbly attired in the Portuguese mode'. Her gown is gold brocade, which glows under a mantle of black silk gauze. She comes riding in a palanquin, seated on a Persian carpet and propped on velvet cushions. On foot behind are a score of maid-servants, slave girls from middle or upper India or negroes from Mozambique, bought for their looks and dressed to set them off in coloured smocks falling to the navel and wide silk pleated scarlet petticoats, some carrying a mat, a carpet, a prayer book, others a handkerchief or a fan. Escorting the palanquin are two Eurasian footmen, handsome and sleek, who at the church door help the lady to alight or, if she prefers to be carried into the nave, are ready there to hand her down.

When such a lady was on her feet, she seemed very tall, for she would be wearing chopines, a patten with a cork sole six inches thick, an extravagant fashion which was carried to fantastical extremes in Venice, and had even reached England, as is evident from Hamlet's exclamation to the actress: 'By'r Lady, your ladyship is nearer Heaven than when I saw you last by the altitude of a chopine.'

The progress down the aisle then began. Owing to the height of the chopines, and because it was undignified for a person of rank to walk otherwise than slowly, the passage to her seat took some time, as she paced along, leaning on the arms of the two footmen, her air languid, an assumed lassitude. Her maids were gone ahead to get ready her place, spreading her carpet, with a mat on top for coolness, arranging her cushions or sometimes setting a chair. There she would sit in the semi-darkness, for the churches in Goa had mother-of-pearl in place of glass window-panes, which suffused a soft yellowish under-sea light, sit there with her rosary of great gold beads, her pale olive face much painted, watching under her eyes, while her handsome maids fanned her nor dared smile back at their lovers who were signing to them in the shadows.

The life we are describing was the decadence into which the Portuguese fell when, no longer adequately reinforced and supported from home, they were losing the original energy which had driven them east. An oriental conquest, the wealth it brought, mixed marriages on a grand scale, and, perhaps, most deadly, the extensive use of slaves, had transformed the hard-bitten Portuguese of early days, the paladins of the Lusiads, the intrepid navigators, into a luxurious society, still able to hold what it had taken from ill-armed native kingdoms, but losing ground to the Dutch, who were coming upon the scene animated with the same pristine virtues that a century earlier had sustained da Gama and Albuquerque.

4

SLAVES

Many of the slaves in Goa were household slaves. Their treatment was probably no worse than in Indian households. Rather, it was their influence upon their masters that was deplorable. If you walked up the Rua Direita, the great street which ran south from the main wharf at the Arch of the Viceroys, you came after a quarter of a mile to the principal square, the Terreiro de Sabaio, in which were the Cathedral, the Senate House, and the Inquisition. On most days of the week a sale of slaves was here taking place. They stood so that you could examine them at your leisure, the dealers drawing attention to the points of their physique and detailing their skill in arts and crafts. 'You see there very pretty and elegant girls and women from all countries in India,' writes Pyrard. 'Most of them can play upon instruments, embroider, sew very finely, and do all kinds of work, such as making sweet-meats, preserves, etcetera.' In spite of their accomplishments they were very cheap, thirty shillings being the average price.

These slaves were docile. Not only did they do all the work of the house for their Portuguese owner, but they helped to support him, in some cases seem to have wholly supported him. They were trained to engage in retail trade on his behalf, selling in the bazaar the fruit and vegetables raised in his garden, or weaving, dyeing, and tailoring materials, from the sale of which a steady income was derived. The female slaves might become his concubines. Pyrard says negresses imported from Africa, 'wondrously black with curly hair', were the favourites in this respect. A grand lady might also make money by letting out her slaves as prostitutes. A certain class of Portuguese and Eurasians specialized in kidnapping for this market young people resident in the Indian states. The slave population in Goa was very great. For Latins the city was a paradise, a lotus-eating island of the blest, where you could sit on your veranda listening to music as the breeze blew in from the sea, with humble folk within call to minister to your every wish. No wonder it was called Golden Goa.

Pride, idleness, luxury, and vice had so demoralized the Portuguese that Pyrard, though he tried hard to accommodate himself, found them intolerable. 'I cannot tell all the affronts, insults, and ill-usage I suffered there,' he says. 'If they had believed that I so much as thought of recording anything about them, they would never have allowed me to return. I have but little of a high spirit, yet did I lead them to believe that I had much less for fear of giving them a bad opinion of me.'

5

A VISIT TO THE VICEROY

Pyrard's testimony is very valuable because it is not that of a mere traveller. Having lived for two years among the lower classes he knew what he was talking about. If you had good introductions, however, and were making a short stay, you might be dazzled by your reception and by the splendid palaces and churches, the richness of their baroque façades blending with the tropic scene and startling you with their beauty. For instance, Albert de Mandelslo, a handsome young gentleman of the Court of the Duke of Holstein, who visited Goa in 1639 in company with Mr. Methwold, the President of the East India Company's settlement at Surat further up the coast, has left us a pleasing impression of a viceregal reception. On landing at the wharf Mr. Methwold and he found 'many Hidalgos or Gentlemen of the Viceroy's retinue, who conducted us into the Hall, where he was to give the President audience. The guards, who were all clad in the same livery, had taken their arms and stood in two files in the Anti-Chamber, through which there was an entrance into the hall, which was richly furnished and full of the pictures of several Princes of Europe.[1] The Viceroy (Pero da Silva) who was all in black, as were also his Courtiers, rose out of his chair at the President's coming in, and sat not down again until the other was set. . . . The President, having despatched his business, took leave of the Viceroy, who brought him to the hall-door, where he stood bare till we were all gone out.'

Pyrard occasionally caught sight of the Viceroy of his day, Ruy Lourenço de Tavora, who succeeded the formidable de Menezes, the Governor-Primate. Loiterers in the Terreiro do Paço, the square to the south of the viceregal palace from which there was a flight of steps leading to the Hall of Audience, would see arrive a cavalcade of gentlemen, some four hundred strong, mounted on Arab stallions, attended by Moslem grooms, who flicked away the flies with horse-tail whisks. The guard, a hundred men in blue uniforms, carrying halberds, would be lining the steps. Presently the Viceroy would emerge, mount his horse, and with the gentlemen set off, their palanquins being carried behind, for show or in case they tired, footmen holding over the head of each rider a

[1] These actually represented the Viceroys and Governors of Portuguese Asia from the time of da Gama. The Resende MS. in the British Museum contains a coloured copy of each of these portraits. The originals are still to be seen in the viceregal palace, now situated on the mainland some miles distant. Richard Burton saw them in the eighteen-forties, but restorers had damaged them. Pyrard also saw them, being allowed one day to peep into the hall.

great parasol. And each of them had in personal attendance twelve pages dressed in silk, and six very tall negroes carrying drawn swords, fierce and devoted, made bulkier still by their padded mantles. It was in such guise that Pyrard saw Tavora pass, not to dine out, for he dared not do that in a city where the use of poison was so well understood, but to attend a fête at one of the great religious houses. Like all the viceroys, he was a very rich man, far richer than are our viceroys, for his salary was £14,000 a year—a sum that may be multiplied by ten or more to give twentieth-century values—and every viceroy hoped to make £300,000 during his three years of office by presents, bribes, and the sale of offices. But before they could enjoy their fortune, they had to get home, and, as Pyrard notes, 'it happens often enough that, as all this wealth of the Viceroys accrues to them from pillage and robbery, so the sea inherits it and all is miserably lost.'

One of the religious houses which viceroys were wont to visit was that of the Jesuits. Several of the monastic orders, the Dominicans, the Franciscans, the Carmelites, the Augustinians, had sumptuously appointed churches and monasteries, which had begun to be built from about 1550. By the beginning of the seventeenth century religious houses had increased so enormously that Fonseca, in his *Historical and Archaeological Sketch of Goa* (1878), the only full account of old Goa in existence, describes more than forty principal foundations, and Captain Hamilton, who was there at the close of the seventeenth century, declares that the clergy numbered 30,000, though the total Christian population was less than 160,000. The Jesuits lived in what was called the Professed House, attached to which was the Church of the Bom Jesus, buildings situated near the top of the Rua Direita. The Professed House, being one of the sights of Goa, was visited by Mandelslo and Mr. Methwold. The former sums up his impressions of the state and luxury in which the Jesuits lived in these words: 'I must confess they gave us the best Canary that ever I drank.' The visitors later climbed the tower of the Bom Jesus, where they took a view 'of all the city, the sea, the river, and all the adjacent champion, as far as the mountain', but it was inside the church that the most interesting sight in Goa was to be seen.

This was the mummified body of St. Francis Xavier.

6

ST. FRANCIS XAVIER

The Society of Jesus has generally been noted for the erudition of its members, but it was founded by two men, Loyola and Xavier, who were essentially ecstatics, men of tremendous emotional force, for whom vision had a much greater value than learning. Both of them had been through a spiritual crisis, after which they abandoned the life of hunting, society, and war to which, the one as a Spaniard, and the other as a Basque aristocrat, they had been born, and conceiving the idea of the regeneration of Catholicism, menaced by its own internal weaknesses, the rise of the new learning, and the appearance of new heresies, they founded in 1540 the Society of Jesus, thereafter dividing the work, Loyola selecting Europe as his field, and Xavier Asia. The conversion of the whole Orient was Xavier's ambition and he felt within him a sufficient force of soul to accomplish this miracle.

Ecstatics sometimes have an aptitude for affairs. Xavier knew that he must get the backing of the authorities in Goa, if his missionary projects were to succeed. King John III of Portugal had, indeed, offered to pay the expenses of a special mission. The Dominicans and Franciscans, who had been sent out shortly after the conquest, had made few converts; and the Portuguese themselves, though not yet as debauched as when Pyrard saw them seventy years later, had become careless of their religious duties. But Xavier saw that to go merely as the king's representative would not give him the ecclesiastical standing he required, and he induced Pope Paul III to appoint him Nuncio. As Papal Nuncio he disembarked at the wharf of Goa in 1542. Many dignitaries of the Church were there to meet him and a large crowd. As he stepped ashore it was noticed that he was barefoot, that his gown was ragged and his hood of the coarsest stuff. Refusing to enter a palanquin and go in procession to the lodging prepared for him in the Archbishop's Palace, he desired them to point out the direction of the then hospital, a primitive institution compared to the later Jesuit hospital. Then motioning them to follow, he led the way on foot, his face turned up to Heaven, his lips moving in prayer. He had black eyes and a black beard and an air of wild happiness. When he came to the hospital, he began at once to wash the sores of the lepers.

Contrary impressions were created by this dramatic entry. Some whispered that a halo had been seen round his head. Already was heard the name, the Heavenly Pilgrim, by which afterwards he was habitually called. But others, particularly the upper class, did not approve of a white man behaving thus in the East. In a contemporary letter quoted by A. Soares in his *Souvenir of St. Francis Xavier* this view comes out: 'Many high folks think it was imprudent to send such a man here, whose manner of life causes scandal. They say the white people will be despised by the natives because of him, for only if they see us as splendid and magnificent conquerors will we be able to impress upon them that we are a superior race.'

Xavier, however, continued to go about barefoot and in rags, tending the sick, comforting the slaves, relieving the needy, even visiting the galley-slaves in the Al Jabir prison and the Sala das bragas and praying with them in the heat and stench of their dungeon. His personality was so overwhelming, a happiness so abounding seemed to flow from him, that presently the grandees forgot they had thought him eccentric. A revulsion of feeling swept the city. In 1542 life in Goa was undisciplined and rough. Neither the civil nor the ecclesiastical authority was well established. Murder was frequent and went unpunished. Excommunication was little regarded. The soldiers in the forts along the coast lived as if the Church did not exist, many with a harem, and none troubling to obtain the Church's blessing on a union. But they were susceptible to the influences of true religion and piety. Nor had they altogether forgotten that one of their objects in coming east was to spread Catholicism. Xavier's saintly life caused them now to feel remorse. They became alarmed about their souls. One form taken by the reformation which followed was a burst of church building. There was already a number of churches and monasteries. These were renovated, enlarged, or entirely reconstructed, while many more were planned and gradually set up, Goa by the end of the century becoming a city of towers and bells. In Pyrard's time the spectacle of Golden Goa was complete, but what had begun as a religious revival had degenerated into religiosity.

The saint's stay in Goa itself was not protracted. The reformation of the Portuguese was but the first step in his vast ambition to convert all pagan Asia. Unlike the later Jesuits, who addressed themselves to the heads of governments and the highly educated, his method was to appeal to the lowest classes, particularly the unfortunate, the oppressed, the suffering, the enslaved. He sought to touch their hearts by goodness, and by his example to make Catholicism seem beautiful. There is no doubt that he loved the native inhabitants. Convinced that without a knowledge of the doctrines of Rome they were condemned to eternal perdition, no conceivable action seemed to him more compassionate than to strive to enlighten them. That their own religion could be of the smallest use did not cross his mind. He made no serious study of Hinduism or of any other oriental cult. He was a holy man, in the medieval European sense and in the sense that still holds in the Orient to-day. Like a flame of the faith, he passed through southern India and on to the Far East. After preaching in Japan, he set out for China, but died on the isle of San-chuan near the mouth of the Canton estuary on 27 November 1552, his mission having lasted in all ten years. In his fiery passage he converted thousands, wearing himself away by his fasts and vigils. Under the tropic sun or in the monsoon rain he would walk without umbrella or hat, at night sleeping on the bare ground of a hut, and that for no more than three hours. The enthusiasm which he aroused, the curious psychic reactions which accompanied his appearance, his fanatical single-mindedness, the absolute genuineness of his emotion, have been the subject of innumerable biographies, which establish beyond question that he was that rare. uncompromising, terrific phenomenon, a mystic and a saint.

7
XAVIER'S CORPSE

Xavier's life represents the lofty side of the Portuguese incursion into Asia. Less well known, and less edifying, is what happened to him after his death. The story is one of the strangest in later hagiology, and its recital here will help to complete the representation of Golden Goa which we are constructing. When he died on the remote fishermen's isle of San-chuan, he was attended by only one follower, the Chinese Christian who on baptism had taken the name of Antonio de Santa Fé. This young man buried him at the place, and because the grave was in the open and unprotected from the jackals, he threw lime on to the body with the object of dissolving it. When the news of the death reached Malacca, the fortress which commanded the strait of that name and was the nearest Portuguese settlement to Sanchuan (Macao, which is quite close, not being founded till five years later), the authorities immediately decided to recover the body and sent an expedition which arrived at the grave on 17 February 1553, nearly three months after Xavier's death. On exhuming the body they were astonished to find it in a perfect state of preservation. Evidently the lime, thrown in at random by Santa Fé, had been of such a quality or strength that it had acted as a preservative and not as a solvent. The Portuguese, however, held the body's freshness to be a miracle, one altogether in keeping with the saint's record, and, taking it to Malacca, there reburied it in a coffin.

When the Viceroy was informed of these events, he sent to fetch the saint to Goa. The reception of the coffin at the wharf by the entire population of the capital, its transport through the streets in state, and its deposit at the Jesuit College of St. Paul, an institution situated about half a mile east of the Professed House and the Bom Jesus, were conducted with a pomp very different from that which had attended Xavier's own arrival as Papal Nuncio.

When the coffin was opened, the body was found to be still perfectly fresh. In the following year it was exhibited, a large number of people being allowed to approach and kiss the feet. On this occasion a lady, called Isabel de Carom, bit off a toe which she carried away in her mouth as a relic.

It became the rule to exhibit the body every year for a few days. Pilgrims came to see it from all over the Goanese territory, an area of some sixty by thirty miles, and alms flowed into the coffers of the Society. Before the end of the century another toe disappeared, though who bit it off was not observed in the confusion and excitement of an occasion when the crowd was very dense and miracles were reported. In 1614 the Pope asked to be sent the right arm, which was duly cut off and forwarded to the Vatican. A few years later Xavier was canonized.

In 1624, when the body had been in St. Paul's College Chapel for seventy-one years, it was removed to the Bom Jesus. The change of sepulchre was celebrated by a Mass attended by every notability in the city. It was witnessed by the Italian traveller, Pietro della Valle, and is described in his *Viaggi*.

The body has lain in the Bom Jesus ever since, having survived the expulsion of the Jesuits in 1759, and the reduction of Goa to what it now is, a little Portuguese settlement, so beggared and insignificant that few people in this country know of its existence. During the seventeenth century the body was exposed to view at regular intervals and all European travellers who visited Goa made a point of seeing it if they could. Captain Fryer, who was there in 1675, states that the saint's cheeks were still fresh and pink. As the years passed his reputation steadily increased, after each exposure there being many to testify that barren women had borne children, that lame persons had danced, and that pagans were converted.

This reputation was by no means confined to India. The saint stood as high, if not higher, in Europe. About 1690 Maria Sophia, Queen of Portugal, asked that his hat, which, it seems, Santa Fé had carried to Goa and which had been on the corpse's head for 138 years, might be sent to her, as she desired to wear it at her next confinement. This was done, and the hat gave her such support in her hour that she dispatched in 1693 a rich vestment for the saint's use on which she had embroidered with her own hand the inscription 'Suo S. Xaverio Maria Sophia Regina Portugalis'.

Hearing of this the Duke of Tuscany ventured to ask in 1695 for the pillow on which the saint's head rested, promising in return to erect in the Bom Jesus a grander tomb than existed at that time. His offer was accepted and the pillow sent. What he wanted it for is not known, but it may have been that he planned to use it on his deathbed. He certainly prized it very highly. His best artists were set to work. A marble tomb with reliefs depicting the chief events in the saint's life was got ready. It was surmounted by a silver and crystal coffin, the silver alone costing £1,000. The whole was sent out and is still to be seen in the southern transept of the Bom Jesus.

By this time the Jesuits had found it necessary to exhibit the body less frequently, for as it dried with the years it became more brittle and could not endure frequent osculation. In 1700 Hamilton, a sardonic sea-captain, who regarded the Portuguese with distaste and was a no-popery man, visited the Bom Jesus, saw the tomb, and wrote that he supposed the saint to be 'a pretty piece of Wax-work that served to gull the people of their money'.

Years passed. In 1859, after all the orders had been expelled from Goa and the monasteries closed, when the city had fallen into ruin and the finances were so low that an admiral's pay was not more than a boatswain's elsewhere, the Viceroy, Dom Antonio Cesar de Vasconcellos Correia, Viscount (later Count) of Torres Novas, appointed a committee of doctors to examine and report on the saint. This they did very thoroughly, finding in the first place that he had shrunk from five to four and a half feet. They enumerated the missing toes, noted the missing arm, and testified that the alleged early pinkness of his cheeks was faded. The face was now covered, they submitted, with 'a dark dry integument'. His hair, however, was still in place. On the whole, indeed, he was in good condition and had weathered remarkably well three hundred years of tropical heat and damp, particularly as he had been mummified as it were by mistake.

When the autopsy was concluded, the inhabitants were allowed in. Altogether 200,000 persons paid to enter the building. The Heavenly Pilgrim had lost none of his popularity. They declare that on this occasion he wrought more miracles than at any time since his death. Besides Catholics, Hindus of many sects kissed the feet, and some of them, finding their diseases alleviated, demanded baptism, a boon which was accorded. The festival lasted a week and at the end of it, when the coffin was closed, all the bells in the city pealed and a salute of ordnance was fired. Having survived so long we may assume that the body will continue indefinitely to be the most noteworthy and the most potent relic of Portuguese Asia.

8

THE JESUITS AND THE GREAT MUGHAL

As has been stated, Xavier was not a typical Jesuit. His approach was more emotional, his aims more popular, than was usual with the members of the Society, whose speciality was learning, diplomacy, and administration. After his death, though the conversion of the rank and file continued to receive attention, the Jesuits' main energies were directed to winning over rulers and the ruling classes, the argument being that could these be gained, the commonalty would follow. This was the same course which the Jesuit, Matteo Ricci, was following in China at the time. It took the double form in India of an attempt to convince the Moslem Court of the Mughals and the Hindu intellectuals of Southern India.

Akbar, the third Mughal Emperor, who came to the throne four years after the death of Xavier, unified under one administration the greater part of upper and central India before his death in 1605. It was essential for the Government of Goa to keep on good terms with him, and it was generally represented at his Court by Jesuit diplomatists. These men, besides conducting the ordinary business of their appointment, strove to interest the Emperor in Catholicism.

Akbar was a person of insatiable intellect. He searched for truth like an alchemist for the elixir. He was delighted to hear what the Jesuits had to say. Had they been able to persuade him that they possessed the secret of ultimate truth, he would have been enchanted. Nominally a Moslem, he was really an eclectic. The Emperors of China as Confucian pontiffs were as convinced as the Popes that they knew the truth. But Akbar had no such conviction. His mind was open. All his life he sought truth. The Jesuit Fathers Aquaviva and Monserrate had an ideal opportunity. Such notice did he take of them, the patience with which he would listen to their discourses was so flattering, that they were continually writing to Rome of his imminent conversion. But it all came to nothing. The fact was that Akbar's mind was superior to Aquaviva's or his colleague's, it had a wider sweep, he was a stronger intellectual. It would have required a philosopher of greater talent than was either of these particular Jesuits to match him. The Society was never able to do it.

9

THE STRANGE CASE OF DE NOBILI, S.J.

More interesting is the Jesuit attempt to confront the higher Brahminism, the great Sanskrit philosophy of the Atman, the most profound and the most fecund metaphysic in the Orient. The ordinary run of Portuguese clerics, though in the course of the hundred years since the time of da Gama's farcical *mal entendu* they had learnt a good deal about popular Hinduism, knew nothing of its esoteric depths. Xavier occasionally met Brahmin philosophers, but the records of his conversations with them show that he was completely ignorant of their system. Towards the end of the sixteenth century, however, it became known that remarkable ideas were current in Hinduism. The Dutchman, Linschoten, writing in 1583, observes: 'The Bramenes believe that there is a supreme God above, which ruleth all things, and that men's soules are Immortall, and that they go out of this world into another, both Beasts and Men, and receive reward according to their workes, as Pythagoras teacheth, whose Disciples they are.'

This not on that the Sanskrit sacred writings had some connection with Pythagoras was still popularly current in 1670, when the English traveller, Thomas Bowrey, wrote of the Brahmins: 'They are reputed to be very great Philosophers, and doe really and with Zeale study the Pithagorean Philosophy. . . . And by the wisest Europeans that Sometime doe converse with them with great freedom, they are said to be great Astronomers and Philosophers, as before mentioned.'

These quotations show that, though the Brahmin doctrines were not generally understood, a faint perception existed that they had some relationship with Greek transcendentalism. So unaccountably serious did they seem by all accounts that Bonhours, the French Catholic and scholar who wrote Xavier's life in 1682, opined that 'it may be inferred that in former times the Indians heard of Christianity, and that their religion is an imperfect imitation or corruption of ours'. Only so could he explain certain affinities between Catholic and Brahmin philosophy, speculations which Jesuit studies earlier in the century had brought to light, and of which plain men like Bowrey had vaguely heard. Their alleged origin in Christian doctrine had the supposed historical support of St. Thomas's visit to India.

Not till the early years of the nineteenth century were translations of Sanskrit classics to become available in Europe. Their revelation of the doctrine of the Atman caused an immense sensation Many eminent thinkers were carried away by enthusiasm. The German poet Schlegel's impassioned outburst after reading the Bhagavad-Gita is well known—as is Schopenhauer's heartfelt remark: 'It has been the solace of my l fe, it will be the solace of my death.' And Wagner, writing to Matilde Wesendonk in 1857, could say of the same: 'Yes, child, it is a world view, compared with which every other dogma must appear small and narrow.' Our own Matthew Arnold was no less profoundly moved. But any analogy between the Gita and Christian mysticism was not yet suspected.

In the twentieth century we have become better informed. The *Upanishads*, the *Vedanta*, are on the shelves of our libraries, along with the works of the monk who styled himself Dionysius the Areopagite, with those of St. John of the Cross, St. Teresa,

Master Eckhart, and of the English author of *The Cloud of Unknowing*. It has become clear that the vision of truth, which these European mystics record having seen, transcended their dogmatic beliefs and was analogous to the Brahminic vision.

The seventeenth-century Jesuits were among the few at that time who saw that Brahminism was more than the horrid tangle of superstitions which some of its outward forms suggested. In order to apply their method of proselytizing from the top, they tried to find out more precisely in what it consisted, so that, by force of superior dialectic, they could show how it fell short of the truth they could reveal. Like Ricci in China who was assuring the Confucians that the step from their theism to Christianity was an easy one, so they in India, after mastering the Brahminical books, must devise a similar acceptable transition. A *Summa* would be required, reconciling Catholic and Brahmin philosophy, as Aquinas had reconciled Catholic and Greek, a reconciliation acceptable to both the Brahmins and the Pope, not an easy book to write but one of which they believed themselves capable. The reader will perceive that a syncretism of sorts was to be offered, a reconcilement not by a demonstration of the transcendental resemblance between Christianity and Brahminism, but by means of a dialectic which would convince the Hindu philosophers that Catholic revelation was needed to amplify their knowledge. Christianity would be introduced to them as a supernatural confirmation of truths, some of which, it was allowed, they had apprehended by natural means.

Knowing, as we now do, the nature of the Atman metaphysic, it goes without saying that, while a syncretism of Brahminism and Catholicism might be possible on the transcendental levels common to the mystical saints of both religions, it was not possible to bring that about by dialectical pyrotechnics. The Jesuits' attempt to accomplish this impossibility is a very curious episode in the history of the West's assault upon the beliefs of the East.

At the beginning of the seventeenth century the most important centre of Brahmin learning was at Madura, the university city of Malabar, a triangle of country which forms the toe of India. The Mughal had not penetrated so far south. It was the very hub of the Brahmin world, a Hindu kingdom of an immemorial kind. Thousands of students attended the university. The curriculum was a long course in the Sanskrit classics, in its first stages concerned with their grammar and literal rendering into the spoken language, which was Tamil. The later stages, to which but few attained, were an increasingly difficult exposition of the metaphysic. Besides the university, Madura possessed one of the largest and most gorgeous shrines in India, a temple where the ritual side of these studies was demonstrated.

If they were to master Brahminic philosophy, the Jesuits perceived that one of their number must go to Madura. But how could they count on his being received? The Government of Goa was detested by the Hindus. In 1567 all Hindu temples on Portuguese territory had been destroyed and their revenues diverted to support Christian foundations. Brahmins resident in the city were obliged by law to listen on Sundays to sermons delivered by Dominicans. It even appears that under the more fanatical viceroys Hindus were not allowed even to worship in private. Thus Father Dalmeida writes in November 1559, describing how he and other Fathers were empowered to enter private houses by night, and, if the inmates were found practising the rites of their faith, to arrest them.

To effect their purpose the Jesuits selected a certain Italian aristocrat, Robert de Nobili, who had joined the Society and come out to Goa in 1605. The instructions they gave him will best be appreciated by relating what he actually did.

De Nobili set out for Madura dressed as a Brahmin, just as Ricci made his way in China dressed as a scholar. On arrival at the city he declared that they should not mistake him for a Portuguese, for he was an Italian nobleman, and one, moreover, who had renounced his family and his estates to become an ascetic in the Asiatic manner. This ensured him a good reception, for in India a sage, no matter what his denomination, is always respected.

Settling in the town, he was careful to conform strictly to the usages of his adopted pose. He ate but one meal a day, and that consisted only of rice, vegetables, and milk. His first step was to learn Tamil, which with its rich vocabulary and elaborate grammar is one of the most difficult of Indian vernaculars. By concentration and enormous industry he mastered it in two years. But this was only the beginning. The Brahminic texts were not available in Tamil. No-one who was not a Sanskrit scholar could read them and no-one who was not a Brahmin could aspire to learn Sanskrit. Moreover, the key texts were reserved for the inner circle of the hierarchy.

In the East, however, patience and a go-between will procure almost anything. De Nobili's scholarly way of life won him a Brahmin friend, who eventually obtained copies of the secret texts and helped him to decipher them. Gradually he worked his way through the intricacies of the metaphysic. Armed at last with Tamil, Sanskrit, and a knowledge of the *Vedanta*, he dared to begin expounding his syncretic system. His reputation increased. As a sage from overseas, a strange rarity in those lands, he aroused curiosity and secured a following. Deliberately cultivating a mysterious legend, he never went out and, shut in his room, was so difficult of access that only after the third attempt could anyone hope to be received. This reserve, his fragile and emaciated appearance due to austerities, his aristocratic air, his imposing presence as he sat in turban and yellow robe, drew to his room eventually most of the pundits, with whom he remained closeted for hours, arguing them indefatigably round to his view.

In 1609, four years after his arrival, he published a book in Sanskrit, so elegantly phrased, so brilliant in its dialectic, that it compelled the admiration even of those who had so far held aloof from a man of whose single-mindedness they were not entirely convinced. This work, it is said, presented a statement of Christian philosophy in terms which made it seem a legitimate extension of the doctrine of the Atman. As is well known, the heart of the Brahminic vision is contained in the celebrated refrain in the *Chandogya Upanishad*: 'What that Unknowable is by which this universe subsists, that is the real, that is the soul, that art thou.' This conception is called non-duality. There is only one Real. Therefore the individual is God. And he is aware of this in *Samadhi*, that is, when meditation becomes absorption, subject and object, soul and God, being then so completely blended that the consciousness of the separate subject disappears. The state of *Samadhi* is termed *niratmakatvam*, which signifies the vision of the non-dual nature of reality. How de Nobili contrived by means of dialectic to hinge Catholicism on to this conception is unknown, for no copy of his book exists. On the plane of mystical Catholicism the reconciliation was arguable. If most of the Christian mystics held that in their state of absorption corresponding to *Samadhi* there remained duality, the self having a vision of God as an object, or that if union took place it did not imply identity, some mystics, particularly the Flemish and German, seem to have experienced the sense of non-duality. That was partly the reason why Eckhard in 1235 was arraigned for heresy by the Bishop of

Cologne, for the conception of non-duality had not, nor has it had since, any place in Catholic philosophy. But as de Nobili was not a mystic and sought only a reasoned adaptation within the accepted framework of Catholicism, he made no use of Eckhard's sermons, which might have supplied him with a real adaptation, for Eckhard certainly believed himself to be a Christian. How he presented his syncretism is, therefore, difficult to conceive, unless we suppose that his views impressed, not the orthodox esoterics, but some sect of Hindus who were prepared to dilute an absolute non-duality, allow a union which was not an identity, and so were ready to admit that God, as an object, might have given a particular revelation to one who had been in union with Him, of which person and his message de Nobili had exclusive information. But this is mere surmise. Without his book and fuller information about his Hindu admirers, it is impossible to say how he achieved his adaptation. But achieve it he did to the satisfaction of some of the Madura pundits, for he was able to raise funds and build a church.

This passage from the esoteric to the exoteric, from metaphysics to ritual, was, as one might well suppose, the danger point. As a sage, a teacher, a *guru,* he was assured of tolerance even from those he had not impressed, but to set up a rival place of worship and obtain donations from the local inhabitants was going beyond what was regarded as his legitimate role. Moreover, there was clearly an enormous difference between Catholic rites in a church and the rituals of a Hindu temple. The pundits who had enjoyed his speculations were somewhat startled to see their philosopher officiating at rites which in effect denied the efficacy of their own. The position may be illustrated by an example. Certain Brahmins formally charged him with atheism on the ground that he did not believe in the Trinity, that is to say, in their Trinity of Brahma, Vishnu, and Siva. It is true that they themselves did not believe in these deities esoterically, but exoterically they were the expression in phenomenal form of three aspects of the Absolute, and, so, played an essential part in ritual and doctrine.

Well aware that objections of this kind might wreck in practice what had seemed feasible in theory, de Nobili tried to make things easy for his Brahmin supporters by various concessions to Hindu usage. Relying on the precedent that in the past the Church in Europe had taken over pagan festivals and turned them into Christian holy days, such as the old Lupercalia of February which became the Carnival of the Virgin, he allowed Brahmins whom he baptized to continue to paint caste marks on their foreheads and to wear the cord they held sacred. Nor did he look too closely at their rural feasts, though it seems he could not bring himself to allow offerings to the *lingam* in time of drought.

But these concessions, made solely to prevent friction and the ruin of his plans, got him into difficulties with the heads of the very Church whose doctrines he was striving to make palatable. If the Brahmins considered he did not go far enough to meet them, the hierarchy of Goa thought he had gone too far. His immediate chiefs of the Jesuit Professed House were satisfied that he had made the best accommodation possible, but the Primate, an Augustinian named Dom Fr. Christovão de Sa, sent for him in 1616 and expressed his displeasure. What had been done at Madura did not accord with the policy adopted towards the Hindus inside Goanese territory. In defence of his concessions de Nobili submitted a memorandum detailing the delicate nature of such a conversion as he aspired to bring about. He obtained, curiously enough, the support of the Grand Inquisitor, Dom Almeida, who agreed that in the interests of a wide conversion it was necessary, certainly at first, to distinguish between civil rites and religious observances, precisely the point which Ricci had raised in China a few years previously. The matter, however, was of such importance that reference had to be made to Rome, and in 1623 Pope Gregory XV decreed that Brahmins converted to Catholicism might wear their sacred cord and use caste marks, provided these were blessed by a Catholic priest.

So dissolved into comparative trivialities de Nobili's dream of converting the Brahmin hierarchy by means of a grand syncretism. But his experiment was an interesting one, perhaps the most interesting missionary experiment which has ever been undertaken. Its intellectuality shows the Jesuits to have been in this respect a long way ahead of the other religious organizations in Goa.

10

AN *AUTO-DA-FÉ*

About a quarter of a mile north of the Jesuits' Professed House, in the principal square, the Terreiro de Sabaio, was an institution of a very different kind. Occupying the whole southern side of the square stood a palace which all travellers of the period have described as superb. This was the palace of the Holy Inquisition.

Its baroque façade, built of black stone, 'a fit emblem of the cruel and bloody transactions that passed within its walls', as Captain Franklin, a later traveller, puts it, had three doors, the two side ones leading to the private apartments of the Inquisitors, the central door opening upon a great hall, the Mesa do Santo Officio. Here suspected heretics were examined at a table, fifteen feet long and four feet broad, which stood on a dais in the middle of the apartment. The walls were hung with green silk and against one of them was an immense crucifix, the figure more than life-size and so elevated that the face was almost under the ceiling. Accused persons were required to gaze up at it, and so horrific was its appearance and terrible the occasion that many, it is said, fainted from fright. Behind were the cells, two hundred in number and ten feet square. These were whitewashed and clean, lighted by a grated window high up, and had double doors, food being passed through an aperture in the inner door, which always remained shut. The food and sanitary arrangements were good, but the imprisonment was solitary, no exercise being provided for nor any books, writing materials, or work allowed.

The Inquisition was established in Goa in 1560. It is an interesting fact that St. Francis Xavier urged that this should be done. Humane, loving, and devoted though he was, he was also a disciplinarian. In a letter dated the 16th of May 1546 to John III, King of Portugal, he describes the Portuguese at Goa and the forts with their Indian or half-caste wives and concubines, and points out the evil influence of these women, many of whom were Catholics in name only, for they worshipped simultaneously the Hindu deities. An ecclesiastical court to prevent those baptized from lapsing into heresy was essential, if the pure Europeans were to retain their faith and not be swallowed up in heathendom. 'For these reasons your Highness should send out the Holy Inquisition,' he concludes.

The New or Spanish Inquisition had been established sixty-eight years previously in Castile and Aragon at the instance of the Dominican, Torquemada. It was directed particularly against the Conversos, Jews who had been baptized under pressure of penal laws, but were suspected of practising their old rites in secret. These Jews were the richest and most industrious people in Spain. Their plunder was one of the objects of the Inquisition, an object which appealed strongly to Ferdinand and Isabella, who were in need of money. The reader will be acquainted with the history of the Inquisition in Spain and Portugal; he will know that it was not identical with the medieval Inquisition, an ecclesiastical tribunal created to check the heresies and superstitions, the witchcraft and sorcery, which threatened to muddle and brutalize Catholicism. He will recall that, less a reforming body than the earlier institution, it represented from one point of view an alliance between the Crown and the Church for secular objects. Besides serving to rob the Jewish Conversos, it was used to terrify the nobility and the people. A lord too independent or a peasant agitator would be tapped on the shoulder one day by its Familiars and informed he was arrested on a charge of heresy. The events of these latter days have made us acquainted with secret police, with espionage in the home, with the breaking of morale by torture and solitary confinement. These were the methods of the Inquisition, and though they have been excused on the ground that they had their counterpart in the criminal procedure of the law and so must have appeared less unjust than they do nowadays, they were more efficient and so more cruel than the methods of the judiciary. A lay judge took action on public complaint or after a factual breaking of the law, but the Holy Office often selected its victims and hunted them down, concocting a process against them afterwards.

The lovable Francis Xavier may in his saintly simplicity have pictured the Inquisition as an honest disciplinary tribunal reforming the licence of colonial life. By Pyrard's time, forty-eight years after its introduction into Goa, it bore a dreadful reputation. Pyrard, a good Catholic, has left this in no doubt. After stating that its procedure was even more severe than in Portugal, and that it continued its old policy of hunting converted Jews, in this case oriental Jews who to obtain the advantage of a trade residence in Goa had declared themselves Christians, he goes on: 'The first time such Jews are taken before the Holy Inquisition, all their goods are seized; they are seldom arrested unless they are rich.' Speaking generally, he then declares: 'Nothing in the world is more cruel and pitiless than the procedure. The least suspicion, the slightest word, whether of a child or of a slave who wishes to do his master a bad turn, is enough . . . they give credence to a child however young, so only he can speak. . . . When a man is arrested there is no friend will dare say a word for him. . . . If a chance word should escape a man, having the smallest reference to the Inquisition itself, he must forthwith go and denounce himself, if he suspect that any has heard him. . . . It is a terrible and fearful thing to be there even once, for you have no advocate, while they are prosecution and judges at once.' Speaking of its attitude to the native inhabitants, he states that though not subject to its jurisdiction unless they turned Christian, they might be arrested should they be accused of hindering one of their fellows from professing Catholicism. 'It would be impossible,' he concludes, 'to calculate the numbers of all those put to death.' To ascertain this, the records were examined in the middle of the nineteenth century by José da Fonseca, author of the above-mentioned *Sketch of the City of Goa*, but he was unable to make a complete computation. He found, however, that seventy-one *autos-da-fé* were held between 1600 and 1773, and that the number of persons burnt averaged twelve on each occasion, which gives an estimated total of eight hundred and fifty-two.

There exists an inside account of an *auto-da-fé* at Goa written by a Dr. Dellon. It is contained in his book *Relation de l'Inquisition de Goa*, published in Paris in 1688, and translated into English the same year. The events it describes took place between 1673 and 1676, some sixty years after Pyrard had left Goa, but the tribunal had not changed in the interval, and the *Relation* provides with approximate accuracy a picture of an *auto-da-fé* in the first quarter of the century.

Dr. Dellon, who was a French traveller of twenty-four, was staying at Daman, one of the forts north of Goa, when he was arrested on 24 August 1673. He had offended the Governor, Dom Manuel Hurtado de Mendoza, by visiting his mistress. And he had imprudently made critical remarks about the Inquisition, and about matters of faith, such as baptism and the adoration of images, which those who heard them considered heretical, though he, also a Catholic, believed them justified by the theological books it was his hobby to read. These lapses gave Dom Manuel his chance of revenge. The Commissary representing the Inquisition at Daman was informed and a Familiar was sent to take him into custody.

His book provides a very full account of the dreadful misadventures which then befell him. To relate them in detail here is tempting, but would overbalance our narrative, and only his description of the *auto-da-fé* itself can be given. After two years in a cell of the Inquisition at Goa to which he had been removed from

Daman, he became convinced in December 1675 that an *auto-da-fé* was about to take place. By this time his nerve was broken by solitude, by the raising of hopes which his tormentors dashed with cruel deliberation, by dark threats, silence as to the precise nature of the charges against him, or the time when he would receive his sentence, and by frightful forebodings about his possible fate. Acts of faith were ordinarily held on the first Sunday in Advent, now very close. The previous Advent had been without one. The dread celebration was never omitted in two successive years. Though the Inquisitors in the course of one of their many interviews with him had said he was liable to be burned, he felt a mixture of longing and fear. If he were not burnt, perhaps he would be released. He was almost eager to take the chance. The prospect of another year in solitary confinement was horrible.

But the first Sunday in Advent came and went. Strange, when the prison was so full. Surely a gaol delivery must come soon. Another sign was that a new Archbishop, Dom Francisco da Assumpcão e Brito, had arrived, the Cathedral bells having been rung for nine days together. What more fitting than that this prelate's installation should be made the occasion of an Act of Faith?

But the second Sunday went by; Dellon began to despair. When the third and fourth were gone, his hopes went with them. He resigned himself to suffer for another year.

But, 'on Saturday the 11th of January 1676,' he writes 'being about to give my linnen after Dinner to the Officers to be washed after the usual Custom, they would not receive it', but put him off till the next day. This departure from routine or maybe something about the manner of the warders set him wondering. Could it be that after all an *auto-da-fé* was at hand, that it would take place, perhaps, the very next day, Sunday, a day always used for that ceremony? In the evening he became certain that something was in the wind, for, as he explains, 'after I had heard it ring to Vespers at the Cathedral, it immediately rung to Matins, which was never before done while I was a Prisoner, except upon the eve of Corpus Christi day'.

These two unusual events convinced him that an *auto-da-fé* was imminent. With the ordeal facing him so close he now became frightened. They had given him no intimation whatever regarding his fate. For all he knew, it might be the stake for him next day. 'They brought me my Supper, which I refused and which contrary to their ordinary custom they pressed me not very much to receive. As soon as the doors were shut upon me, I entirely abandoned my self to those melancholy thoughts which possessed me; and at last, after many tears and sighs, overwhelmed with sorrow and imaginations of death, I fell asleep a little after Eleven a Clock at Night.'

He had not been long asleep when he was awoken by warders entering his cell. They carried lights—he had never seen a light during all the nights of his imprisonment—and the chief gaoler, who accompanied them 'gave me a habit which he ordered me to put on, and to be ready to go out when he should call me'. Leaving a lamp they withdrew without any explanation, but Dellon knew that at an *auto-da-fé* a special costume was worn by the victims.

If he had been frightened before he went to sleep, he was now terrified. 'I was seized with an universal and so violent a trembling that for more than an hour it was not possible for me so much as to look upon the habit which they had brought me.'

At last he summoned courage to get up and kneeling before a cross, which he had painted on the wall, committed his soul to God's protection. Then he put on the dress. It was black stuff, striped with white, and consisted of a blouse and a pair of loose trousers.

At two o'clock in the morning the warders returned and conducted him to a long gallery. 'There I found a good number of my Companions in Misery, ranged round about against the Wall; I put my self into my place, and there came yet divers after me.'

When all the prisoners were assembled, there seemed to be some two hundred, of whom only twelve were Europeans, though in the faint light of the few lamps, and as all were dressed in the same dark clothes, it was hard to tell. Dead silence reigned. 'One might easily have taken all these persons for so many statues set against the Wall, if the motion of their eyes, the use of which alone was permitted to them, had not testified them to be living creatures.' Or it might have been they were come to attend some funeral, so sombre and melancholy was the company.

No women were amongst them, though there were some women prisoners. These were in an adjoining gallery, 'vested with the same stuff', and Dellon caught sight through a door of two more prisoners, beside whom stood monks in black habits and holding crucifixes.

Having no knowledge of the Inquisition's procedure on such

occasions he was unable to glean a hint of what his impending sentence was likely to be from the clothes in which he and the other prisoners were dressed, but as they and he all seemed as yet to be dressed the same, there being nothing about the blouse and trousers which had been allotted to him to distinguish his case from the others, he took a little courage, arguing it unlikely that so many people were for the stake.

But now the warders began to bring in more garments. These were like scapularies or large capes, of yellow stuff with a St. Andrew's cross painted on them before and behind. Dellon knew enough to recognize them to be *sanbenitos*, the penitential grab worn by prisoners of the Inquisition during their procession through the streets to the place of sentence. The *sanbenitos*, of which there were twenty-two only, were distributed first to twenty Indians and negroes, the twenty-first to a Portuguese, and the last one to Dellon. 'My fears redoubled when I saw myself thus habited, because it seemed to me that, there being among so great a number of Prisoners, no more than 22 persons to whom the shameful Sanbenitos were given, it might very well happen that these should be the persons to whom no mercy was to be extended.'

While he was in this state of dreadful apprehension, five 'bonnets of paper', like dunces' caps in shape, were brought. These were painted with devils amid flames and bore the legend 'Sorcerer' in bold letters. Instinctively he realized that such caps must denote a greater degree of guilt, and narrowly watched the warders as they began to fix them on the heads of shrinking prisoners. One of those to receive a cap was standing next to him, and when Dellon saw the warder approach with the cap in his hand, he felt certain it was for him that the emblematic horror was intended. When it was put on the other a sigh of agonized relief escaped him. The face of him upon whose head it was set was drawn and haggard, as if he 'believed his destruction to be inevitable'.

No more garments or accoutrements being produced, word was passed that the prisoners might sit down. The parade had been so early—so unnecessarily early as by deliberate intention to cause the greatest possible suspense and fear—that dawn was still a long way off. So they sat there in utter silence, the light of the lamps so weak that they seemed no more than shadows in the vast gallery. At four o'clock the warders came with baskets of bread and figs. 'But altho I had not supped the night before, I found in my self so small an appetite for eating, that I had taken nothing, if one of the Guards coming near me had not said: "Take your Bread, and if you cannot eat now, put it into your Pocket, for you will be certainly hungry before you return."'

Dellon did not venture to ask the man to be more explicit, but the remark, if it were to be believed and was not another deception, gave a faint hope which, taken with the other, that a sorcerer's cap had not been set on his head, heartened him a little.

At last, after they had waited what seemed a dark age, the first greyness of dawn began to creep into the gallery. The light strengthened and looking round Dellon was able to observe 'upon the faces of everyone present the diverse motions of shame, of grief and of fear, wherewith they were then tormented'. Yet he thought too that he could also detect relief, as if they were glad, though they might be going to their deaths, that their horrible captivity was at an end.

As the sun rose they heard the deep note of the cathedral's big bell, a bell which was only tolled on such occasions and was a signal for the inhabitants, Portuguese, Eurasian, and Indian, to line the streets through which the procession was about to pass.

The prisoners were then ordered to file out into the great hall, and when Dellon entered it he saw the Grand Inquisitor seated by the door with his secretary standing beside him, a list in his hand. To one side was a crowd of residents from the city, and as each prisoner stepped in a name would be called, when one of the residents came forward and the prisoner was allotted to him. These were known as Fathers in God and it was their duty to accompany their penitent throughout the procession, stay beside him during the ceremony of the Act of Faith, and produce him at the end of it. Dellon's Father in God was no less a personage than the Admiral of the Armada, a Portuguese nobleman, for it seems that the duty of attending upon penitents was regarded as an honour, not only by ordinary citizens but by the aristocracy.

When the business of appointing each his keeper was done, the whole concourse left the palace of the Inquisition and descended the wide flight of steps into the great square in front of the cathedral. With the January sun gaining height about him, Dellon stood and sniffed the air of morning, which seemed to blow from paradise, so fresh and sweet it smelt after his long captivity.

Now the procession began to form. At the head of it were the Dominicans, who had this privilege by the right that St. Dominic had been the founder of the first Inquisition. Before them was borne the banner of the Holy Office whereon was embroidered a picture of St. Dominic, holding in one hand a sword and in the other an olive branch, to which a legend was attached, 'Justitia et Misericordia'.

The Dominicans moved off, behind them following in a long line the penitents, each with his godfather beside him and a taper in his hand. About a hundred had entered the procession before the officers of the Inquisition commanded Dellon to do so. His head was bare as were his feet. The procession was so long that he had passed out of the square before the end of it was complete and so was unable to tell who formed the tail.

There was a very large crowd, the inhabitants, European and Indian, not only of Goa, but of the districts in the neighbourhood, lining the route, business being abandoned for that day. As he walked Dellon's bare feet were so cut by loose flints that they were bleeding profusely by the time the procession reached its destination, the Church of St. Francis, actually quite close because it was behind the Cathedral, but which was approached after parading all round the town. The staring crowd he had found an ordeal; unaccustomed for so long to exercise he was exhausted; and his godfather, the Admiral, would answer no questions, remaining cold and distant throughout the progress.

On entering the church, which was the most gorgeous in Goa—the Italian traveller, Gernelli Careri, who visited it twenty years later, says: 'It has a roof curiously adorned with fretwork and is like one entire mass of gold, there being so much of this metal on its altars'—Dellon perceived that it had been made ready for the ceremony, for the great altar was spread with black 'and there were upon it six Silver Candlesticks with so many tapers of white Wax burning'. On each side of it was a dais, where, to the left, sat the Grand Inquisitor and his staff, and to the right Dom Furtado de Albuquerque, Count of Lavradio and Viceroy of the Indies. Dellon walked up the aisle, pews having been placed on both sides for the members of the procession, those entering first being placed nearest the altar.

When he had taken his allotted seat, with the Admiral beside him, he looked round to watch the rest of the penitents march in. Following had been many more in *sanbenitos* of the kind he was wearing, and behind them at last came the five with pointed caps, a lofty crucifix bringing up the rear. But this was not the end, for he now saw a man and a woman behind the crucifix, as if by design the face of the Saviour had been turned away from them. They were both Indian Christians and along with them were carried four effigies and four boxes. The significance of this—who were the two penitents, what the boxes, and the effigies—Dellon was to learn later on. At the moment he noted that these two were differently dressed from all the others, their *sanbenitos* being of grey, not yellow, stuff, and painted not with a St. Andrew's Cross but with devils, flames, and burning firebrands, in the midst of which was a portrait of the wearer. The face was on the chest and repeated on the back, with the name below and the crime in large letters, the words in both cases being *crimen magicae*. They also wore the pointed caps, similar to those worn by the five who preceded them. Dellon had not seen these two persons in the gallery nor, therefore, had he witnessed the bestowal upon them of their costumes, and he surmised them to be those of whom he had caught a glimpse through a door, with black-stoled monks holding out to them crucifixes. These monks attended still, marching instead of godfathers.

The symbolism of the whole pageant was becoming clearer to him. If he were not mistaken, these were the victims destined for the stake. He shuddered, believing, yet not daring to be sure, that he had escaped an awful death. As for the effigies and the boxes, he did not yet guess what they signified, but it was strange that the former, borne aloft on poles, wore, too, the flaming habits and the tall pointed caps.

The divine service of the *auto-da-fé* began. Everyone was in his proper place, the last mentioned unhappy pair seated at the extreme back, and the crucifix, which had faced away from them, now set on the altar between the candlesticks. The Provincial of the Augustinians, the head of that Order in the East, ascended the pulpit. Besides the two hundred penitents, and the like number of godfathers, there were present as many of the public as could push their way in, the Franciscan monks also having their set place, grey friars, with cords about their middles, sandalled and, on their backs, the broad-brimmed hats they wore over their cowls.

The Augustinian prelate opened his discourse.

In spite of Dellon's anxiety—for if he now hoped to escape death there were many other severe punishments which might be inflicted on him—he listened carefully to the sermon, a short one for those times, for it lasted only an hour. Among the Provincial's points was a comparison of the Inquisition with Noah's Ark 'between which yet he found this difference that the Animals, which entered into the Ark, went out again after the Deluge, invested with the same Nature which they had when they entered it, but that the Inquisition had the admirable property to change in such sort those who are shut up in it, that in coming out we see those to be Lambs who when they entered it had the cruelty of Wolves.' This was hardly a correct description of his case, thought Dellon, who had been as mild, if as foolish, as a lamb from the beginning.

The sermon being finished, two clerks of the Holy Office entered the pulpit and began to read in turn the judgements passed upon the prisoners. During the reading, the head gaoler led each man into the centre of the aisle, to stand with a lighted taper in his hand. In due course Dellon was called. He heard the clerk read a summary of the allegations, his remarks about baptism, images, and the Inquisition, all of which he had made argumentatively, carelessly, for he was an ingenuous, talkative fellow. But it was held he had spoken with deliberate malice. For these crimes he was declared excommunicated, his goods were confiscated, and himself condemned to five years in the galleys, the sentence to be served, not in Goa, but in Lisbon.

How monstrous this sentence was he did not fully realize at the moment, so relieved was he to have escaped the stake or further imprisonment in the Santa Casa. To be a galley-slave seemed to him almost a happy prospect, for no matter what his treatment he would be out of the hands of the Church.

When the sentence had been pronounced he was taken to the altar, at the foot of which was a missal, whereon he was ordered to make a confession of faith after a clerk, who read it from a breviary. He then returned to his place and listened while the rest of the judgements were pronounced. As there were two hundred this took all day. After a while he noticed that the congregation was eating and, remembering that he too had food in his pocket, made a meal with good appetite.

At last the reading of the judgements came to an end, that is of those relating to the penitents who had walked in front of the crucifix. Their punishments had been various, but none were sent to death, not even those with the flaming caps of sorcerers. Judgement upon the two who had been behind the crucifix was reserved for the moment. The Grand Inquisitor left his dais and put on alb and stole. Then accompanied by twenty priests, each carrying a wand, he took up a position in the middle of the church, where after praying for a while he absolved the convicted penitents from the excommunication which had been passed upon them, his attendant priests striking them one by one a blow on their breasts. When Dellon had been so absolved by the touch of a wand, he was surprised to see a sudden change in the manner of his godfather, the Admiral. This worthy's stiffness had been due wholly to fear and not to any coldness of heart. When he heard his godson's absolution pronounced and knew that he had been taken back into the bosom of the Church, he wept, called him his brother, though he was a galley slave, and embracing him warmly, offered him tobacco.

This part of the ceremony ended, the Grand Inquisitor returned to his place on the dais and directed that the man and the woman should be brought before him. Their judgements were then read out: they were indicted of the crime of magic: and they had both relapsed, this being their second offence. As Hindus by birth this may have meant no more than that they had practised such arts as astrology or divination or engaged in one of the many occult practices connected with Hinduism. But they had had the temerity to enter so strict an association as the Catholic Church of seventeenth-century Portugal, perhaps for reasons of temporal advantage, and now were paying the penalty of their rashness. Their judgements ended with the words always used when condemned persons were to be burnt, to wit that they be delivered to the secular authority, which was earnestly requested to show mercy, but that if, indeed, the penalty of death were imposed, it might at least be inflicted without effusion of blood. 'At the last words of the Inquisitor's a sergeant of the Secular Justice approached and took possession of those unfortunate persons, after they had received a light blow on the breast from the hand of the Alcaide of the Holy Office, in token that they were abandoned by him.'

Their burning was to take place at a selected spot on the river bank, and thither Dom Furtado de Albuquerque adjourned with his glittering Court, as did the Inquisitors, for, of course, everything had been arranged beforehand; there was no appeal nor conceivably would the civil authorities dare to show mercy, in spite of the apparent earnestness with which it had been demanded of them. Dellon did not see carried out this last cruelty, this abominable stupidity, for stupid it was if the Holy Office desired to commend to the enlightened attention of Asia the Catholic Church and the message of compassion which it had received from its Founder. No Church of the Orient inflicted such punishments. If there were disgraceful practices in Hinduism, they were immoral rather than cruel, or if cruel, the cruelty was self-inflicted. To find a parallel one must leave Asia and go to the America of the Aztecs. Yet there is no parallel even there, for the victims of the Aztec priests were sacrificed not in punishment but oblation.

The Inquisition's dark fanaticism had also its ludicrous aspect. The four boxes above-mentioned contained bones, the remains, in three of them, of prisoners who had died in the Inquisition, and in the other those of a man who, never accused in his lifetime of heresy, had been found guilty of it after his death, when his corpse was 'plucked from his Grave after they had formed a Process against him, as he had left very considerable Riches'. The effigies carried on poles with the boxes represented these four deceased. The bones and the effigies were burnt at the place where the man and the woman suffered death.

Dellon records that the portraits of all those burnt at the stake were hung in the Dominican Church. Each face was painted surrounded by flames. 'These terrible representations are placed in the Nave of the Church as so many illustrious Trophies consecrated to the Glory of the Holy Office', he adds with bitter sarcasm.

While the execution was being carried out, he was back in his cell. 'I was so weary and so sore at my return from the Act of Faith,' he writes, 'that I had almost no less desire to re-enter my Lodging to rest my self than I had before to go out of it.' Indeed, the head gaoler on taking charge of him again from the Admiral only led him as far as the gallery, leaving him to walk on alone and shut himself in. He lay down on his bed, hoping for supper. This came at last, but instead of being fish or curry, the usual evening meal, consisted only of bread and figs, for the cooks had taken a holiday and were still out watching the burning.

He slept better that night than he had for a long time. At six o'clock the next morning the head gaoler came to get the clothes he had worn at the *auto-da-fé*, not the *sanbenito*, for that he would have to put on when he left the prison, but the striped blouse and trousers which had been underneath it. At seven his breakfast appeared and he was told to pack, an order which he obeyed 'with all possible diligence'. At nine o'clock his door was opened for the last time and with his luggage on his shoulder he was taken to the hall with the green silk hangings and the huge crucifix. Most of the convicted prisoners were already assembled there. Some had received sentences of whipping, the hangman having already carried them out. The Inquisitor appeared and took his seat at the great table. 'We fell upon our knees to receive his blessing, after we had kissed the ground near his Feet,' says Dellon.

The prisoners then were disposed of according to their sentences. Numbers of them, it appears, were not Christians at all, but Hindus or Mohammedans who had incurred the displeasure of the Inquisition on one or other of the grounds we have previously noted. Of these some were ordered to leave Goa (a happy sentence one would think, though if they were shopkeepers and all their goods were confiscated, it may have meant ruin). Others were condemned to hard labour in the Arsenal, and a few to the local galleys. The Christians, both European and Asiatic, were to go to a house in the town, there to undergo certain preliminary instruction. Dellon, with his sentence of deportation to the galleys of Portugal, was sent along with them. An Indian shouldered his trunk for him, which was light enough, for though they had made a careful inventory of his possessions on arrival, anything of value had been confiscated.

It was January the 13th and he remained in the house for ten days in semi-imprisonment until the ship on which he was to embark for Portugal was ready to sail. It is interesting to note that the Prior of the Dominicans at Daman, a monk with whom he had actually been staying when he became involved with the persons who informed against him, came to see him now, embraced him tenderly, and wept at his disaster. This prior apparently considered that he had been harshly treated, and had even interceded with the Procurator of the Inquisition on his behalf at some period during his imprisonment. But though a leading Dominican he had no influence whatever with the Inquisitors. The tribunal had absolute power to take action in defence of the Faith and not even senior members of the Order with which it was so closely connected could hope to move it in favour of prisoners. The only information vouchsafed to this kind monk when he went to see the Procurator, also a Dominican, was that Dellon still lived.

Now he showed his good heart by procuring for him provisions for the voyage, without which he might never have reached Lisbon alive.

On 23 January he was summoned finally before the Grand Inquisitor and made to swear that 'he should keep exactly the secret of all which he had seen, heard or said or which had been acted concerning him either at the Table or at any place of the Holy Office'. It was this oath, taken on the Gospel, which made him hesitate for ten years to publish his history.

That night, preparatory to embarking, he was lodged in the Archbishop's prison, the infamous Al Jabir, a dungeon similar to the Salle to which Pyrard was sent, dark, stifling, and filthy, crowded with galley slaves. But now he himself was a galley slave, and such a horror had he taken of the Inquisition and his solitary cell, clean though it was, that the Al Jabir seemed human, and, so, happy in comparison. After being there forty-eight hours, he says, 'An Officer of the Holy Office, clapping Irons upon my feet, carried me to a Ship which was in the Road'. They weighed anchor on 27 January and making a very fast passage reached Brazil in May, remaining until September, awaiting a good wind. Dellon was shut up at night in the local prison, but allowed in the daytime to stroll about the town.

On the passage from Brazil to Lisbon he had a narrow escape, not from drowning or other mishap of shipboard, but of being declared a relapsed heretic. A certain friar was celebrating Mass. When Dellon approached the Holy Table to receive the Sacrament he shut his eyes out of devotion. The friar, who had a prejudice against him because he had been convicted by the Inquisition, sent for him afterwards and declared that his conduct smelt of heresy, 'since I vouchsafed not so much as to look upon our Lord, when he was presented to me in the Communion'. Dellon was much alarmed at this accusation. On arrival at Lisbon he would be in reach of the Inquisition again. If this friar chose to lay a complaint against him he might find himself charged with relapsing, when nothing could save him from the stake. He hastened to apologize in the most contrite manner, assuring the friar that his motive in closing his eyes had been wholly that 'of humbling myself in the presence of God'. It was with difficulty that he succeeded in soothing the fanatic, who accepted the explanation with very bad grace.

Galleys, in the proper sense of that term, had been abolished in

Portugal some time before this date, and when Dellon was handed over to the authorities at Lisbon he was not, as he would have been some years earlier, chained to an oar and sent to sea to row a man-of-war in some expedition against pirates, but was consigned to a prison near the docks called the Galley, in which all criminals, who had received from either a lay or ecclesiastical court the old-fashioned sentence of so many years in the galleys, were incarcerated and sent to hard labour. On arrival there, he was chained by the foot to another victim of the Inquisition, a Portuguese who, he learnt, had escaped the fire by confessing the evening before he was to be burnt. Most of the other prisoners, he found, were either fugitive and incorrigible slaves or Turks who had been taken prisoner on the pirate ships of Barbary. He was later to meet a few educated men of his own class.

The work was hard and the overseers brutal. Every morning early, except on a very few festival days, the slaves were marched from the Galley to the docks and there set to unloading ships, stowing cargoes, and collecting ballast. All the prisoners, no matter what their rank in life, were employed on such labours 'unless they have money to give the Officers who conduct them and who exercise an unheard-of cruelty upon those who cannot mollifie them somewhat from time to time'.

The hours of work were from dawn till eleven, and from one o'clock till the sun set, when they returned to the Galley, chained in couples, and slept chained in dormitories. Their rations were a pound and a half of ship's biscuit a day, and six pounds of salt fish a month with vegetables, though they could supplement them from charitable persons outside. Priests would call to give spiritual comfort. In short, the Galley was less rigid than a modern prison, and, if it was managed with more brutality, there were compensations that prisoners do not find to-day. You were not cut off from outside succour; private benevolence could have its way; and if you wanted to visit the town, a warder would take you there if you paid him. 'The liberty of seeing and speaking to the whole world rendered it much less troublesome to me than the horrible Solitude of the Inquisition,' says Dellon. The day after his arrival he was shaved, given prison clothes, and set to work with the other galley slaves. Five years of penal servitude had to pass before he could hope to see his country again. 'There was no great appearance that any favour would be showed to a man who had spoken against the Integrity and Infallibility of the Holy Office.'

Yet he began at once to cast about how he might obtain the ear of influential persons.

Inquiring whether any fellow countrymen lived in Lisbon, he was delighted to learn that the Queen of Portugal's physician was French and, moreover, that he was popular with the grandees of the Court. He appealed to him at once, begging his protection, which he gave 'in the most obliging manner in the World, offering not only his interest in all things which lay in his power, but also his Purse and his Table, where he did me the honour to give me a place, enchained as I was, whensoever Liberty of going to him was granted me'. Here again we have the human element mitigating the barbarity of the law, which had lagged behind the best public opinion.

All this was pleasant enough, but it did not produce immediately any practical result. The Queen was approached but apparently nothing could be done at the moment. Dellon also wrote to his relations in France, acquainting them for the first time with his situation and beseeching them to use what interest they possessed.

Later, on the advice of his friend, the Court Physician, he presented a petition to the Inquisition of Lisbon, setting out his case and asking for a reduction of sentence. But no answer was given, though he sent several reminders. Eventually he learned that a new Grand Inquisitor had only recently been appointed and had not yet taken up his residence.

Three months passed. Then towards Holy Week, 1677, the Grand Inquisitor arrived. But during the Easter celebrations no official business was done, and it was not until after Quasimodo Sunday that the Tribunal opened. Whereupon Dellon immediately presented a fresh petition, which reached Dom Verissimo de Lancastre, such being the Grand Inquisitor's name, and to which he gave answer that he could not believe what was stated in it, 'there being no appearance that they would have condemned a man to serve 5 years in the Gallies for matters of so little consequence'.

Dellon then wrote entreating him to read his process, for it seems that a copy of the proceedings relating to his condemnation in Goa had been forwarded with him. On this application the secretariat of the Inquisition noted that, as no appeal lay from a decision by the Grand Inquisitor of Goa, his status being equal to that of the Grand Inquisitor at Lisbon, it would be improper, indeed illegal, to review the process.

That would normally have been the end of the matter had Dom Verissimo been a bureaucrat. Though at first he declared it impossible for him to do more, his niece, the Countess of Figveirol, 'who had a very particular esteem for the first Physician of the Queen', talked him round till he assented, with the charming smile for which he was noted, to have the process read aloud to him. Finding that no further charges than those stated in Dellon's original petition were contained in it, he repeated his view that the sentence was excessive. As he was not an appellate authority, he carefully refrained from passing any order on the process, but calling for the last of Dellon's petitions wrote at the bottom: 'Let him be set at Liberty as he desireth and let him return to France.'

This good news was conveyed to Dellon by a Familiar of the Holy Office on 1 June 1677. Nearly four years had elapsed since his arrest in Daman. He felt 'a joy which persons who have not suffered Captivity will scarce be able to conceive'.

But he was not yet completely out of the clutches of the Inquisition. For another whole month he was to remain in chains. As often happens in an office, the secretarial staff were not too pleased at their chief having taken the law into his own hands, contrary to the legal opinion which they had submitted. Accordingly, they decided to put an interpretation on his hastily scribbled order which it was not intended to, but might, bear. Instead of the words 'let him return to France' being allowed to stand for an additional favour, they were declared to be mandatory and, moreover, to mean that Dellon was not to be set at liberty until he had actually embarked for France. When, therefore, he asked the Familiar to inform the Governor of the Galley prison that he was free and desire him accordingly to strike off his irons, the fellow expressed surprise, drew his attention to the proviso, and admonished him to seek a ship with all expedition.

At the moment Dellon did not fully appreciate the malice of the trick which had been played on him. It was not until he had obtained leave of absence and gone to the wharves from which ships sailed to France that he discovered how difficult it was, dressed in prison garb, dragging his chain and with a limited time at his disposal, to get the shipping clerks to listen to his request for a passage or, indeed, to find out when a ship was sailing. The gaolers refused to let him hang about the pier and he soon perceived that unless he were first liberated he could not arrange the matter of his departure. He therefore memorialized the Inquisition to that effect.

Days, weeks passed and no answer was received. Finally, on 28 June he was informed that if he entered into recognizances with one surety in four hundred crowns for his early departure, he would be released.

Knowing at last exactly how he stood, he went to his good friend the Court Physician (he does not give his name out of discretion) and asked him to finish what he had so kindly begun. 'Some urgent affairs hindered him from going the same day to the Inquisition, but going thither the 30th of the same month in the morning gave caution for me.'

That afternoon they sent a Familiar to the Galley and Dellon's irons were at last struck off. He was then taken to the Inquisition and formally declared at liberty. 'I answered only with a profound reverence,' he says, 'and as soon as I had set foot out of this terrible House, I went into the next Church to render thanks to God and the Holy Virgin.'

His second action was to call and thank the French doctor, who wept and embraced him with tears of joy. Thence he returned to the Galley to collect what little luggage remained to him and to say good-bye to 'these poor afflicted Persons, who had been the companions of my Misfortune', with some of whom he had become warm friends. Dressed in his own clothes again, he went to the pier, and it was not long before he found a ship willing to take him 'and', he writes, concluding his narrative, 'I had the happiness to arrive in my Country in perfect Health'.

The reader of Dr. Dellon's story will have been struck by the difference between the Inquisition and the Society of Jesus. The second with its modern hospital, its up-to-date college, its attitude towards the Hindus exemplified in the careers of Xavier and de Nobili, has a pleasing freshness compared with the haunted atmosphere of the Santa Casa. Yet, perhaps, the first was more characteristic of the Goa we have been describing. That city of fidalgos and slaves, with its murders, its adulteries, its poisons, its ignorance, was of a piece with the spectral hall where under the crucifix reared to the ceiling the Grand Inquisitor sat at the giant table.

11

THE AUGUSTINIANS

There is one further visit to make before we can leave the baroque city and set out with Friar Sebastião Manrique on his travels. This is to the Augustinian monastery, the Convent of our Lady of Grace as it was called, where Manrique lived for many years.

The Augustinians arrived at Goa later than the Dominicans and the Jesuits, and began to build their monastery in 1572. This occupied some time, for to the monastery proper they added a church, a college, and a novitiate. These buildings were situated two or three hundred yards to the west of the Jesuits' House on a slope which commanded a view of the harbour. Albert de Mandelslo called there a few days subsequent to his visit to the Professed House in 1639. It was, indeed, one of the show places in Goa. Coltineau, another traveller of the period, declared the monastery itself to be the best building in a city of magnificent buildings. Mandelslo, taking a palanquin at the wharf, was carried to it in the cool brightness of a January morning. He was much impressed. 'It is seated', he writes, 'upon a little eminency, so that, seeing it at a certain distance a man would take it for one of the noblest palaces in the world. The Friers carried us all about it and shew'd us particularly the rich copes and other priests' vestments.' The Augustinians still retained their original name of Hermits of St. Augustine, by which they had been called when they were begging recluses in the eleventh century. In the thirteenth they were organized by the Pope under a General and during the next three hundred years their monasteries spread over Europe and into Asia, and from being begging friars they became a rich community. In Goa they lived in great state. The group of buildings was like a small university. There were a fine library, an excellent picture gallery, vast dormitories, and a great number of cells, resembling, rather, private studies. The chapel, with its Gothic choir, was surmounted by two towers, which contained the largest bells in the city, one of them weighing 4,800 pounds. The pillared cloisters round the quadrangle, and the garden outside, completed the appearance of a college.

The Augustinians were, after the Dominicans, the most influential body in Goa at this period. Dom Fr. Aleixo de Menezes,

Archbishop and first Primate of Asia from 1595 to 1610, was of their Order. Their Provincial was a prominent grandee. We have seen one of them preaching at an *auto-da-fé*. If the Dominicans can be described as the police of the Church in Portuguese Asia, and the Jesuits as its diplomatists, by the same analogy the Augustinians may be spoken of as its preachers and missionaries. The reader will immediately think of exceptions to this classification. Xavier the first Jesuit was pre-eminently a missionary; the Jesuit College of Santa Fé was largely an establishment for educating the children of converted Asiatics; Menezes on the other hand was a man of affairs, and by his persecution of the Nestorians had something of the Dominican fervour; and as we shall see, Manrique had his diplomatic triumphs. On the whole, however, particularly at this date, the Augustinians were distinguished above the others for their missionary organization. They had an important monastery at Cochin, in Malabar, the clergy of the place being all under their control and the right to evangelize restricted to their Order. And they were the leading Order in Bengal, where they had churches and monasteries at a number of towns, the most important of which was Hugli, a trading post some twenty-five miles north of the site of the present city of Calcutta, which the Mughal Emperor, Akbar, had permitted the Portuguese to build in 1580.

From Hugli missionary settlements had spread to Chittagong and eastwards along the coast of the Bay of Bengal. These activities had as a rule nothing dramatic or spectacular about them. The Augustinians sought to convert the local inhabitants in a manner which did not differ from that of modern missionaries. They were more practical, more prudent, and more modest than the Jesuits. They do not seem to have expected a grand conversion of the Orient, and were content to labour in their Master's vineyard and gather such fruits as they reasonably might. Yet sometimes it fell to their friars to undertake duties of an extraordinary kind. Such was the experience of Fr. Sebastião Manrique.

IV

Friar Manrique Sets Out

In 1628 Manrique, as he says, 'was a member of the community of our monastery at Cochin', a fort and settlement near the toe of India, within the dominions of the Hindu King of Cochin. The date of his transfer from Goa is unknown. In this year he was selected by the Provincial of the Augustinians to proceed to the Order's monastery at Hugli in Bengal. In May a passage was booked for him and another friar, Gregorio de los Angeles, on a merchant vessel, by chance named the *St. Augustine*, which was sailing to Hugli with a cargo of conches, those great shells which, made into trumpets, are blown in Hindu temples, and which, cut into suitable shapes and decorated with gilding, were then widely used by women as ornaments. The consignment was worth eight lakhs of rupees, between £60,000 and £80,000 at the modern exchange. The captain, the master, and the pilot were Portuguese, the crew Moslems, the passengers Indians of various types, some of them being the wives of the crew. They numbered altogether more than two hundred.

On 6 May the vessel, having crossed the bar, was ready to sail and a message was sent to the monastery, requesting the two friars to embark that day. The monks assembled in the chapel to pray for a safe voyage, the Office for such occasions, the *Itinerarium*, being chanted. Manrique and his companion, de los Angeles, then rowed off to the *St. Augustine*, which shortly afterwards weighed and stood out. The south-west monsoon had not yet established itself and the wind was variable. It failed them altogether before they reached Cape Comorin, and for a fortnight they lay becalmed on a glassy sea, the sun beating upon them with all the force of the Indian hot weather. But this calm was a prelude to the breaking of the monsoon. A stiff breeze came at last, which carried them round the Cape and up the Bay of Bengal at such a steady pace that they found themselves in a fortnight at the mouth of the Hugli river, a branch of the Ganges delta.

This river is used to-day by all steamers going to Calcutta. The pilot service of that city is composed of men who have specialized in its navigation, which is notoriously dangerous with shifting banks and quicksands that have swallowed many a ship. In the seventeenth century it was known in English as the Braces of Bengala, the word having, it is said, the meaning through the Portuguese of 'embrace', the fatal embrace of the quicksands. But it also has to do with sounding the depth, and as Manrique's ship cautiously entered the wide mouth, the lead was cast without intermission.

Here, of course, it was calm, the monsoon blowing like a yachting breeze over the tidal water. The friars arranged an altar on the stern and made ready to celebrate a thanksgiving Mass. But shortly before noon, 'while we were going thus agreeably under a serene sky and counting the fathoms', the *St. Augustine* slid silently on to a bank.

It was the bottom of the ebb and, provided the bank were not a quicksand, there was no reason why the flood should not refloat the ship. But the shock of running aground had strained her timbers. The seams opened and she began to fill with water. Pumps were set to work, but now a curious state of things was revealed. The sea got into the conches and though the pumps cleared the hold they could not suck the water out of the shells. The weight of the cargo was thus enormously increased, and when the tide rose the ship was too heavily laden to lift, and remained lying on the bank. Luckily it was not a quicksand, but the situation was bad enough. If she did not lift before the water reached the decks, they would all be drowned. There were no lifeboats. The flat western shore was just visible a mile distant. But they had no means whatever of reaching it.

The pilot, who had been that way thirteen times before without mishap, was at his wits' end. To lighten the ship's burden he advised the captain to have the masts cut down. All hands were employed to throw as many of the shells overboard as possible. But still the ship showed no signs of lifting. In a desperate state of mind the pilot begged the friars to pray.

As the narrative proceeds Manrique's character will emerge. In the present crisis he remained perfectly calm. On learning from the pilot of the dangers which threatened them, he decided to confess those of the passengers who were Catholics. 'Placing myself at the bow and de los Angeles going to the stern, we confessed them all as far as it was possible in the limited time, amidst the lamentations of the women and children, and the noise and confusion caused by the cutting of the masts,' he writes.

When this was done, it occurred to him that here was an opportunity of making some converts. Humanity in a crisis is a prey to ghostly fears, and as there were no Hindu or Moslem priests on board to give spiritual succour, he hoped the passengers would accept what he could offer. Accordingly, taking his crucifix from his neck and holding it before him, he went to the cabin where the wives of the Moslem sailors were huddled. Speaking to them in Hindustani, a language he knew tolerably well, he pointed out the hideous fact that they were in anger of losing, not only their lives, but also their souls, and adding, as he says, 'whatever God inspired me to in that extremity'. But it was no good. Favourable though the circumstances were, he failed to make any impression. He opines that this lack of success may have been due to his own sins; perhaps he was not thought worthy to be an instrument of divine solace. But there seems also to have been a practical reason, for he states: 'an accursed old creature started dissuading them and reminding them of the promises of their false prophet.'

In spite of the cutting of the masts and the jettisoning of part of the cargo, the ship remained grounded. If she lifted at all, the tide only drove her further on to the bank, the swell bumping her along the bottom and increasing the leaks. It looked as if she must break up, and panic increased among the passengers. While some people were hastily tying planks together to make rafts, others attacked them in the mindless way that men behave when their reason is numbed with fear. There was a horrible scene of screaming and devilry. The captain was unable to do anything with them. Manrique tried to help him, crucifix in hand. 'In the end the mob quieted down, for there is great respect in those parts for priests', he notes.

But things were very bad; the wind freshened and the ship, which now began to float, the decks nearly awash, became unmanageable and struck another shoal. It seemed impossible that her timbers could hold longer. Then de los Angeles remembered that they had in their baggage a relic of one of the Augustinian saints, Juan de Sagun. It was decided to try what this would do. In order to bring the saint into direct contact with the water, the element which threatened them, de los Angeles attached the relic to a tape and threw it overboard. The passengers, who had reached the limit of terror and despair, experienced now an extraordinary relief of mind. They began to hope, for they knew well that nothing was so potent as a holy relic, and readily believed, when los Angeles declared it, that the morsel of the saint now trailing in the water, would drag the ship safely to the shore. So intense was their relief that most of them, says Manrique, knelt silently weeping. And, sure enough, the saint did drag them ashore. It seems that at the top of the flood they were swept clear of the shoals and stranded on the west bank of the river. De los Angeles then pulled in the relic, and, undoing the tape, put it back in his luggage.

That a relic was charged with occult force was not a delusion of the ignorant but the view held by everyone at that date. For instance, in 1632, four years after the events here described, Cardinal Richelieu, the leader of France, sent to Meaux for relics of the seventh-century Irish hermit, St. Fiacre, under the impression that they would cure his piles. They were applied, but failed, though this did not hurt their reputation: evidence to prove the efficacy of relics was too overwhelming. Had not the dried corpse of St. Isidore, placed in Philip III's bed, saved that king from death a few years earlier? And soon Philip IV would be held to have died bewitched, because among the authentic relics which he wore round his neck certain images made by a sorcerer had been feloniously inserted, which annulled the good influences emanating from the relics, and themselves radiated an evil influence. On the other hand, the Chinese Board of Rites, a body composed of highly educated Confucian scholars, took the view that relics of Christian saints were possessed of powers likely to be malignant, and in 1600 advised the Emperor Wan Li not to accept bones presented by Ricci, the Jesuit. Similarly, the Goanese ecclesiastical authorities considered so highly dangerous to them a tooth-relic of the Buddha which came into their hands in 1560, that they ground it to powder and threw it into the sea.

It was, therefore, no reflection whatever upon Manrique's intelligence that he believed St. Juan de Sagun's bone saved the ship. The Catholic Indians, of course, shared his view, and no doubt the Moslems on board found it natural that St. Juan, a patron of the Augustinian Order, should exert himself on behalf of the two friars.

V

riar Manrique in anger of Decapitation

Night had fallen when the ship stranded. At dawn they took their bearings. Orissa was the name of the territory thereabouts. It had recently become part of the Mughal dominion. The chief town of the immediate district was Hijli, distant about nine miles It was a lonely, flat, and marshy shore.

The first thing the Captain did was to order the crew to arm themselves and load the small cannon which the ship carried. The powder, however, was found to be damp, and the pieces, probably one-inch falconets, were charged with what dry powder the passengers had in their flasks. These precautions were very necessary, for as soon as the news spread that a merchant ship was ashore every rascal in the place would arrive eager for loot.

Before this could happen, they were observed by a river patrol belonging to the Governor of Hijli. The officer in charge anchored his galley close by. There was a standing custom, common to all countries in the Bay of Bengal, that the cargo of a wreck became the property of the local authority. The Captain, whose name was Pires Comacho, was aware of this, but he also knew there was room for bargaining. When the officer of the patrol raised the point, which he did immediately on coming aboard, Comacho replied that, of course, the Portuguese would abide by the custom. His intention, however, was to bribe the officer to let him proceed up the river to Hugli, as soon as he could refloat the ship and rig her with a jurymast. How much or how little was the officer prepared to take and what assistance would he give—that was the real point.

When the tide ebbed towards midday it became possible to wade ashore. Manrique and de los Angeles immediately did so, because they wished to get in touch with a certain Emmanuel de la Esperança, the Vicar of the Augustinian monastery at Hijli.

Accordingly they wrote him a letter, describing what had happened and asking him to arrange transport for them to Hijli and thence on to Hugli, as it was impossible to say what might happen to the ship. A man was found to take the letter.

This turned out, however, to have been an unfortunate move. Had the Captain and the patrol officer been left to arrange matters between themselves, all might have been well. The letter had the effect of bringing a third party on the scene. The man carrying it was stopped before he got to Hijli by the Commandant of Military Police, who happened to be on tour with a mounted force. When this officer gathered from the messenger that a Portuguese ship was ashore, he immediately decided to cut out the river patrol and himself do the squeezing he guessed was in progress. As his force consisted of three hundred men, he should be able to frighten the Portuguese effectively. Giving the order to gallop, he arrived within the hour.

His methods were more brusque than those of his colleague, who no doubt thought it prudent not to provoke the Portuguese past bearing, having regard to their firearms. Directing his men to board the ship, open the hatchways and the luggage of the passengers, he himself sent for the Captain and the friars.

Opening the conversation in an insinuating manner, he asked Comacho to be good enough to let him have the keys of the chests on board. Comacho replied that the chests were private property and the keys were with their owners, adding sarcastically that in any case the Commandant had no need of keys, seeing that his men had already broached the chests and hatchways.

The Commandant then played his next card. With apparent ferocity he gave orders that the Captain and one of the friars should be decapitated forthwith. 'Thereupon, they seized the Captain and myself, who stood nearest to him,' writes Manrique. 'I was seriously frightened, but took heart when I saw the Captain laugh.' Comacho was a man of great experience. He knew the methods of the Mughal officials. He also knew that the Commandant could not proceed to extremities. If he made too much noise, his superior officers would hear, and if they heard, they would take charge and he would get nothing.

However, he made a great effort to intimidate the Captain, so as to be able to raise his price, telling his peons to bind both him and Manrique. Shouting and threatening, the fellows dragged them away as if to immediate execution. In spite of the Captain's reassurance, Manrique found the experience unnerving. The pantomime was so realistic. He was stripped except for his underwear, and when a certain spot was reached, the peons brandished their scimitars and made as if to behead him.

But all the time bargaining was actually going on. Comacho would make an offer, which was conveyed to the Commandant, who would indignantly refuse it and tell his henchmen to begin threatening again. Comacho would then increase his offer. This went on all night, Manrique never being sure that the next moment might not be his last, for he does not seem to have fully grasped the situation. The point was that the Commandant was an official, not a bandit. While it was his duty under the law to seize the cargo in the name of the government, what he wanted was a bribe to let it go through. The Captain was quite willing to bribe him. The whole bother was about the amount.

Just before dawn the figure was agreed on. The peons' manner to their two captives immediately changed. They became all politeness, cut the bonds, returned the clothes, offered betel, a token of good fellowship, and intimated that the Commandant was expecting them for breakfast.

Adjourning to his tent, they found the table spread. Nothing could have been more charming now than the Commandant's smile. With the utmost cordiality he invited them to sit down. The servants loaded their plates with food, the meal lasting nearly an hour.

But the comedy was not yet over. Though the Commandant had intercepted Manrique's messenger to Friar Emmanuel at Hijli, the letter appears to have reached him in the end. He immediately went to the Governor and explained the situation. Now if the Governor's subordinates wished to pass the *St. Augustine* secretly through to Hugli, he for his part, as subordinate to the Viceroy of Dacca, had a similar ambition. The first step was to take the matter out of the hands of his underlings.

Not long after breakfast the Commandant was disagreeably surprised to receive from his chief written instructions to send the Captain, the friars, and the ship's papers to Hijliwithout delay. He could only comply. His night-long bargaining had come to nothing. The plum which he had snatched from the riverine police had in turn been snatched from him.

Friar Emmanuel had himself come down with the Governor's emissaries so as to be able to assist his brother Augustinians. Palanquins were provided for the Captain and the ecclesiastics. But as the passengers also wanted to go to Hijli they felt obliged to let certain ladies travel in these vehicles. The nine miles to the town was no easy walk. The monsoon had converted the flat country into a swamp. 'To me these three leagues seemed three thousand,' wrote Manrique. 'The roadways were like bogs and in places the water was up to our waists.' They reached their destination at nightfall, covered with dirt and exhausted with the heat. The friars went straight to the Augustinian monastery. Bedraggled as they were, they entered the chapel to return thanks. Then in a pond in the garden, the monks' washing-place, they got rid of the mud with which they were caked.

Three days later they were all summoned to appear before the Governor. Friar Emmanuel took them to the audience-hall of the palace. Here they waited for a while, watching some gentlemen play chess. Presently a gong was sounded and the Governor, coming in, took his seat on cushions under a canopy. Friar Emmanuel with a low bow presented Manrique and de los Angeles, who were invited to sit among the local notabilities. Comacho was present with the ship's papers.

It is clear from what follows that not only had the Vicar of the Augustinian monastery some standing at Hijli, but also that the Governor was on good terms generally with the Portuguese at Hugli. No doubt the existence of that trade emporium up the river, where goods carried in Portuguese ships from Malacca and China were exchanged for Indian products, provided him and his merchants with an excellent market. The prosperity of Hijli must at that time have largely depended upon amicable relations with Hugli. It would be stupid to invoke the letter of the law and confiscate the cargo, particularly as the Viceroy of Dacca would then claim it. Far better to let it through, taking his private percentage. However, he had too great a sense of his own importance to bargain directly. After polite inquiries for the health of Dom Francisco da Gama, the then Viceroy of Goa, who, in point of fact, had recently been recalled to Lisbon to answer charges of peculation—a misfortune to which no reference was made—he withdrew, directing officials of the Treasury to talk business with the Captain, and genially expressing the belief that a settlement quite satisfactory to both sides could be reached.

But just as he had intruded so unseasonably upon the Commandant, so now his own chief, the Viceroy of Dacca, intruded upon him, for a dispatch-runner arrived from that city, which was over two hundred miles away. These runners, called Jalabdārs, were able to cover enormous distances—it is said fifty miles a day—but even so it is an astonishing thing that the news of the grounding of the *St. Augustine* should have reached Dacca and that the Viceroy should have acted upon it, all in the span of about a week. Yet this was so, for the runner seems to have arrived the day after the audience. His dispatches were such that the Governor had no option but to order the Captain and the friars to proceed to Dacca at once. We can only suppose that, the cargo being so valuable, hope of reward had urged the informers, and greed the Viceroy, to more than ordinary exertions and dispatch.

A warning that the friars might have to travel to Dacca was sent to Emmanuel de la Esperanza by a friend of his, a eunuch employed at the palace. Such a journey would be an intolerable inconvenience. The Vicar resolved to get his guests off to Hugli that very night before the Governor's order was served on them. A boat was hired; Manrique and Los Angeles both disguised were smuggled on board; and four armed Portuguese and two slaves were provided as an escort. After dark they rowed down to the main river and in this way reached Hugli, a hundred miles upstream. What eventually happened to the *St. Augustine* and its cargo we are not told.

VI

Demonism

The town of Hugli was not properly part of Portuguese Asia. It did not come into the scheme of that line of fortresses from Aden to Malacca and beyond, with Goa as their central point, which guarded the flow of trade from Asia to Europe. It was not a fort at all nor was it subject to the jurisdiction of the Viceroy of Goa.

Though a Portuguese settlement of importance, its creation was rather a private venture, and the trade it handled was Asiatic trade, that is to say, the exchange of one kind of Asiatic product for another, not the exchange of Asiatic for European commodities. Such trade was later called by the English the country trade.

Hugli came into existence in the most natural way. With the establishment of the Mughal capital in Upper India in the middle of the sixteenth century—a rich and luxurious Court, and like all such societies with a liking for novelties—there arose a brisk demand for certain Chinese luxury products, like porcelain, jade, silk, and embroideries. The Moslem traders, who had previously supplied these goods, having been driven off the sea, a lucrative opening awaited any Portuguese merchants with the enterprise to provide what the Court wanted.

This opening was not taken up by the Lisbon merchants who handled the commerce between East and West. But adventurers saw their chance. They began in a small way. Sailing into the Braces of Bengala and past Hijli, they obtained permission from the local authorities at the village, afterwards to be the town, of Hugli, to unload their cargoes and erect warehouses. The articles they brought were calculated to attract the attention of the Court, and in due course did attract it, the Emperor Akbar in 1577 sending for the leading Portuguese merchant adventurer of the day, a gentleman by the name of Pedro Tavares. It was the perfect business opportunity and Tavares made full use of it. He guaranteed an annual delivery of such Chinese *objets de luxe* as might be required, provided that he was allowed to build a substantial town at Hugli for the permanent residence of his nationals and their priests. Akbar gladly consented and gave instructions to the Viceroy of Dacca, within whose jurisdiction Hugli lay, that every possible facility was to be provided, hinting at the same time that should there be any obstruction in the flow of supplies, the Viceroy would probably lose his appointment.

In such fortunate circumstances it was small wonder that Hugli went ahead very rapidly. The Augustinians arrived in 1599 and raised the necessary money to build a monastery, called after St. Nicholas of Tolentino, and a church, named Our Lady of the Rosary. Trade was by no means confined to the supply of the Court. Articles in general demand were also imported. But, besides genuine merchants and ecclesiastics, men of an undesirable type began to flock to a town where money was so plentiful. Criminals and fugitives from Portuguese Asia found asylum there, as the Governor was neither appointed by, nor subordinate to, Goa, being elected by the inhabitants. It became also a place of resort for pirates and slavers. Soldiers of fortune, who found residence in Goa too restricted for their tastes, arrived in substantial numbers and from thence spread down the coast eastwards to Arakan and Pegu. It was such men who had founded some years earlier, with the permission of the Arakanese king, the trading port of Dianga close to Chittagong, then the frontier town of the Arakenese dominion. Some joined the Arakanese and Burmese service, and there were cases of them setting up independent principalities on islands in the great Bay. We shall hear a great deal more about them, for it was among these bravoes that Manrique was shortly destined to pass the strangest and most exciting years of his life.

For the moment he settled down at the monastery of St. Tolentino to the strict and narrow life of a missionary friar. He continued his study of Hindustani, a language not spoken in south-west India, and was able to become acquainted with the practices of Hinduism far more directly than at Goa, where the Hindu temples had been destroyed. Unlike de Nobili, however, who at this date was still at Madura, he made no attempt to understand its philosophy or to converse with any Brahmin pundits. He was content to observe, and like many others before and since was profoundly shocked by what he saw.

It will not be out of place to hear his description of some of these practices, so that the reader may be in a position to judge whether they were more deplorable than those of the Inquisition at Goa.

Of the appearance of the Hindu temples, he cannot withhold his admiration, and speaks of their majesty, their splendid workmanship, and the riches they contained. The more notable of them are, of course, among the most extraordinary edifices in the world. It was their festivals that he found horrible. 'The most important temple in the kingdom of Bengal,' he observes, 'is that of Jagarnath in Orissa: it stands on the seashore.' He goes on to describe the festival which took place in June, the crowds of pilgrims, the rich offerings, the curious processions of triumphal chariots, the maniacal excitement, the yogis and devotees heavily manacled who on reaching the temple door freed themselves of their chains as if by occult power, the shouting, the wild chants, the scurrying naked mob. As the great car of Jagarnath approaches, the hysteria reaches its climax, and some of the yogis and pilgrims, seized with frenzy, a foam on their lips, fling themselves beneath the wheels and are crushed to death; others thrust into the muscles of their back hooks attached by ropes to a wheel on the top of a pole and are whirled round, like flying boats at a fair, swinging out over the roadway, their blood dripping on the worshippers below, and continuing thus to swing until they are dead.

Such a scene, witnessed in the heyday of Hinduism, before modern legislation, introduced by alien conquerors, had transformed it from a spectacle for the alienist into a bit of local colour for the globe-trotter, must have been horrific in its subliminal force, nor is it surprising that in his description of it Manrique should have referred to the Pit, to the Rebel Angels, and to their Captain, the Devil. Certainly, had Rubens, who was alive at the time, been tempted to make it the subject of a great canvas, his baroque composition would have whirled with demons.

But what the Friar has to say of a festival he witnessed on the island of Saugar, which lies opposite Hijli at the mouth of the Hugli river, is stranger still. At one time Saugar was full of flourishing temples, but had been so frequently looted by Portuguese pirates from Dianga, raiders in the employ of the Arakanese, who kidnapped its inhabitants and sold them as slaves, that when Manrique was there the buildings were in ruins, and it was only on the occasion of a festival of great antiquity and importance that for the time being it was frequented. Then great crowds came from all parts of Bengal, though at the risk of being caught in a pirate raid. Their mood, however, was one of extreme exaltation. Danger of pirates would have seemed a trifle compared with the self-immolation they contemplated.

The pilgrims on reaching the ruined temple, whose festival it was, first had their heads and beards shaved; then they washed in the temple tank and anointed themselves with oil. So purified, they entered the shrine, both men and women, where in the half-light they prostrated themselves before a deity. The music, the conches wailing, hot wafts of scent from flowers or incense, worked on minds open to bewitchment. It seemed that the god would take them if in utmost humility they offered all they had. Prone on the ground they offered him their lives, their tears gushing as they begged his acceptance. Certain at last that he would accept, they rose from the ground and wild with happiness rushed to the beach. Close in, waiting, were a multitude of sharks. In an ecstasy, men and women waded out into the sea. The sharks immediately darted among them. 'Since these are accustomed and thus encouraged by constantly tasting human flesh, they become so bloodthirsty that they rush up fiercely even at a mere shadow,' comments Manrique.

This scene has all the horror of an hallucination. But sometimes it was anticlimactic. Towards the end of the festival the sharks would be so gorged that either they did not wait by the beach or if, indeed, they were there, they swam idly about, at the most nosed the offered victim and rejected him. For him so rejected by a shark it was as if God had rejected him, and he would leave the water overcome with grief, and be inconsolable, for if God had turned away from him, where could he go, what could he do? He was alone in the vastness, there was nothing, the supreme horror of nothing, in front of him.

Now, what can we make of such a scene? To Manrique it was demoniac and that word had then a definite meaning. But for us it has no meaning or we do not know precisely what its meaning is. But we can say, at least, it is the opposite of the reasonable and that it carries with it the sense of extreme evil. Yet were these weeping humble worshippers possessed by what was evil? Yes, says Manrique, and the evil which had invaded them created in their minds a ghastly delusion. The modern psychologist would phrase it differently. Some alienists would explain the Hindus' suicide as due to an uprush of the autonomous psyche. Definitions change with the centuries, but the shift from one set of terms to another leaves the mystery still a mystery. The autonomous psyche can no more be explained than the Devil. In truth, we cannot tell what ailed these poor people, but all our instincts, as sane and reasonable men, tell us that in some way they were grievously deluded.

It will be interesting here to take the view of another traveller, not a Christian, and not a European. Hsüan Tsang, the Chinese metaphysician, who toured India in the middle of the seventh century, visited Allahabad, then called Prayāga, a Hindu town at the confluence of the Ganges and the Jumna. He himself was a Buddhist. At that date in China Buddhism was held in esteem by many Chinese thinkers. But he was also a Confucian in the sense that the sanity, the reasonableness, and the moderation of that ancient system of behaviour, which was part of his country's heritage, ran in his blood. His object in visiting India was to collect Buddhist documents, for Buddhism, though a Hindu revival was gradually sapping it, was still the chief religion in the country. Much of his time had been spent conversing with Buddhist doctors of divinity, and though he was a more civilized, a more balanced, a more—one might almost say—modern thinker than any of those he met, he had enjoyed his disputations, particularly at the University of Nalanda.

His journeys took him, as we have said, to the town of Prayāga, a noted Hindu place of pilgrimage. Like Manrique, he goes out to observe the people, and what he sees was as strange, and he finds it as distasteful.

In the sacred river poles were fixed, each with a peg near the top. He watched devotees climb these poles at dawn. They would place one foot on the peg, hold on with one hand, and stretching out the other hand and foot, hang there all day in mid-air, following the sun with their eyes till at last it set. Then they came down and ate, to recommence next day, and so to continue with no respite.

Demented as such behaviour appears, it was a kind of austerity, though more mindless than the mortifications of a recluse who seeks to subdue the flesh in order to contemplate God. The Hindus seem to have thought that the action itself, useless, exhausting, and unreasonable though it were, would ensure Heaven; but to believe that Heaven could be secured by such an action was hardly less extravagant than that suicide could secure it. Some devotees, says Hsüan Tsang, hung from a pole every day for fifty years. The state of mind of a person when he came to be old, who had thus passed his life, is impossible for us to imagine. No novelist has described such a character, no painter has discovered for us the strange face and eyes of such a creature. His expression would not be wholly that of a madman, for these people were not idiots. Rembrandt, perhaps, might have laid bare his soul. No-one but a great master of oil paint could interpret for us the mystery of his long vigil.

But we have brought in Hsüan Tsang because of his account of the Tree of Death, a story yet more curious than that of the sharks. In the city of Prayāga was a temple to which many people went, but from which all did not return. In front of the principal hall was a great tree. To right and left of it were piles of human bones. Worshippers would climb the tree and, becoming curiously obsessed, would throw themselves from it, in the belief that suicide at that particular spot guaranteed them eternal happiness When Hsüan Tsang was there, a Brahmin philosopher desired to demonstrate the falsity of this superstition. We are not told why he had this desire, whether he was a reformer, a humanitarian, or a publicity seeker, but that he was a metaphysician of repute, a person belonging to the inner circle of the Brahmin hierarchy, is not in doubt. He entered the temple accompanied by his friends. The presiding priests led him respectfully to the foot of the tree; heads shaven, their foreheads painted with symbols of life and death, they waited, not much perturbed that anything he might say or do was likely to put an end to practices which went back to the remotest antiquity.

The philosopher began to address the worshippers. There was an immense crowd of yogis, saddhus, pilgrims, beggars, firm believers that in the tree dwelt a spirit and that if you heard him whispering as you perched among the leaves, then you should jump, for he would carry you to Heaven. The philosopher was encircled by this crowd. He began to speak against the spirit, telling them they were the dupes of a murderous fable. When he had been talking a little while, he was observed to falter, his expression to be abstracted. He stopped and in agitation looked up into the branches. His friends, concerned, laid hold of him, begging him to leave the precincts. The priests and the people waited silently.

Suddenly he was seen to shake off his companions, and turning quickly, to climb the tree and mount into the higher branches. Looking down he again addressed the crowd. 'I hear the spirit,' he cried, 'and I hear his musicians. They are calling upon me to follow them to paradise. They hover about me. What I said was a lie. The spirit is here. It is no criminal fable. This tree is the very gate of Heaven. Only from here can one enter in. Oh! The spirit whispers to me again! He speaks of salvation, eternal happiness.'

In this way he continued to rave. The saddhus, the yogis, the pilgrims, the beggars, sat on their haunches, their faces turned up, waiting confidently for the event. There was an underflow of drumming from the main shrine. Three vultures perched on the topmost bough. Then the Brahmin jumped.

Hsüan Tsang's attitude towards this extraordinary scene does not differ superficially from Manrique's in the matter of the sharks. It was clear, he wrote, that the tree was haunted by a demon and that anyone who climbed into it was tempted to commit suicide. That the author of the *Vijñapti Matrata Siddhi*, the greatest work of Buddhist idealist philosophy produced in seventh-century China, an eclectic *Summa* of immense intellectual force, should have believed in demons may puzzle the reader. Had he been taxed with this, the Master of the Law, as he was called, would have pointed out that there was a difference between relative and absolute belief. A demon had no absolute existence, but in the relative sphere it might be held to exist and to embody that mental disequilibrium which he found to be characteristic of popular Hinduism. Demons there were in popular Buddhism, he would have admitted, but that religion, in its greater sanity, never gave habitation to one in a temple nor allowed that its counsel was sound and it a good spirit.

The judicious reader will perceive that the difference between Hsüan Tsang and Manrique was the difference between an idealist philosopher and a dogmatic theologian. But he will also notice that they agreed in practice and, further, that their practical objection to a demon was that it caused evil delusions, the same objection which the modern psychiatrist has to the inroads of the force labelled the autonomous psyche.

As the history of Manrique proceeds it will be found that he always stands for sanity. He may express himself often in theological jargon and clearly believes in the absolute validity of his jargon. But his terms provide a working hypothesis. We shall return to this point as occasion requires.

The reader was invited earlier in this chapter to consider, on the evidence here adduced—and that evidence necessarily is much circumscribed—whether the practices of the Goanese Inquisition compared well or ill with the practices of Hinduism. In another place the *obiter dictum* was thrown out that if there were cruelties in Hinduism they did not include the condemnation to torture and death of heretics by an ecclesiastical tribunal. That comparison remains sound for there was no such thing in Hinduism as heresy and, consequently, no priestly body empowered to punish it.

Yet it is precisely here that the point of view of the Inquisition merits our attention. Its duty—in theory at least—was to oblige Catholics to follow rules of belief and conduct, which had originally been drawn up to embody what was fair, reasonable, sane, and proper, and so to behave—as Confucian China was admonished to behave—with propriety, consideration, docility, and benevolence. But mankind has always been attracted to commerce with demons. This commerce has taken the form everywhere of sorcery, witchcraft, and black magic. The Catholic Church frowned on such cults for the practical reason, among others, that their devotees ceased to behave like normal men should and became bad citizens, and a danger to society. A great deal of the Inquisition's attention was directed against the crime of magic. We have already seen that the persons condemned to be burnt at the *auto-da-fé* in Goa described by Dellon were sorcerers or persons who had dabbled in the occult. The Hindus, on the other hand, did not discourage such acts. Indeed, as Hsüan Tsang and Manrique show, practices which were nothing but demonology could flourish in a temple or at a temple festival under the very aegis of the priesthood. Suicide was one of the results which the Catholic Church by long experience knew was likely to follow demonry. Other results were moral licence, murder, cruelty, insanity, rebellion, and disorder. All these evils could be checked by forcing the people to abide by Catholic rules and beliefs. If the Inquisition abused its power, becoming corrupt and tyrannous, in principle it stood for moral and mental equilibrium, as did the Church which had set it up.

Nowadays, though belief in demons has faded, the demons themselves, or the hidden force which the term covered and rendered anthropomorphic, ignore their alleged non-existence and—so say the psychologists—invade our consciousness, there being no Inquisition to force it to keep them out, and drive us to the madness and mass suicide which is total war.

This is the real case for the Inquisition and against the kind of Hinduism whose practices we have seen described. If burning heretics kept demoniacism at bay, the most subtle, the deadliest plague that can afflict the human mind, why, then, we were justified, argue the Inquisitors. It is for the reader to bring in the verdict.

VII

Among the Slavers of Dianga

The monastery at Hugli 'stood a shining light in the midst of the vast Paganism of Bengala', says Manrique. He had arrived in June 1628, and a year and three months now went by. When, as it seemed to him, he was just beginning 'fully to appreciate the sweet association of those godly men', the Prior ordered him to go to Dianga to relieve a certain Friar Domingos de la Purificação, who was vicar of that district.

Dianga lay in what is now Eastern Bengal, but then was the North-West Frontier viceroyalty of the Arakanese monarchy. The viceregal capital was Chittagong near the mouth of the Karnaphuli, Dianga being close by on the other side of the river. As for the kingdom of Arakan itself, let it be said for the moment that it was a Mongolian Buddhist state, similar to the Burmese, and had occupied the Hindu territory of Chittagong in the previous century. It stretched some six hundred miles down the littoral of the Bay of Bengal, the north-east frontier marching with the Burmese domain.

On the 11th of September 1629 Manrique embarked on a Portuguese galley which was lying in the river at Hugli. The galley had come from Dianga to sell a cargo, possibly of slaves, for one of the occupations of the Portuguese at Dianga was to make slave raids on the delta villages of the Sundarbans—we have seen how they had made Saugar Island uninhabitable—and sell the Bengalis so kidnapped at Hugli and other ports of India, or to the Arakanese who used them to plough, and to reap the rice crop. Dianga, originally leased by the Arakanese to Portuguese private merchants as a port, had long ceased to be such a place of normal trade. We need not give its history here. Suffice it to say that its merchants turned pirate and gave the Arakanese a great deal of trouble. It had been necessary some years before to reduce them by force of arms. But instead of destroying or driving them out, the King of Arakan had enlisted them in his service as a force to guard his north-west frontier. Their slave raids westwards he encouraged, for it was his policy to harry the Mughal and so discourage him from penetrating further eastwards.

Manrique does not state the route he took to reach Dianga, but as the monsoon was in full force and the sea at the mouth of the Hugli would have been rough, we may safely assume that advantage was taken of the innumerable deltaic waterways. By following their winding courses it was possible to get from the Hugli, the western Ganges mouth, to the main eastern stream formed by the confluence of the Ganges, the Brahmaputra, and the Meghna, and thence, under cover of the islands at its mouth, to skirt along to Dianga in comparatively calm water. The journey was over 350 miles in length and occupied a fortnight, halts included.

The Vicar, Friar Domingos de la Purificação, hearing that a boat was in with a Religious on board, hastened to the wharf, guessing that his relief must have arrived, though who he was or whether an Augustinian he had not been informed. 'When he found out,' writes Manrique, 'that I was a Brother of his own Order, such was his joy that he threw his arms round my neck and for some time was unable to speak to me, so shaken was he with sobs.' When somewhat recovered, he said: 'Beloved Brother, you are most welcome. It is seven years since I last saw a Brother or a Priest. Now God our Lord in His infinite mercy has seen fit to grant me my dearest wish.'

Anyone who has been stationed for a long time in a lonely place in the East will understand the Vicar's emotion. Seven years with no-one to talk to except bravoes of his own nation and the native inhabitants; seven years of tropical sun and rain, of illness—for he was very ill—of a separation from all friends and relatives, much more complete than could ever happen now—that was what he had endured and that was why he wept.

Presently, all animation and happiness, he began to see to Manrique's luggage and took him up to the Residency, close to which was the little wooden church. In accordance with the regulations, a report of the arrival was made to the Arakanese Viceroy. Later, when Friar Domingos came to open the letter which Manrique carried from the Prior of Hugli, he found instructions to proceed to the Augustinian head monastery at Goa for medical treatment, as soon as he had made his relief familiar with the business of the Mission. Manrique learnt from him during the following days something of the circumstances under which he would be working. There were 750 Portuguese, of pure or half blood, resident in Dianga and the neighbouring villages. These men were organized into companies under their captains, to whom the King of Arakan had granted estates. The Arakanese had been watching for generations the gradual expansion over India of the Mughal's power. Before its imperial administration was extended to Bengal, they used to lay claim to large parts of that region. But the Mughals, by overthrowing in 1576 the Moslem dynasty whose capital was at Gaur, had established themselves in western and central Bengal and now confined the Arakanese to the province of Chittagong. This province was purely Indian, nor was it geographically part of the Arakanese kingdom. It followed that the Mughal should hope one day to absorb it. That was the solid reason why the King of Arakan had seen fit to retain the Portuguese in his employ, for these adventurers were the most formidable fighting men in the East, their knowledge of firearms and cannon being more advanced than, and their seamanship superior to, those of the forces of the Mughal.

During the fifty years before Manrique's arrival his compatriots had become more and more closely associated with the Arakanese. A regiment of the bodyguard at the capital, called Mrauk-u, was entirely composed of them. Some had risen to high rank in the Arakanese service: Philip de Brito, for instance, was appointed in 1600 Governor of Syriam, the port of Pegu, after the most successful incursion the Arakanese ever made into Burma, when they carried off the King of Burma's White Elephant and his regalia. There was in the opposite sense the case of Dom Martim, an Arakanese prince, who had fled the country, and been baptized under that name by the Augustinians at Hugli, later residing at their monastery in Goa at the time when Manrique was living there. And Gonsalves Tibao, one of the Dianga Portuguese who had turned pirate, made himself King of Sandwip, an island off the Chittagong coast, and became so bold that in 1616 he attempted to raid the Arakanese capital.

In sum, for the best part of a hundred years the Arakanese had had to do with this particular class of adventurers from Portugal, had seen the good side of them and the bad, had suffered from their treacheries, but had derived profit from their science, until now in 1629 they held them under their thumb.

The Portuguese of Dianga had never acknowledged the Viceroys of Goa as being competent to give them orders, though both de Brito and Tibao liked to treat with them as equals, the former marrying the famous Eurasian beauty, Luisa de Saldanha, the niece of the Viceroy of that name, and the latter persuading the twentieth Viceroy, Dom Jeronimo de Azevedo, to join him in the raid on Mrauk-u. Now their only connection with Goa was through the Augustinians. In point of fact, as mercenaries of Arakan who kidnapped subjects of the Mughal, they were an embarrassment. The Viceroy's policy was to maintain friendly relations with the Empire. He did not want to be accused of collusion in the slave raids.

We have an excellent description of what these raids were like, written by the Mughal nistorian Shiab-ud-din Talish. 'The Arakan pirates, who were both Portuguese and native, used constantly to come by water and plunder Bengal,' he writes. 'They carried off such Hindus and Moslems as they could seize, pierced the palms of their hands, passed thin slips of cane through the holes and shut them huddled together under the decks of their ships. Every morning they flung down some uncooked rice, as we do for fowl. . . . Many noblemen and women of family had to undergo the disgrace of slavery or concubinage. . . . Not a house eventually was left inhabited on either side of the rivers leading from Chittagong to Dacca. . . . The sailors of the Bengal flotilla were so terrified of the pirates that if a hundred armed boats of the former sighted but four of the latter, their crews thought themselves lucky if they could save themselves by flight. . . . Half the pirates' booty went to the King of Arakan.'

These were the ruffians among whom Friar Domingos had lived for seven years; and we can well understand the reason for his loneliness. Manrique was a man of tougher fibre. As will later appear, he was able to win the confidence of the mercenaries and undertake on their behalf important responsibilities.

But at first he was very homesick. On Friar Domingos' departure he was alone at the Residency. It is true that for a time he had as companion a certain Friar Manoel, who must have followed from Hugli. This Brother fell foul of the local Hindus, not on account of the Mission's activities as such, but because on the occasion of a festival he forbade the native Christians, of whom there were a considerable number, to lend carpets and hangings for the decoration of a temple. As we have said, Hinduism has no intolerance in it, so that Friar Manoel's objection to Christians allowing their things to be used in a Hindu shrine seemed preposterous: the Hindus would have lent anything required for a Christian festival. So badly did they take this priest's interference with what had, no doubt, been an established practice, that they put something into his food which killed him after an illness of fifteen days.

It was subsequent to this that Manrique felt the loneliness. He had been accustomed for twenty years to the ordered life of a monastery, where every hour had its planned duty, with the brothers about you and the Prior above, a life of friendship, of studies, of happy discussions, like at a university, and no anxieties, no responsibilities, the evenings so pleasant, those evenings he now found interminable, silent except for sounds in which he had no part, men singing strange choruses, the thudding of temple drums, the voices of the 'vast Paganism' in which he was lost. 'My heart failed me,' he writes; 'I was so overwhelmed with melancholy that, though I tried hard, I could not conceal it. It was terrifying, this new sensation.' The Evil One sought to drive him to despair, making him think how far away he was from home, how never again would he see his parents and brothers. 'Thus assailed I sought the one true remedy, beseeching God to console and use me in His holy service.'

But these were night fears. In the day he was busy enough. The pirates, the slavers, who were his countrymen and co-religionists, helped the Mission in a curious way. When a captain returned to Dianga after a raid, with the holds of his galleys full of Hindu and Moslem peasants, these unfortunates were visited by the friar before they were sold into slavery and, he claims, he was able to convert a very large number of them to the religion of the cruel men who had pierced their hands, and fed them like fowl. The ironic comedy of such a proceeding did not strike him or, if it did, he justified it in this way: the Portuguese in defending the frontier of Arakan against the Mughal were, in effect, continuing the agelong crusade against the Moslem infidel, which had been the glory of Portugal for so many centuries and had inspired da Gama in his voyages eastward. That fact excused the raids in principle. It was true that many, indeed most, of the kidnapped persons were Hindus, but they were resident in the Mughal's dominion and the loss of their labours was a blow to his prosperity. Furthermore, the catastrophe suffered by these innocent persons was only temporal. Their abduction, ruin, enslavement, degradation, were spiritually an extraordinary piece of good fortune for them. Had they remained in their villages, tilling their fields, tending their cows, passing their lives in industry and thrift, happy, simple, but ignorant of the essential truth, they were doomed to eternal punishment in hell. This was the consolation he now was able to bring, as he went among them holding out his crucifix. Let them dry their tears, cease to grieve that they had been torn from their homes, would never see their families again, would pass the rest of their lives in servitude; let them rather rejoice because, when he had baptized them, as baptize them he would if they confessed their errors, their happiness in the next world was certain.

Manrique gives statistics of interest in this connection. He states that on the average 3,400 persons were kidnapped annually and brought to Dianga. Of these he was able to baptize some 2,000 a year. He goes on to say that it was easier to convince these wretched beings than the residents in the Chittagong province, among whom the annual average of conversions was not more than 400. Indeed, this was his experience in general: shock made people more open to reason. His claim that he was causing them to see reason has to do with his experiences at Jagarnath and Saugar Island. He says: 'When the Gospel story was planted in their minds, the extravagances of Hinduism became apparent to them. For Christian truth is so consistent with our natural reasoning, that no-one who has made acquaintance with it can deny its validity.'

This standpoint shows an instinctive grasp of realities. When we compare him with de Nobili, he seems very limited, yet in a way he had a sounder apprehension of the mental dangers to which the great metaphysic of the Atman, in some of its popular forms, exposed the masses. It does not seem that the Jesuit perceived in Hinduism anything demoniacal, that is, in modern phraseology, anything likely to induce psychosis, or he would never have believed it practicable to arrange an adaptation between it and Christianity. But the Augustinian instinctively felt that such an adaptation was impossible, for the only manner in which a man could be cured of the tension which urged him to such hysterical acts as swinging on a hook or giving himself to sharks, was for him to realize that he had been suffering from hallucinations. Having once seen that he was mentally diseased, he cured himself. He could never cure himself unless he recognized that it was a disease, and that recognition would not come to him if he were allowed to believe that an accommodation was possible.

During the year 1629 a raid was undertaken which so annoyed the Mughal authorities that three years later it was cited as one of the reasons for the drastic revenge they took on the Portuguese. The circumstances were as follows. A certain Captain called Diego da Sa, a young man and one of the most daring of the slavers, rowed his galleys to within a few miles of Dacca, the seat of the Mughal viceroy of Bengal, and attacked a village so far beyond the range of the usual Arakanese raids that, though on the river bank, it was considered perfectly safe. A great booty and many prisoners were taken, including a Moslem lady of Sayad family, the family which traced its origin to the Prophet himself. This lady, who was the wife of a senior military officer, a General in command of two thousand horse, had come down from Dacca a few days before with her young daughter to stay with her mother-in-law who had property in the village. As soon as the raid began the two women and the girl got into a covered cart and, attended by some retainers on horseback, tried to escape. As luck would have it, they were detected in their flight by a party of Portuguese and taken to the galleys. The lady herself was a woman of great beauty.

The loot and captives were quickly stowed and the raiders turned for home before the Dacca fleet could come up and attack. Manrique was on the wharf at Angaracale, a village close to Dianga, when da Sa's ships came in. It was a joyful occasion. The galleys were dressed with flags and fired broadsides to announce that the raid had been a particular success. A large crowd collected. The slavers came ashore shouting, singing, gesticulating, and dancing. The prisoners were roughly tumbled out, blinking in the sudden light after the dark holds and, chained together, were marched into Dianga. Their misery and despair did not shock Manrique because his mind was fixed on saving their souls. The Moslem lady, her mother-in-law, and daughter, though not herded with the captive villagers, were exhibited to the crowd. They were weeping.

Among those looking on was a certain Captain. At sight of the lady he became infatuated and approached da Sa to allow her to stay at a friend's house. Da Sa made no objection—his intention was probably to hold her to ransom—and the Captain conducted her and her mother and daughter to the house with every show of respect and consideration. But that very night he induced his friend to let him into her room. She resisted him as long as her strength held out, begged him to kill rather than dishonour her. When it was clear that she would have to submit, she resorted to a stratagem. Pretending that he had persuaded her, she began to return his kisses, and suddenly, when his tongue was between her teeth, she bit off the end of it.

The Captain fell back, the blood pouring from his mouth. He shouted and his friend rushed into the room. It was a terrible scene. The woman was now screaming. The Captain was in agony. They tried to staunch the wound but the blood still gushed out. It seemed that he might bleed to death and a messenger was sent to call Manrique to confess him. In a fury the friend bound the woman's hands and told his servants to take her down to the sea-shore and drown her.

On receiving the message—it was nearly midnight—Manrique set out with his assistants for the Captain's house. It was bright moonlight and as he hastened along the road, which lay beside the beach, he saw some figures walking by the edge of the sea and heard as if one of them were weeping and moaning. Approaching to find out what was happening, he noticed two men slinking away. A woman, her arms tied behind her back, came up to him. He did not recognize her, but his assistants knew her. He questioned her but she was too distraught to speak. 'On this I had her hands set free and consoled her briefly,' he writes, 'and, asking her permission, left her at the first house we came to, in charge of the Magistrate who happened to be with me. I then proceeded on to give confession.'

When he got to the house the Captain was better. The bleeding had stopped and it was unnecessary to confess him. Indeed, any movement of the tongue was to be avoided. Manrique returned to where he had left the lady. 'As soon as she saw me, she fell at my feet, weeping bitterly. I made her get up and sit on a carpet they placed for her, and begged her to believe that no-one would hurt her.' But it was of her daughter and mother-in-law she was thinking. The Friar told her they were well and safe, and would join her as soon as it was light. The conversation continued for some time, the lady telling him of her husband, the General, of his friendship with the Emperor Shah Jehan's son, and about her father, also a high cavalry officer. But presently the thought of her home and her present predicament so overcame her that she fainted. The Friar was much concerned. Ascribing her swoon as much to want of food as to grief, he procured from the Residency what he calls 'a jar of essence', which had been sent him as a present, and this he persuaded her to eat, as soon as she came to, though it was necessary to assure her first that there was no pork in it.

The lady was very beautiful and very temperamental. The circumstances in which Manrique had met her in the moonlight by the water's edge and saved her from death were highly romantic. There was created a certain human bond between them. He began to see his way towards what was always his single purpose. If he gained her confidence and gratitude a little further, there was a chance he might be able to convert her, though the conversion of a Moslem was always difficult and of a Shayad perhaps without precedent. He therefore continued his kind ministrations. During the day he arranged for her and her two companions to lodge with a captain called Pedro Gomez Ravasco, a married man, elderly and decent as slaver captains went. He personally conducted her to the address and after that called regularly to inquire and console her. Gradually he introduced the subject so dear to his heart. Her capture, the capture of all three of them, had been God's will, for nothing can happen against His will. But why had He been so apparently harsh as to allow them to be snatched from home and friends? Because that was the only way their souls might be saved. 'The ladies listened to these arguments with very bad grace, especially the mother-in-law, who was a bigoted Mohammedan,' he writes. What turned the scale, apparently, was the illness and death of the young daughter. Before she died she was won over and baptized, and almost with her last breath declared her happiness and beseeched her mother to follow her example. The dying wish so moved both mother and grandmother that not long afterwards they desired to become Catholics.

The conversion of these Moslem aristocrats was somewhat of an event at Dianga, for though the Portuguese there were bad men they were good Catholics, in the sense that they firmly believed that the Church could save them from the hell they deserved for their evil deeds. The Moslem lady, whose favours had been violently sought by one captain on the day of her arrival, was now, as a Christian lady, courted respectfully by several. Eventually a young Portuguese, the son of noble parents resident at Santaren near Lisbon, won her consent and they were married.

This story came in due course to the ears of the lady's husband and father, and appeared to them so monstrous and disgraceful an affair that they petitioned Shah Jehan to avenge them on the Portuguese of Hugli, whose situation put them wholly at the mercy of the Mughals. This was one of the causes of the attack upon that town in 1632, as will be related.

Busied in this way, Manrique banished the nostalgia which had assailed him at first. The cold weather of 1629 passed into the spring of 1630, and in May the monsoon broke. Shortly after that, when he had been nine months at Dianga, an event occurred which sent him on a journey, the most interesting of his life.

VIII

Startling News

When Manrique came to Dianga the King of Arakan was called Thiri-thu-dhamma, and a cousin of his was Viceroy of Chittagong. This man died and was succeeded in his appointment by a grandee whose name Manrique does not record.

Soon after his installation in the viceregal palace, the Portuguese Captains decided to call and pay their respects. It was the custom on such occasions for the Vicar to accompany them and accordingly Manrique was asked to attend. Dressed in their best clothes the Captains presented themselves at the gate of Chittagong. Slavers though they were, in costume, in swagger, in punctilio of manner they yielded in no way to the gallants Pyrard has described sauntering in Goa. The Viceroy had sent his band to meet them and an escort of elephants. They were conducted to the palace in state, royally entertained to dinner, at which His Excellency declared that he looked to them with confidence to continue their harrying of the territories of the Mughal. The entertainment lasted all night, and included juggling and a ballet. At dawn the Portuguese returned to Dianga, quite satisfied that the new Viceroy was all that he should be.

It appears, however, that he had personal reasons for disliking the Portuguese nation. Manrique states this dislike dated from thirty years earlier. That was the period when the Portuguese were more independent than they were now. Between 1600 and 1617 they had had dreams of making and unmaking the rulers of Mrauk-u. But the Arakanese kings had seen this danger and taken the precaution to engage additional mercenaries, such as Japanese, Afghans, and Burmese, and had, moreover, developed their own fleet. These measures enabled them to keep the Portuguese in their place, though on two occasions, after they had accepted the position of frontiersmen, it had been necessary to send a force to Dianga and punish them for treachery.

It was not difficult, therefore, for the new Viceroy, who, in addition to a personal dislike, had designs of his own, with which the presence of the Portuguese at Dianga interfered, to concoct a story sure to alarm the Court of Arakan and cause it to send another punitive expedition.

The story was that the Portuguese had written to the Mughal Viceroy at Dacca offering in consideration of certain payments to let his troops enter Chittagong that August. This story, supported by a forged correspondence, was embodied in a dispatch and sent to Mrauk-u in May.

As the Viceroy had calculated, King Thiri-thu-dhamma accepted the report without further inquiry: the treachery was so thoroughly typical of the Portuguese. Orders were issued to the Admiral-in-Chief to assemble five hundred galleys and proceed to Dianga before the Mughal could move. If possible he should take the Portuguese by surprise; if he failed in that, he must beleaguer Dianga.

The inhabitants of Mrauk-u very soon noticed that the fleet was mobilizing. This seemed very curious, for the monsoon had begun. To send an expedition at such a time was most unusual and argued a situation of grave urgency. What could it be? It was observed that no Portuguese and Eurasian mercenaries of the capital were being drafted aboard, though these men were the backbone of the navy. The Portuguese community, which was fairly large, became anxious. Could anything be preparing against Dianga? They set about to make inquiries. Some had wives with friends in the palace-city, which, like the Forbidden City in Peking, was the core of Mrauk-u, and where the Court resided.

These women had very little difficulty in getting the truth. The Court was buzzing with it; the numerous princesses, the lesser consorts, their many attendants were talking about nothing else. It was hardly necessary to tip; the story was imparted for the sheer pleasure of telling a secret, though of course on condition that it went no further.

As soon as the Portuguese were sure of the facts, they sent a messenger to Dianga with two letters, one addressed to the Vicar and the other to the Captains, warning them of the danger which threatened from the King. The messenger left on June the 19th and reached Dianga on the 30th, a remarkable feat in the monsoon, as Manrique notes: 'the road lying for over ninety leagues across rough mountains and heavy swamps.' During the open season, from October to May, the route from Mrauk-u to Dianga was by sea along the coast, but in the monsoon the sea was too rough for most boats, and communication was by mountain track. That being so, it may be thought that the Arakanese fleet could not have set out for Dianga until October and accordingly that the messenger need not have hurried. But during the monsoon there are lulls, when the sea subsides for as much as a week. The open sea-passage, being only a hundred miles, could be navigated between storms. Moreover, some of the Arakanese war vessels must have been large ships, as capable of keeping the sea in all weathers as were the Portuguese ships that crossed the oceans.

Manrique was at the Residency when the messenger arrived. He read the letter and was puzzled what to do. The captains and the whole fleet were away on a marauding expedition. There was hardly an armed man left in the place. Then he remembered—one captain had stayed behind, being ill with fever. This was Gonsales Tibao, a nephew or relative of the pirate Tibao who twenty years before had made himself master of Sandwip Island. The young Tibao was one of the principal leaders. Manrique directed the messenger to go to him at once.

When Tibao read the letter he got out of bed, though the fever was still on him, and calling for a palanquin was carried by his negroes at a trot to the Residency. He told Manrique flatly they were in great jeopardy and that some way of meeting it must be devised. Three old Portuguese, long past the fighting age, were sent for, three old slavers who had seen much in their time.

Presently they came in their tarnished finery, curiosity on their creased and sombre faces. What did the Father want of them? They were told of the predicament and asked to advise. One of them urged sending a fast galley after the fleet and getting it to return at once. But there were objections to this proposal. For one thing, a single galley might well be attacked and not reach its destination. The ships, moreover, probably split up among the creeks in the Sundarbans, would be difficult to locate. A long time would elapse before they all were collected. Then another of the old men made a suggestion. The best course, he said, would be for the Vicar himself with Captain Tibao to go to the Court of Arakan and represent to the King that the charge of treachery was groundless, that the Captains were not even in Dianga, but all away serving His Majesty as zealous frontiersmen, burning, robbing, kidnapping, and enslaving. When His Majesty heard this and saw that the Vicar, an Augustinian of age and standing, deeply respected and liked, had come as a surety, he would be satisfied or at least ready to direct the Admiral to wait pending an inquiry.

This advice appeared so sound that it was adopted, and as there was not a moment to be lost, Manrique and Captain Tibao resolved to start next day. It was the Eve of the Visitation.

IX

The Tiger

With the greatest haste the boxes were packed. It was not necessary to bring food; that would be available *en route*; but money and presents were indispensable. And there was another matter. Though a number of Catholics lived in Mrauk-u—the mercenaries, their wives and families, traders, prisoners, and some native Christians—there was no church, no Catholic priest. The kings of Arakan had not been as accommodating with permission in this respect as had the Mughal. Manrique guessed there would be a rush to the Mass as soon as it was known that a priest had come. He must therefore bring what would be required: the wine, the vessels, the vestments, and the books.

It was decided to leave after dark in case the Viceroy's spies noticed what was afoot. During the afternoon the Catholics assembled at the church. After the celebration, Manrique addressed them. Let them pray for him and Captain Tibao. The journey in the monsoon would be difficult. There were many dangers on the way, and when they reached Mrauk-u, who could say how the King would receive them? Yet it was essential they should go. The lives of all present, and, more important, the preservation of religion at Dianga, depended on a successful issue to their journey.

At nightfall the last farewells were said and they embarked in a galley. The first part of the journey could be made by boat, because between Dianga and Ramu, on the edge of the mountains which divide India from the Arakan homeland, there was a flat littoral, intersected with creeks. By keeping to these creeks it was possible to avoid going on to the sea. As the crow flies, Ramu is little more than sixty miles down the coast, but the creeks wind about in such a fashion that it took Manrique and his party three days to get there.

The town had an Arakanese Governor, but as he was known to

be friendly to the Portuguese, they called, after sending ahead a handsome present of Indian muslin. On being received with cordiality, they did not conceal from him the object of their journey. He told them they were wise to go, but when they asked questions, trying to ascertain what he knew of the Government's intentions, he discreetly turned the conversation. It was a terrible journey in the rains, he said. The galley they had was too small for the sea passage. At the moment it was raining and blowing hard. It might continue to rain without pause for three weeks. How did they propose to get to Mrauk-u?

He was not exaggerating. In Arakan three hundred inches of rain often fall between May and October.

The Portuguese replied that by walking down the coast they hoped to cover the hundred miles, which lay between them and the mouth of the Kaladan river, and from thence get up to the city of Mrauk-u. The Governor asked his bodyguard whether one could pass that way. No-one could pass, they said; every few miles there were torrents pouring down from the mountains, so deep and rapid that elephants could not ford them.

The only alternative, said the Governor, was to take the route over the mountains. (That was the track the messenger had taken.) It came out at the town of Peroem on the Mayu river, from where inland waterways led to the capital. Tibao protested that the mountains were full of tigers, and the track hard to find. That was so, admitted the Governor, but he could provide them with guides, for in a couple of days he would be sending under escort to Arakan fifty-three Indians captured in the raids. The best course would be to join the party. Risks from wild animals would be greatly reduced and there would be no danger of losing the way.

This entailed a halt of two days. But they agreed with alacrity. It was a lucky chance. They might have perished, otherwise.

On the second evening the prisoners arrived with a guard of thirty soldiers. They were manacled and had iron collars to which a chain was attached, binding them one to the other, like the twelve galley-slaves whom Don Quixote saw 'inserted like beadstones in a great chain of iron'. The men were old and young, some Hindus, some Mohammedans, innocents going to perpetual servitude.

Next day early in the morning the company set out. Manrique had with him two catechists and a servant, Tibao a number of servants and slaves, all of whom were Catholics, for at that date servants took the religion of their masters. The Governor had provided two elephants, one to carry the luggage, and the other, which had a comfortable howdah with mattresses and curtains, for the use of the Friar and the Captain. They did not, however, mount at once, but took a boat, for the first six miles could be done more comfortably by water. On disembarking, they were at the edge of the tree-covered foothills. The elephants met them there and it was while the boxes were being transferred from the boat to the baggage-elephant that they experienced their first misadventure. Suddenly a tiger, as large as a young bull, burst from the undergrowth and before a shot could be fired, seized one of the escort and dragged him away. The Arakanese was as helpless in his mouth as a dog. His companions immediately gave chase with spears, shouting all they could to frighten the beast. But the tiger continued towards the high jungle and it was not until Tibao's servants fired a volley that he dropped his prey and disappeared. But the man was terribly mauled; he was disembowelled, they found, besides bleeding fast from wounds in the back.

His comrades wanted to carry him at once to the boat, but Tibao's servants suggested getting the Friar: perhaps he would be able to do something for him.

'On this I hurried there with all speed,' writes Manrique, 'and found him living and in full possession of his senses.' Nothing, of course, could be done in a medical sense, but spiritually everything could be done: a soul could be saved. It was pouring rain. The Friar knelt beside him in the mud, and, speaking in Hindustani, gently told him he was dying, yet that he need have no fear; it was not too late for him to become a Christian. The man seemed to listen. Though a rough soldier he was mild and respectful. Manrique begged him to believe and so escape the dread fate which otherwise was inevitable. 'I added other suitable arguments and pointed to Heaven,' he explains.

The soldier—his religion is not given, though if he were Arakanese, it must have been Buddhism—either could not hold out against such pleading or frightened by his approaching death, clung to the straw of this stranger's guarantee, and, saying he was convinced of the truth of Christianity, humbly inquired how to become a Catholic. Deeply pleased, the Friar removed from his neck the metal crucifix he always wore 'and placing it in his hands I explained its mystery, how through love for us Christ had voluntarily placed himself in that predicament'. The story moved the dying man: he began to weep and raising his hands to heaven, as it were in supplication, asked the Friar to give him baptism.'After making him recite the Creed with me I baptized him, choosing the name Buonaventura, the Lucky.'

It only remained now to make him comfortable. His comrades, who had stood by during the scene of his conversion and baptism, watching with curiosity and saying not a word, carried him wrapped in a sheet to the boat, and settled him under a mat awning. 'He was by this time unconscious,' says Manrique, 'and I ordered a candle to be lighted and placing this divine symbol of our redemption near his face, commenced with those Christians present to recite the prayers for the dying. Just at the words "suscipe, Domine, servum tuum" he passed away.'

The rain was still falling hard when they dug the grave, near a great tree, a full fathom deep, for the tiger would return to look for his kill, and they laid the body there and put a cross at the head. Losing one of their number thus to a wild beast on the very threshold of the journey had unnerved them, all except Manrique, who was quite undismayed, nay, certain that the rescue of a soul was a happy augury for the success of his mission. He mounted the elephant and, giving the sign to march, set his face joyfully towards the mountain and the gloomy forest.

X
The Colloquy in the Jungle

The waste of gorges and swamps, of woods and mountains, dividing Chittagong from Arakan, is formidable to cross during the monsoon. The writer has been on its fringes and can declare that nothing would have induced him to attempt it in July. Our travellers were to take eleven days to get over.

At first they advanced cautiously, firing shots at random, in case the tiger should seek to replace the victim he had dropped. 'We travelled on thus through the heavy forest,' says Manrique, 'with our muskets in our hands, afflicted by the rain and sinking in the mud.' At four o'clock they came to the edge of a rice plain some miles wide. Such forest clearings do not necessarily mean a village. Here, not a hut was to be seen; the clearing was a swamp no longer cultivated. They decided to camp beside it for the night. The grass was lank and wringing wet, but the elephants cleared a space at the foot of a tree. It was raining too hard to light a fire and, so, impossible to cook supper. Tibao had taken the precaution to bring a quantity of hard cakes, a sort of biscuit, and these were distributed, the captives even getting a share. The howdah was then pitched on the ground like a tent, and some of the party huddled inside and others lay under the lee of it. When the moon rose, an invisible moon that diffused a faint light under the dripping trees, a gale suddenly blew up, carrying away the curtains of the howdah and finally its roof. Dawn found them all drenched to the skin. But so violent was the gale that the rain had ceased.

Manrique and the Captain mounted their elephant. They had now no protection against the weather. The swamp was crossed. Beyond it was a ridge, which they climbed painfully. At the summit the wind dropped, and down came the rain again, heavier than ever. 'But God was pleased in His infinite mercy to ordain that it should not rain quite all night,' records the Friar. They were able to light fires, dry their clothes, and cook a meal. Then they climbed trees, to be safe from the wild beasts. Trees in the tropics are infested with ants, particularly with the large red kind whose sting is worse than a bee's. In 1926 an aeroplane, among the first to fly that way, fell in July into this jungle further to the south, and its occupants, lost and exhausted, were eaten by ants. But Manrique says the night seemed comparatively a pleasant one, for no rain fell until after dawn.

In the morning they descended the ridge and at the foot came upon some deserted huts, made of bamboo and thatched with palm-leaf. A tremendous thunderstorm now raged up and they took refuge in them. The downpour was so intimidating that they abandoned the march for that day, resting fairly snug for twenty-four hours.

During this halt Manrique had a conversation with one of the Moslem captives. The Friar was reading his breviary when the man spoke to him. Capture, the miseries of the march, his bleak future as a slave, did not seem to have quenched his spirit.

'Father,' said he, 'is the book you are reading a scripture?'

Manrique: No, it is the book of our prayers and supplications.

The Slave: To whom do you Christians pray?

Manrique: To the one true God.

The Slave: Bravo, I say; but how is it that your churches are full of images? We see you bent in supplication to them.

For answer to this question Manrique laughed.

The Slave: You laugh? It is a Christian custom to laugh when sacred matters are being discussed?

Manrique: I laugh, not at sacred things, but at your question. Do you imagine that we worship idols like the Hindus?

The Slave: Why set idols in your churches if you do not worship them?

Manrique then explained the difference between a crucifix, or an image of the Virgin or of the saints, and an idol. The reader here will recall that one of the counts against Dellon was that he had spoken slightingly of the adoration of images, and will be able to understand the honest bewilderment of the Moslem slave.

The conversation had drawn others of the chain-gang and these, sitting a little back from the talkers, listened with solemn faces. Manrique says that they seemed satisfied with the distinction he drew, but now his interlocutor began cross-examining him again. There was something brusque and hardy about the fellow, who was evidently better read than his present state suggested. One is reminded of the indomitable Gines of Passamonte, with whom Don Quixote had an enchanting wrangle, the most incomparable in all literature between a knight and a galley-slave. But, of course, Cervantes himself was captured by Moslem pirates and enslaved for five years. He knew the life, he knew the galleys, and by his art has told us in those pages what it meant for a man of fire and mind to be a slave.

But to return—the Moslem prisoner asked how many religions God had set in the world. Manrique told him three, 'adding explanations in his own tongue as best I could, God helping me.'

Christianity, Judaism, and a third. Whatever the third was, it was not Mohammedanism, for the enslaved Moslem said: 'For a man of your attainments you are surprisingly ignorant. Do you not know that God ordained four religions and caused them to be revealed in sequence, the revelation becoming more perfect on each occasion? The last, by the Prophet Mohammed, is therefore the most complete. Your religion is good as far as it goes and you may be saved by it, but ours goes further and so is to be preferred.'

Manrique: Is that all you have to say?

The Slave: Is it not enough?

Manrique: Quite enough. Let me then accept your admission that Christianity gives salvation, but warn you that not only does your cult not give it, but that it leads to utter damnation.

At this insult to their religion the captives who sat listening put their fingers in their ears and murmured, deeply shocked, *taubah*, *taubah*, repentance, repentance. The Friar silenced them, and saying he would prove his words, preached them a sermon upon their errors.

When they had listened patiently to the end, they uttered a phrase from the Koran, *Allah karim*, *Allah mihrban*, God is Compassionate, God is Merciful, and getting up from their places left the hut.

That Manrique could have hoped to convert them shows how tightly he was encased in his period and in his dogma. What were the facts? These men, Moslem residents of the riverine villages of eastern Bengal, had been kidnapped by Christian slavers and sold by them to the King of Arakan for labour in his rice-fields. On the way to their servitude they are invited to adopt the religion of their kidnappers on the ground that it is a higher religion. God is compassionate and merciful, they reply; how can we prefer your religion which permits you to act so cruelly against us? St. Francis Xavier would not have gone about a conversion in that way. Had he been travelling to Arakan with a gang of slaves, he would never have ridden an elephant while they went in chains, but have walked beside them, weeping, comforting, suffering with them, and pleading, as he looked up to Heaven, his face radiated with joy, and beyond doubt would have convinced some of them that he had a secret of salvation which they had not. But Manrique did not seek to convert by playing on the emotions. He was calm, normal, plain, steady. He told a simple story, showed how comforting it was, how homely, how safe, how full of common sense, how it gave you hope and peace and content. It was quite unnecessary to do anything extravagant. Enough if you believed and acted with propriety. Certain that he was offering those Moslem captives a thing of the greatest value, it did not cross his mind that it could be suspect because Christians had made slaves of them. But we are the last persons to blame him for that; have we not taken away the liberty of all Indians and at the same time invited them to believe that our civilization is superior to theirs?

Yet, this little drama, played in the middle of a tropical forest with the monsoon pouring upon the roof, was not quite over. The captives departed, quoting the Koran, but the one of their number who had spoken so sharply and with such assurance now began to doubt. That night as he lay chained with the others and thought of his predicament, he went over the arguments which Manrique had advanced. Could it be that after all he was wrong? If so, not only had he lost everything which made life worth living, but had nothing to hope for after death. For all his devotion to the Prophet he had fallen into this misery; perhaps his faith was not as sound as he believed. Might it not be that God had allowed him to be taken as a slave so as to bring him by the road of suffering to truth?

He was so agitated by this cruel doubt that early next morning before the march began he went to Manrique. 'All last night my mind refused to rest,' he said, 'with turning over what you spoke of salvation. Will you discuss it with me when we reach the capital?'

Manrique: When we halt to-night, I will speak with you again.

The Slave: If my companions see us together, they will be suspicious and angry. At the capital there will be opportunity.

Manrique: But you may die on the march. Maybe the Devil

knows you will die and strives to prevent you finding the truth, so that your soul may not escape him.

But the slave was afraid to risk embroiling himself with the others and turned away, muttering, 'No man can escape his fate.' Manrique was never able to speak to him again. 'Though I strove to find him in Arakan, I could obtain news neither of him nor of his companions,' he writes.

XI

The Image on the Pass

When they left the huts, it was still raining but not so hard. The way led up a lofty and rock-strewn mountain. About six miles on they were confronted by a herd of wild buffaloes, very dangerous beasts—even tame buffaloes are dangerous. To fire at them would, they knew, precipitate a charge, and they fired over them, the reports and the whistle of the balls frightening where a hit would only have irritated.

Crossing the summit, a high gale blustering after them, they clambered down the other side in the failing light and after sunset were in a gorge at the bottom of which there roared a swollen river. By its brink they passed the night in trees, for the forest was full of beasts, tigers mewling and elephants shuffling by. With the dawn they essayed to pass over the river, but the current was too fierce and it was too deep. A raft was made and ten of the more experienced tried to paddle it across so as to fix a rope from bank to bank, but were driven downstream and had to be hauled back. Again and again they tried, with no better success.

There was nothing for it but to wait until the water's force abated. How long that would be no-one could say. But exposed to the fury of the rain, without shelter at night, with no possibility of lighting a fire and the food they carried sodden and uneatable, they were in evil case. Luckily, an Arakanese had some dried boiled rice, which he had protected from the weather, and this sufficed for a very light meal, to which the prisoners were not invited. So miserable did they all become that on the third day Manrique broached the wine which he had brought for the Mass. Two bottles were drunk. On the morning of the fourth day the situation seemed desperate. Besides wet, cold, and hunger, there was constant danger of tigers. Manrique called the Christians to prayer, 'begging God by His passion not to allow us to be buried in the bellies of wild animals'. After taking their confessions, he turned to the prisoners, both Moslem and Hindu. 'I explained to them,' he says, 'what they should do so as not to lose their souls as well as their bodies. On this they all began to weep, but not one was converted.'

That evening, when the moon rose, the sky cleared and the stars came out. A fire was kindled with the help of gunpowder; they dried their clothes and passed a better night. In the morning the torrent was less swift. The raft made the other bank; the rope was fixed to a tree and they all crossed, the two elephants swimming over.

Another deluge now came on, but they pressed up the opposing ridge, so steep that Manrique and Tibao had to dismount and climb hand-over-hand. The elephants, in spite of their bulk, were as agile as goats, collecting themselves and stepping from rock to rock. By nightfall they were over the pass and, descending a little way, slept as before, tied to the branches of trees, after they had recited the Litany of the Blessed Virgin.

The town of Peroem was now one day's march distant. At the thought of the journey's end, their spirits rose with daylight. An early start was made, the track leading them first to a valley and thence to another ridge, rugged and precipitous like the former. Hereabouts they came on a river, which was part of a canal project, so Manrique was told, to join Arakan with India. Judging from the nature of the ground, this hardly seems likely, but it is interesting that as early as the seventeenth century there was talk of such a land connection, for the matter has been discussed ever since, taking the form when I was there in 1924 of a railway connection. Had this been constructed it would have greatly strengthened the British military position in Burma against the Japanese invasion of 1942. Manrique states that in his time the proposal was abandoned in case the Mughal should use the waterway for an invasion of Arakan.

At the summit of the ridge to which they now climbed was a shrine cut in the rock, in which was seated a stone image with the legs crossed. This image was of Buddha, for they were on the threshold of a Buddhist kingdom. Though Manrique uses for it the Arakanese word for Buddha, he had never seen a Buddha before, nor did he know the differences between Hinduism and Buddhism; for him both religions were confused in the general term of paganism. But, indeed, at that time there was no knowledge of Buddhism anywhere in Europe.

That Arakan was a Buddhist state requires a word of explanation. From very early days it had been associated with that religion. As most people are aware, there is an early and a later Buddhism. The first—it might be called Apostolic Buddhism—derived from the attempt made by the Master and his disciples in the sixth century B.C. to combat the superstitions of popular Hinduism by teaching that a plain, decent, humane, and reasonable way of life was wholly sufficient for a man's salvation It had its great day in India: the Emperor Asoka (260–226 B C.) made its code the basis of his administration. But it was not sufficiently exciting to hold India for ever. On the popular side, the level common sense of its rules seemed dull beside the dark intoxications of Hindu rituals; on the esoteric side, it discouraged metaphysics and the mystical vision which made the Hindu philosophy of the Atman so attractive to intellectuals. To meet this craving of the Indian mind for ritual and mystical speculation, the later Buddhism developed, the Mahayana or the Greater Vehicle as it was called by its followers, who gave to the original Apostolic Buddhism the name of the Hinnayana or the Lesser Vehicle. The Mahayana had rituals for the people which often were hardly distinguishable, except by their terminology, from Hindu rituals; for intellectuals it had a splendid metaphysic whose differences from the philosophy of the Atman were so subtle that a lifetime might be happily spent in disengaging them. When Hsüan Tsang, the T'ang dynasty intellectual, visited India in A.D. 630, he found the Mahayana, the Hinnayana, and Hinduism flourishing simultaneously under the benign rule of the Emperor Harsha. Arakan was then an Indian land, its inhabitants being Indians similar to those resident in Bengal. It is safe to say that Hinduism and both forms of Buddhism were to be found there, as they were to be found throughout the continent. The country was noted, however, for a colossal statue of Buddha known as the Mahamuni, which was reputed to be of great antiquity, being considered a contemporary likeness of the Master. The possession of this particularly sacred sculpture was sufficient to identify the Arakan area more with Buddhism than with Hinduism.

In 957 the country was overrun by Mongolian barbarians, who must have been early Burmese, for the Arakanese language to-day is an early form of Burmese. Meanwhile both the Mahayana and the Hinnayana had ceased to exist in India, which returned wholly to its original cult of Hinduism. The Mahayana was carried to

Tibet and China, the Hinnayana to Ceylon and Burma. The Hinnayana had an especial attraction for the Burmese, who in the eleventh century developed at their capital, Pagan, a version of it, more pleasing, more humanitarian, and more genuinely religious than is known to have existed in any other part of the Buddhist world, a sort of reconstruction of the Apostolic age. In about the year 1060 the Pagan dynasty extended its authority over Arakan, become, as we have seen, a state inhabited by a mixture of Mongolian and Indian races. As a result, Arakan was brought into the orbit of the Hinnayana as practised in Pagan. The Mahamuni, though it had been overgrown by the jungle, was still in its place, and was now cleared and repaired. It was a religious carving of far greater antiquity and fame than anything in Burma. The cult was centred upon it and it became the palladium of the country. The Pagan kings had as great a veneration for it and tried to take it to Burma. Failing in this, they made pilgrimages to its shrine. Arakan became the land of the Great Image.

During the six hundred years which elapsed between these events and the arrival of Manrique, Arakan had remained Hinnayana Buddhist and continued to regard the Mahamuni as her most important possession. Long since she had become politically independent of Burma. The Mrauk-u dynasty began to rule in 1430, and by 1530, under King Min Bin, the country was developing into the chief maritime state on the Bay of Bengal. It was during the reign of Min Bin that the Arakanese fortified Mrauk-u, engaged foreign mercenaries, particularly Portuguese, and extended their territory over the mountains to Chittagong. As we have seen, they were enabled to do this because the Mughal, who had been gradually creeping eastwards, had weakened but not yet overcome the then existing native governments. When Manrique sighted the image of Buddha on the pass above Peroem, he was therefore entering Arakan proper, an area which for many hundred years had been associated with the Hinnayana or Apostolic form of Buddhism. He was also making acquaintance for the first time with a Mongolian state, the inhabitants of which spoke Burmese or a dialect of it but who had a certain admixture of Indian blood in their veins. The state as such went back to the year 957, somewhat in the way that England goes back to the year 1066, and the hundred years between Min Bin (1531–53) and the reigning king, Thiri-thu-dhamma, had been the most progressive in its history. These are all very relevant facts for readers of this book, and they would have been very relevant also for Manrique, though he cannot have known any of them.

But to return to his narrative. 'On reaching the high place where the carved Idol sat,' he says, 'all the pagans in our party prostrated themselves and touched the ground with their foreheads thrice, thanking it for their safe passage over the dangerous mountains.' By pagans he means the Hindu slaves and the guards, who were Arakanese Buddhists. That the Hindus should have returned thanks to the Buddha was not out of keeping with their conception of the Master as one of the many deities belonging to India.

While Manrique was viewing their prostrations with distaste, the Moslem slaves came up and assured him in a confidential aside how much they also condemned worship of images. But as prisoners they could not interfere and stood silently by, looking their disgust. Manrique, however, did not hesitate to protest. 'I approached somewhat to those who were idolatrizing,' he writes, 'and told them that we had all to give thanks to the true God and not to that statue of stone, and added many other considerations on the subject.' The Hindus were too timid to abuse a priest who was riding with the captain of a gang of kidnappers, though one man made bold to say that what was not evil must be good and that as no-one could say there was harm in giving thanks it must pass as a righteous act. Manrique records this retort without comment.

When the march was resumed, one of the Moslem slaves, an old man, became so exhausted that he stumbled and seemed about to fall. The Arakanese guards drove him on, but Manrique, in spite of their protests, had him unmanacled and gave him a seat on the elephant, an act of pity which so pleased his co-religionists that they warmed to the priest with whom they already had in common a hatred of idols. But this did not show itself except in flattering remarks. He was no nearer converting them than before. Nor did the man, whose mind he had swayed, dare to speak further with him that evening.

During the afternoon they struggled through the waterlogged fields of rice outside Peroem and very tired entered the town at nightfall. The Governor, as soon as he knew of their arrival, sent them to a rest-house. There, Manrique at once recited the *Te Deum* and the Litany of Our Lady, standing before the assembled Christians, crucifix in hand. This first duty done, they changed their clothes. An invitation to dinner was now received from the Governor, but they were too worn out to accept it and sent word they would call on him early next day. On getting this message, he sent them the dinner, a huge dinner which the servants set upon so greedily that they had to be restrained for their health's sake. It was nine o'clock when they had finished. Another thunderstorm came up, the lightning blazed by the windows and it poured as if after a drought. But the roar of the storm seemed like a lullaby as they fell exhausted into a deep sleep.

XII
The Admiral

The arrival at Peroem was on July the 17th. As Ramu was left on July the 7th, the passage of the mountain divide had taken eleven days, four being spent waiting for the river to fall. If twelve miles for each marching day were averaged, a reasonable average in the circumstances, the distance covered was eighty-four miles. A march of that length would have carried the party down to near the mouth of the Mayu river. It is therefore assumed here that Peroem was at no great distance from its mouth, which is a wide gulf open to the monsoon. It is marked in that position on my map, and will be seen to lie some forty miles in a direct line from the capital.

When the Portuguese woke up next morning, they found the rain still falling. Presently two palanquins came to fetch them to the Governor. His affable attentions can be accounted for by the fact that they were on their way to Court. It was the duty of officials throughout these kingdoms to forward distinguished strangers with dispatch, especially when they were bearing presents for the king. Tibao and Manrique had no doubt made this plain on arrival and as an additional inducement now sent the Governor himself a present of four gilt Chinese trays piled with cloves, cinnamon, pepper, and cardamoms, spices locally unprocurable, which had been imported into Dianga by Portuguese vessels from Java or Sumatra. This done, they got into the palanquins and set out for his residence.

The Governor, who was very pleased with the present, seated them beside him, offered them betel and provided spittoons. These formalities over, they set to business. To get to Mrauk-u it was necessary to cross the mouth of the Mayu river, known then as the Gulf of Maum, whence the capital could be reached by rivers and creeks. Unfortunately, said the Governor, it would be impossible to cross the gulf in such wild weather. They would meet there the full force of the monsoon. But the new moon was due in four days' time. A fine interval might then be expected. To this Tibao replied that their affairs were so urgent they dared not delay. The Governor accordingly directed a galley with thirty-six oarsmen to get ready, the start to be made early next morning, be the weather what it might.

On returning to their lodging, they learned that the Arakanese fleet, which was under orders to attack Dianga, was assembled in the Kaladan river at a place called Urrittaung, about half-way between them and the capital. This news suggested that when the expected lull came with the new moon it would leave the shelter of the river and make for Dianga. Speed was therefore even more necessary than they had believed.

During the afternoon a return present arrived from the Governor of fifty hens, two deer, four bags of scented rice, which was a speciality from Cheduba, an island further down the coast, together with butter, fruit, and sweets. This was followed up by a call from the Governor's son, a charming youth of about fourteen. He came to the rest-house mounted on a richly caparisoned elephant, attended by a guard of thirty men and by servants who held a state umbrella over his head. On hearing his runners calling his name and styles, Manrique and Tibao hastened out to meet him, being careful to employ the courtesies usual in the country. On his coming in, they would have provided betel, had they possessed any, but in default offered him sweetmeats, made in European fashion, marzipans in fantastic shapes which amused the young gentleman. 'But I am sure his real enjoyment was in eating them,' writes Manrique. At the conclusion of the visit he was presented with a length of green Chinese damask embroidered with yellow flowers, and went away on his elephant, very delighted. At nightfall a lavish dinner arrived from the Governor with a message that the galley would be standing by at dawn.

Half an hour before light they were up and making ready. When they were about to start, the Governor sent, asking them to call and take leave. While porters carried the boxes to the galley, they hurried round to his house. Apologizing for not conducting them himself—he was too old to wait about in the wet—he directed his son to see them aboard. Elephants with gilt howdahs were provided; the send-off was in style. But on reaching the water's edge, they were somewhat dismayed. The estuary or gulf was far rougher than they had expected. Waves were breaking heavily on the shore, while further out great rollers were driving up from the outer sea. When the boy saw their faces, he suggested they should postpone their departure. 'My father said all along it would be better to wait,' he urged, genuinely concerned for their safety. Hearing him speak in this way, the pilot in charge of the galley came up and added his entreaties.

But there was no help for it. Delay was impossible. Tibao signed to his men to carry the Friar on board. At this, the pilot, almost in tears, exclaimed to the crew: 'We are lost; these Portuguese are sons of the sea; even death does not frighten them on the water.' It looked as if the crew were going to desert. Tibao saw it was a moment for action. He stripped off his clothes and, in only a loin-cloth, jumped on to the poop, flourishing a cane, and ordered the rowers with curses to start at once. Frightened but obedient they bent over the oars.

The crossing was a terrible one. Rough as it was near the shore, it became far worse as they approached the centre of the estuary. Here they met the full force of the monsoon storm. It seemed so probable that the boat would be swamped that Manrique and the servants took off their outer things. The oarsmen became exhausted and had to be helped. Manrique himself, crucifix in hand, prayed for divine help and, though the wind and crash of the waves made it impossible for anyone to hear him, gave absolution to all the Catholics. He did not, however, attempt to convert the oarsmen, as he felt it beyond his power in such a gale to impart the Catholic truths and hopeless to expect them both to row and give attention. The pilot, who up to this had done his work at the tiller manfully, now called out that his strength was failing him. Tibao and Manrique went to his assistance and took over the helm. In this exposed position they were battered by the waves. 'The seas were coming over the stern with such force', says Manrique, 'that whenever they struck me on the shoulders I was forced forward on to the nob of the tiller-post, which was most painful and resulted in my spitting clotted blood for some days after.'

Several hours elapsed before they began to get the protection of the land on the other side. The visibility was so low that it was hardly possible to see a boat's length ahead, and to find the opening of the Kudaung creek, the place they were making for, was extremely difficult. However, late in the afternoon they made it. Running up a little way, they secured the galley to the bank. The crew, in an ecstasy of relief, went ashore and 'kissed the ground, muddy though it was'. Then, completely exhausted, they returned on board and threw themselves down, remaining in a sort of torpor for over an hour.

The creek was fringed with mangrove, behind which was a rice plain and low hills. Lying a little back was a rock face on which to-day are still to be seen the reliefs which King Min Bin had carved a hundred years before when on his way to invade Bengal. Urrittaung was twenty miles to the north-east. By climbing a tree they might have seen, had the weather lifted, the spire of its pagoda which is on a hill. Evening came on. The boatmen, though somewhat restored, were unable to do more than eat their rice and fall asleep. But the place being notorious for tigers, so bold that they would board a galley lying close to the shore, even swim out a distance to pull a man off, it was necessary to mount a guard with muskets, and this the servants did, taking their turns all night.

Dawn saw them upon their way. Turning into a creek on their right, they sped along on the tide, the monsoon cloud still shrouding the landscape. In the course of the morning they reached the Urrittaung custom-house. From there a messenger was sent to the Admiral of the Fleet, for they had decided to call on him before proceeding to Court, tell him their mission, and beg him to delay his departure pending the King's decision.

The Admiral sent a guardship to bring them to his camp, which was on the bank of the Kaladan river, the fleet being moored just off shore. It was a comfortable camp, the various quarters being small pavilions of bamboo, thatched with palm leaves and walled with mats, clean and smart, for they were quite new. In the most elegant of these pavilions they found the Admiral.

The Augustinian friars had a certain reputation in those regions, arising, no doubt, from their strict life and genuine piety. The present king, Thiri-thu-dhamma, it is true, had allowed none to settle at his capital, not for reasons of religious intolerance, but because, it would seem, he thought it politically undesirable that the various Catholics in his dominion should be united as a body, with a church and so, possibly, an organization, which might be used for spying. But an individual friar, particularly of the standing and education of Manrique, could count on a more respectful reception than could a layman. This explains why in the first instance the Catholics of Mrauk-u had written direct to him and why Captain Tibao had insisted on his coming.

The interview with the Admiral opened with the presentation by the Portuguese of Chinese silk and spices.

'How did you get here in such weather?' he asked. They explained the route they had taken, the trials they had undergone, and coming to the pith of the matter told him frankly the object of their mission.

'The allegations made against the loyalty of the Portuguese Captains in Dianga', Manrique assured him, 'are wholly without foundation. They invite the fullest investigation into their conduct and in proof of their innocence and of their belief that His Majesty will hold them innocent, they have sent me, their Vicar, and place me unreservedly in his hands.'

This was uttered with such warmth, and Manrique looked so imposing in his black habit, that the Admiral was convinced a mistake had been made. His quick brain immediately told him that his own position was rather exposed. If this Religious gained the king's ear, as he was quite likely to do, His Majesty would naturally be annoyed at having been misinformed and his indignation might not stop at the punishment of the Viceroy of Chittagong, but could very well extend to him. As Admiral, he had advised an immediate sack of Dianga, when, so the king might say, he should have been well-informed enough to suspect the truth of the allegations. Accordingly he hastened to reply: 'I have no doubt whatever of the truth of what you say, Father, and am equally certain of your good reception at Court. For myself, I never believed that the Portuguese would play traitor. Had I done so, I should have sailed at once for Dianga. If your Reverence was able to brave the monsoon to get here, you can well imagine it would not have stopped me from getting there. No, I was not waiting for a lull or anything of that sort, but because I had my doubts and wanted to be sure of my ground.'

Though Manrique heartily thanked him for his good opinion and declared that throughout Asia he had the reputation of being not only an intrepid seaman but also a man of affairs, who knew whom to trust, and what not to believe, the Admiral thought it prudent to swear to the truth of his statement—though in this we may find he was using too much emphasis—and raising the silk skirt he wore and disclosing a figure tattooed above his knee, he placed his hand on it and took a formal oath.

''His Majesty,' said he, then, 'is not at Mrauk-u, but on a lenten pilgrimage to the Mahamuni, where you will find him. I will place you in charge of one of my captains, who will conduct you and on your arrival arrange for an audience.'

XIII

The Comptroller-General of the Household

At Urrittaung the travellers were inside the rice plain of Arakan, a considerable area, eighty miles, say, from north to south and standing back some sixty miles from the sea. What it consisted of was the wide alluvial valleys of three big rivers, the Mayu, the Kaladan, and the Lemro, which, rising in the wild mountains which enclose the inhabited zone in a semicircle, flow into the Bay of Bengal, their mouths adjacent one to the other. Each of their valleys is a rice plain capable of producing far more rice than there has ever been population in Arakan to consume. Rice being the staple food and the basis of wealth in all that far eastern world, a country producing a superfluity of it was a rich country, better off than India, where food never sufficed for the population. Add the fact that a proportion of the hard work was done by slaves from India, and you have a picture of a comfortable agricultural community.

Another peculiarity of this Arakanese homeland was the network of waterways over the low ground. Besides the three main rivers and their tributaries proper, there was a maze of creeks running in all directions between them. One travelled by them instead of by road, for the towns and villages were on or near their banks. It followed that the country was full of boats, from canoes carved from a single tree-trunk to substantial cargo boats and vessels capable of carrying many passengers. The boatmen formed a large class, able to man, with the help of slaves, the considerable fleet: the Admiral is said to have mustered at Urrittaung no less than three hundred and fifty vessels.

Although so close to India, this curious kingdom was not Indian in atmosphere. The population being predominantly Mongolian, speaking a Mongolian language and with far-off memories of north-western China in its subconscious, constituted the first of that series of Mongolian states—Burma, Siam, Annam, and the Shan Principalities—which reflected, though in what the Chinese would have called a barbarous manner, some glimmer of the civilization of the Celestial Kingdom. These states, with the exception of Arakan, had at one time or another been included, at least theoretically, in the Chinese Empire, having sent envoys to pay homage at Peking. Though Arakan had not done this, it had caught or inherited or copied an imponderable something, which made it more like provincial China than provincial India.

With the change of the moon two days after the arrival of the Portuguese envoys, the weather cleared, as the Governor of Peroem had anticipated, and at dawn they made a start for the Mahamuni. The great image was situated on the top of a little hill called by the Sanskrit name of Sirigutta, about forty miles northwest of Mrauk-u. In the early period before the Mongolian invasion a town had stood there called Dhaññavati. When I visited the hill in 1924 I saw lying there numerous stone sculptures of the Hindu pantheon in the Gupta style of the fifth century A.D., which must have belonged to a Hindu temple in the vicinity. The hill itself was untenanted, for the Mahamuni had been removed by the Burmese conquerors of 1784 to Mandalay, where it is now to be seen in the Arakan Pagoda, if it was not destroyed by the Japanese bombing of that city. But the original shrine was still on the hill and there was a great bell upon which was a magical inscription. Magic was used to guard the Mahamuni, it being held —in the event truly—that its destruction or removal would synchronize with the fall of the kingdom. So the hill of Sirigutta has now a mournful air. I found it forlorn, a holy place that was swept and garnished. Very differently was Manrique to see it, with the whole Court assembled at its foot in attendance upon the Thirithu-dhamma, for strictly this was not the King's name but his title, a term from the classic Pali analogous to our style, Defender of the Faith.

The journey could be made wholly by boat. Manrique, the Captain, their servants, their luggage with the presents, were accommodated on three fast naval vessels under the command of the Arakanese staff officer. The route was up the Kaladan river and later into a creek, whose classical name was Thye-ma-nadi, 'the beautiful river'. By the end of the first day the banks became lined with trees, so tall and spreading that they seemed to meet overhead, a jungle landscape with monkeys swinging on the boughs, peacocks streaming across, and an occasional rhinoceros in the undergrowth. These beasts are seen there no longer, having fled to retreats in the further mountains. On the second day they came to a populated rice plain dotted with villages. Halting at one of these for breakfast, they were astonished at the quantity and cheapness of provisions. For a rupee or half a piece of eight, say two shillings, it was possible to buy thirty good fowls, and eggs were selling at about a penny a dozen.

That afternoon they rowed up the Thye-ma-nadi and when about three miles from Mahamuni were obliged to stop because the river was blocked with houseboats. The staff officer explained. When the King and Court went on a state tour through the country, particularly when they visited the Mahamuni, they did not go in galleys or barges but, far more comfortably, in bamboo pavilions built upon rafts. The pavilions were large and fitted with all the conveniences of the day, the King's being a palace, not only in name but in fact, a miniature of his palace at Mrauk-u, with its numerous rooms for the consorts and suite. The rafts bearing the pavilions could not have been propelled by oars at any pace, but this was unnecessary, for all the rivers and creeks were tidal. Fifteen or twenty miles would be covered in a tide, an ample distance for a stately progress. It was with such houseboats and rafts that the Thye-ma-nadi was blocked, though, said the staff officer, the King himself and his household were ashore, as he possessed a land palace at Mahamuni. In the circumstances he would try and get into communication with the Admiral's brother-in-law, for whom he had a letter. To him was to be entrusted for delivery a report which the Admiral had drawn up and addressed to the King. Let them stay where they were until he returned.

Very early next morning he reappeared, accompanied by the Admiral's relative, a Court official of some importance. This gentleman was affable, and became more so on receiving a present of two lengths of transparent Chinese silk. They could count on him, he said; at the first favourable opportunity he would see that His Majesty received the report, adding, what was perhaps more a hint than a compliment, that persons able to continue to make such agreeable presents would never lack his service. The Portuguese fully understood his meaning, but so polished, so infinitely engaging was his manner, that he left them feeling only gratitude and admiration. 'In such matters these people could give instruction to many European Courts,' observes Manrique, who found his address altogether extraordinary. The fact is that the inhabitants of the area now known as Burma have, and always have had, a happy brilliant charm—when they choose to exercise it—which has no parallel in the East and in the West is to be matched perhaps only in Ireland.

That day they remained in the Thye-ma-nadi. After dark a message came from the courtier. They must not attribute the delay to his indifference. There had been no audience that morning, but His Majesty had promised him private audience at night. He begged them to accept the present of game which the messenger would deliver. The Portuguese sent back their thanks and passed the night in some anxiety. One could never tell how the wind would blow from hour to hour in an oriental court.

However, before sunrise next day the messenger returned in high spirits. 'I have good news,' he declared gaily, 'excellent news, but in case I should omit some item by inadvertence, perhaps your Honours will know how to refresh my memory.'

They gave him a preliminary tip and he continued: 'My master presented the Admiral's letter to His Majesty last night, who caused it to be read and immediately decreed that the fleet should not sail for Dianga until further orders. He also directed his Comptroller-General of the Household to fetch your Honours to audience this very day.'

This news, which was everything they desired, so overjoyed them that they gave the messenger ten rupees, a sum which, as we have seen, would buy three hundred fowls and was therefore equivalent in modern food values to £75. It was a princely tip and the recipient attempted to kiss their feet.

On his departure they got ready their present against the Comptroller's arrival. Meanwhile they received a call of some interest. In the royal bodyguard was a company of Japanese *Samurai*, who now led by their Captain came to pay their respects, for they were Catholics. These men had been converted by the Jesuit successors of St. Francis Xavier, who had had great success in Japan until they aroused the suspicions of the Sogun Ieyasu about the year 1612 and were executed or driven out along with their native flock. As incomparable swordsmen, faithful and valiant, some of these exiles had been engaged as guardsmen by the kings of Further India and were to be found among the household troops of Siam, Pegu, and Arakan. The company of them, who now called on Manrique, was in attendance on King Thiri-thu-dhamma during his annual visit to the Mahamuni. They were in full uniform, their two swords sticking from their belts, and as they came alongside in the galleys which carried them, they fired a salute with their falconets. Their captain then climbed aboard and knelt to the Friar, introducing himself as Leon Donno, the first being his name taken on Christian baptism and the second a Japanese word denoting 'gentleman'. Manrique begged him to rise and only succeeded in getting him to do so on threatening to break off the conversation. As the deck was not large enough to accommodate all his followers, Tibao ordered mats to be spread under a tree on the bank. There they adjourned. 'They all came up to kiss my hand with as much devotion and respect as if I had been a Saint,' says Manrique, adding: 'But in these parts there is more respect for a priest than in Europe for Bishops.' Moreover, they had long been deprived of spiritual succour. No priest, said Leon Donno, had visited them for seven years. They had much to confess and ardently desired the consolations of the Church. And he added: 'We have in addition a special request to make. As your Reverence is aware, there is no Church in Mrauk-u. In spite of our representation to the King, permission has been withheld. We believe that your Reverence will be well received at Court and we urge that you demand His Majesty's sanction to build one.'

'Though I have come primarily to avert the danger which hangs over the Catholic community at Dianga,' replied Manrique, 'you may rely upon my good offices in your every just demand, whether spiritual or temporal.'

They had got so far, when the servants came running to say the Comptroller was approaching. Sure enough, there he was, the official upon whose condescension everything turned. A great elephant was seen lumbering along the bank. In the gilded howdah he was sitting up, attended by the Admiral's brother-in-law. Surrounding the elephant marched a guard of forty men, and behind came servants, active and intelligent youths, says Manrique, one carrying their master's tobacco, another his pipe, a third coals to light it, a fourth his betel-box, a fifth a jug of lemonade, and a sixth a basin of water.

The cortège halted and the Comptroller dismounted. He was begged to come on board the galley, the poop of which had been decorated in his honour, and, consenting with every show of politeness, was ushered to a seat with two velvet cushions. When he had sat down and his servants were grouped behind him, he got to his feet again and spoke in a formal manner.

The Comptroller: The Lord of Life has directed me, the meanest ant of his pantries, to welcome you.

Manrique: His Majesty is very gracious.

The Comptroller: It is hoped that the Viceroy of Goa is well.

Manrique: By God's mercy he is very well.

The Comptroller: I trust that your own healths are unimpaired by the journey.

Manrique: Our healths have been marvellously preserved by the grace of God.

The Comptroller: It is reported that you have come to petition His Majesty?

Manrique: We have come to assure His Majesty that the Portuguese of Dianga are His Majesty's devoted humble servants, as they have ever been in the past, having served him, and his father and grandfather of glorious memory, not only by harrying the Mughal in Bengal, but by fighting his enemy, the King of Pegu. If God grant me the good fortune of being admitted to the Royal Presence, my endeavour will be to convince His Majesty of my nation's continued desire to serve him.

The Comptroller: I am heartily glad to hear your Reverence speak so.

Manrique: Your Benignity is very condescending.

The Comptroller: May it please the Lord Buddha that things turn out as you wish. His Majesty will accord you the favour of an audience in due course. Meanwhile I am to conduct you to a lodging on shore.

Manrique: Your Excellency's condescension is overwhelming.

After this exchange, which was carried out through an interpreter, all standing, they sat down, and Captain Tibao signed to the servants to bring in sweets and cakes, the marzipans which had been so much appreciated at Peroem. The Comptroller, while he ate one, unbent somewhat, assuring them that he believed His Majesty to be well disposed, and that on hearing their statement he would recall the fleet.

The present was now brought in. It resembled that offered to the Admiral, but was somewhat more ample, consisting of four gilt trays of spices and on a fifth three pieces of Chinese silk, two of satin, and one of velvet, each piece large enough to make a skirt. When the trays were set before him the Comptroller was too dignified to examine their contents or use in his thanks anything to suggest an alacrity to accept them. He merely bowed, his hands on his breast, and the trays were discreetly handed over to his servants.

The Comptroller: It is getting very hot. I have dismissed my elephant and am taking you in my barge, as soon as it arrives. That will be cooler for you than going by land.

An extremely handsome vessel was now observed coming alongside, rowed by twenty-four slaves. The bow was lavishly carved with faces, dancing figures, and foliage; the oarsmen sat amidships; and the stern, painted green and gold, was covered with an awning and had side curtains of scarlet and yellow.

During the conversation with the Comptroller, the *Samurai* captain had remained respectfully on the bank. Manrique noticed him while they were transferring to the barge, and feeling it would be a politeness to invite him to accompany them, asked the Admiral's brother-in-law whether there was any objection. The courtier demurred; the *Samurai*'s rank was too low. But when the Comptroller was approached he gave permission. A servant was accordingly sent to call him. The invitation profoundly flattered the Japanese. Tipping the man, he came on board, and going up to the Comptroller saluted him in the Malay manner by joining his hands palm to palm and raising them above his head. Seating himself beside Manrique, he said: 'Your Reverence has procured for me a great honour. As my Vicar, I am bound in any case to serve you, but now my obligation is very much greater.'

In recording this little scene Manrique remarks: 'The Japanese nation is by nature the most ambitious of honour of all oriental nations, and will sacrifice life itself to maintain a punctilio.'

As they rowed up the three miles which divided them from the town, they passed between rows of floating houses moored to each bank. It was like a street in Venice on a gala day, 'the traffic of small craft so heavy that we could scarcely make our way in midstream'. At last they reached the crowded wharf, where the Comptroller's police cleared a space for them to land.

XIV

The Audience

Beyond the wharf elephants and palanquins were waiting. A procession was formed and they went to the Comptroller's house, where a meal was ready, the midday meal, there being some hundreds of dishes simultaneously on the table, so that a guest might help himself to what took his fancy. Most were of a rational character, says Manrique, but there were certain eccentricities like roast snake and fried rat which he personally avoided. Afterwards they were conducted to a house which had been prepared for them. The Comptroller bade them farewell with every promise of goodwill.

They expected the audience to take place next day, the 26th of July 1630, but there was a certain delay, the reason given being that the king was making a lenten fast, and not till August the 1st were they summoned to the palace. The intervening week was spent by Manrique in confessing the Christians resident in the vicinity and in celebrating the Mass. One of the rooms of the house was fitted up as a chapel, the Japanese bringing silks and rugs which made it look very well. Some of the Catholics had not confessed for eight or nine years and their confessions in consequence were exceedingly long. One man came in—he must have been some kind of an Indian—and throwing himself at the Friar's feet said he had not confessed for nineteen years, during which time he had lived with an Arakanese woman, who regarded herself as his wife, though, as he had not been married to her according to the Catholic rites, he knew well that their relationship was one of sin. So sinful had he felt that relationship to be that when, some nine years before, an Augustinian had visited Arakan, he was afraid to confess. But now he dared not outrage God any longer, he said. Manrique led him to the chapel and invited him to begin. 'The good man wept so, from sorrow and compunction, that he was often prevented, by his sobs, from speaking and we passed most of the night in this way. Some time near dawn he became too exhausted to continue. But after resting awhile, he was able to finish and was given absolution: his relief was inexpressible. Later, Manrique married him to the woman and baptized his children. From this man he learnt that though some of the slaves in the vicinity—possibly those dedicated to the service of the Mahamuni—were Catholics, most of that community resided at or near the capital. This information decided him to visit Mrauk-u, when his business with the king was finished, if he could obtain the necessary permission.

On July the 31st it was announced that the king's fast would terminate that night and that the next morning he would release nine captive birds, a symbolical act of mercy, and climb in procession Sirigutta mount, at the top of which was enshrined the famous sculpture. After kneeling there and reciting appropriate verses from Pali devotional works he would descend, breakfast, and then give audience to the Portuguese.

Manrique did not see the procession—the king in his palanquin surrounded by the whole Court, the officials, the astrologers and the principal abbots. The weather had been quite fine; since the change in the moon there had not been a drop of rain. Though hot and damp, the sun shone, and the white and gold parasols, the yellow robes of the abbots, the standards, insignia, the flowers, the brocades, will have shimmered and glowed as they surged up the slope.

When the ceremony at the Mahamuni was over, the Comptroller came to fetch the Portuguese. They were carried in palanquins to the palace, which we can assume to have been a stockaded enclosure containing a number of wooden buildings, carved and gilded, with a pillared audience hall under a spire, a reproduction in cheaper materials and on a smaller scale of the palace at Mrauk-u. All the palaces in the states between India and China have, and have always had, a close resemblance. As we shall see, the palace at Mrauk-u was like the contemporary palaces in Burma and Siam, and, since the fashion has not greatly changed, like the palaces used to-day by the Shan Sawbwas. It will be clear that Manrique was not received in the main hall of audience, which is always the eastern front of the palace and open to view, but in a more private hall further in, such as may be seen at the Mandalay palace.

PORTUGUESE IN GOA
(*From Linschoten, 'Voyages'; Amsterdam*, 1638)

THE KING OF COCHIN
(*From Linschoten, 'Voyages'; Amsterdam,* 1638)

Alighting from their palanquins, the party entered the main building and found themselves in a hall where a company of the bodyguard, in this case Burmese mercenaries, were drawn up. These men conducted them into a second hall, where a company of Upper Indian mercenaries, probably Pathans, was posted. Thence they moved into a third hall in which were waiting a number of courtiers. After salutations had been exchanged, the Comptroller went up to a small door, on which he knocked three times, pausing after each knock. At the third knock, a shutter above was opened and 'an ancient humpbacked eunuch looked out'. He was a hideous creature and he shouted at the Comptroller: 'What do you mean, battering at the door of the Lord of Life!' Somewhat taken aback, the Comptroller replied meekly that he had orders to introduce the two Portuguese strangers now with him. For answer the eunuch slammed the shutter in his face.

This unpleasant reception caused everyone in the room to fall nervously on their knees. Presumably the janitor had received no instructions to admit anyone. What was to be done? There was dead silence. Manrique let his eyes wander round the hall. It looked as if an enchantment held the company. Not a sound was to be heard in the strange place. The kneeling figures, the stillness, the dreadful face at the shutter, recalled to his mind scenes from the romances of the period, stories of magicians and dragons, dwarfs and ogres.

From these dreaming thoughts he was presently aroused by the appearance of a beautiful girl at the shutter. She was dressed in embroidered white silk edged with pearls, and in her black hair was a bunch of white jasmine. With a laughing face she repeated a phrase of verse:

> *Be welcome as the rain farmers long for,*
> *When their ricefields are parched in the sun.*
> *Happy strangers, welcome to a smile*
> *From the mouth of the Everlasting Lord of Life.*

Immediately, the door was opened, not by the disgruntled porter, but by a party of stoutish women, who may have been an Amazon guard. Manrique found himself in another large hall, at the end of which, looking down on them, as it were from a window, he saw a youngish man. Immediately, the Comptroller fell on his knees and elbows, with his palms together, and touched the floor thrice with his forehead—the ceremonial *shi-ko*, very similar to the *kotow*. The Friar and the Captain copied his example to the best of their ability, for they guessed that the man in the window was King Thiri-thu-dhamma himself, who at the time was not more than twenty-eight years of age.

One of the Amazons, if they were Amazons—the kings of Further India used such a guard for the private apartments rather than a corps of eunuchs—one of the stout women, we had better say, led the Portuguese to a place nearer the window, where carpets were spread and a few grandees were seated. There she placed Manrique, with Tibao behind him, for from beginning to end of the mission the Friar was conceded the position of spokesman. At this moment their present to the King was brought in by some persons whom Manrique declares to have been eunuchs, and may have been so, though eunuchs, being repugnant to Buddhists, were not as a rule employed in the harems of Buddhist kings. The present consisted of a crown made of cloves, a hundred half-pint flasks of Persian scent, fourteen packets of Tibetan musk, and four yards of the very finest woollen cloth from Spain. The articles were displayed for the king to see. He made no sign or remark and they were removed.

The royal interpreter now told Manrique that His Majesty desired to know the object of his visit. He also warned him, in an aside, that the correct etiquette, on being thus addressed by the king—a singular honour—was to make a further *shi-ko* before answering. Manrique complied at once, and, when he had sat down again, the interpreter whispered that the moment was propitious for him to make his petition.

What he said to the King did not differ in substance from what he had said to the Admiral. He dilated upon the danger from the Mughal, upon the prowess and loyal service of the Portuguese, and upon their resolve to continue the king's faithful servants. Declaring that the Captains at Dianga never acted except on his advice and that therefore if they had conspired it must have been with his knowledge, he asked how, if he were the chief conspirator, he would have dared to put himself in the King's power.

It is well to remember here that it was not the practice of such kings as Thiri-thu-dhamma to receive a stranger in order to dispute with him. Before the audience all must have been arranged. During the week since Manrique's arrival, the King, who had been fully informed by the Admiral of the object of the mission, no doubt had made his inquiries and already concluded that he had been misinformed by the Viceroy of Chittagong. Reflection, moreover, must have convinced him that the Dianga captains were unlikely in the ordinary course to prefer the Mughal's service to his, for the simple but good reason that they were so well off with him that no credible offer by another could tempt them. They had lands, slaves, mistresses, and the huge revenue from their raids. The Mughal wanted to end the slave raids. But how could he compensate the captains for their loss?

These considerations had predisposed Thiri-thu-dhamma in the mission's favour. Now he was impressed by the Friar's bearing. We can suppose he was well pleased that the Portuguese were innocent. Past history showed how satisfactory was the present situation. When Goa was at the height of her power before Portugal's absorption in 1580 by the Spanish monarchy, a viceroy might well have joined forces with the freelances of his nation in Bengal and have made a descent upon Mrauk-u. That was the real danger period. Later, in 1616, when the Viceroy Don Jeronimo de Azevedo did join the filibuster, Gonzales Tibao, in such a raid, Portuguese power was already on the decline. Soon afterwards it was found possible to bring the freelances to heel, and they had been converted into excellent mercenaries just in time to form a frontier corps against the encroaching Mughal. It was highly desirable to retain their services. They must be given every latitude provided they remained faithful. Further, now that Goa was no longer so powerful as to be dangerous, it would be good policy to enter into direct relations with her, for if at any time he were involved in a more serious clash with the Mughal, a reinforcement of Portuguese war-galleys would be very useful. Arakan was somewhat dangerously isolated. The King of Burma in the south had a savage defeat to avenge, a White Elephant to recover. Statecraft, every prudent counsel, indicated the Portuguese as natural allies. It must therefore have been with profound satisfaction that he learnt there had been no conspiracy at Dianga. So now, at the conclusion of Manrique's speech, it was not necessary to put further questions. He briefly assured the Friar that he did not doubt his word and declared he would issue formal orders for the fleet's return.

As soon as he had said this, a curtain was drawn across the window, hiding him from sight. Everyone performed a final *shi-ko*. The audience was at an end.

XV
The Blessed One

When Manrique published his *Travels* in 1649 he was, as Procurator-General of the estates of his order, an important cleric at the Roman Curia. As such, he strove to make the book as scholarly as he could by quotations from the Fathers and florid passages founded on the Latin classics. But he was not a man of real intellectual curiosity, particularly in the matter of oriental religions. During the days which followed his audience, we do not find him exploring the site of the Mahamuni, the most renowned of all Buddhist sites at that time in Further India.

But we are more curious; moreover, to turn aside from Sirigutta hill without acquainting ourselves with it more closely would leave us almost as ignorant as was Manrique of one of the elements of a singular drama.

The Mahamuni precincts occupied the whole hill, both the top and the sides. There were three walled enclosures, the lowest wall at the base, the second thirty feet up, and the third, enclosing the levelled summit, again thirty feet higher. Covered step-ways mounting from gates at the four cardinal points led to the shrine, the centre of the innermost enclosure. In the first enclosure were a library and a reservoir fed by a perennial spring. In the second were twelve figures of Hindu deities dating from the pre-Arakanese period. These now occupied the position of guardian spirits assigned to them in the Buddhism of the Little Vehicle, which, though it did not strictly recognize deities, had no positive objection to them provided they served and worshipped the Buddha. More important was a great banyan tree, under which the Blessed One had rested while superintending—as legend had it—the casting of his statue. In the third enclosure, besides the shrine, was a bell, the Yattara bell (the bell now hanging there is a copy made in 1734), one of the strangest bells in the world, for inscribed

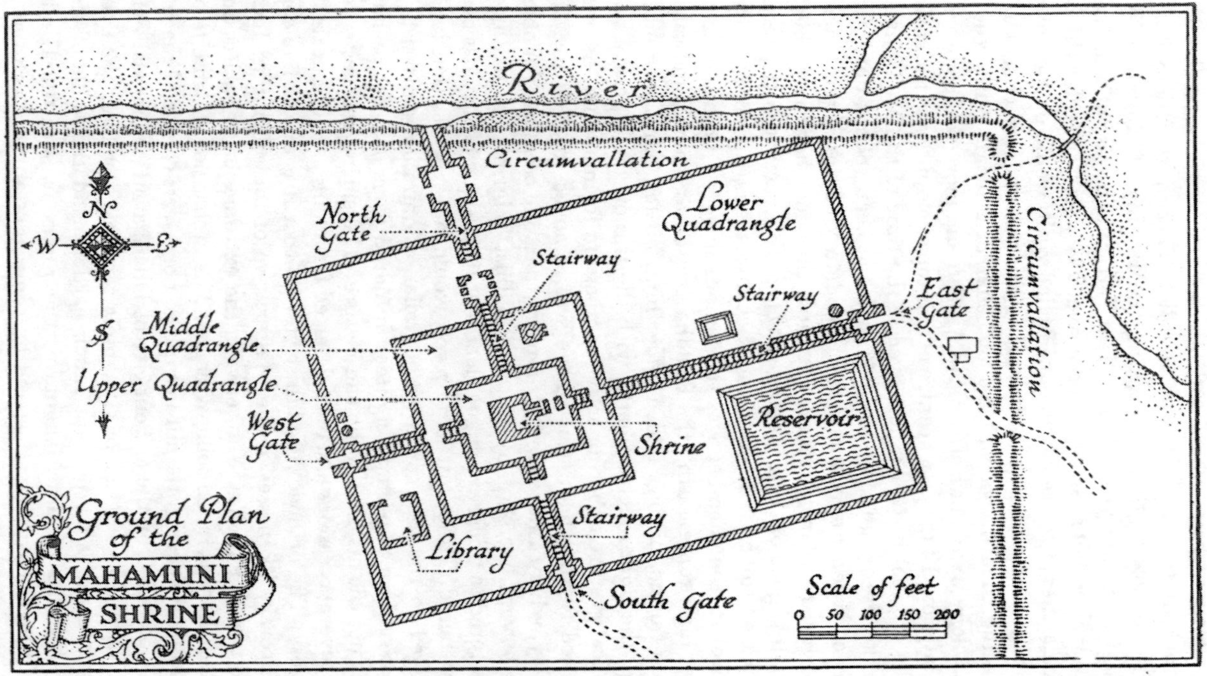
Ground Plan of the MAHAMUNI SHRINE
River
Circumvallation
Circumvallation
N
W
E
S
North Gate
Lower Quadrangle
Stairway
Stairway
East Gate
Middle Quadrangle
Upper Quadrangle
West Gate
Shrine
Reservoir
Stairway
Library
South Gate
Scale of feet
0 50 100 150 200

on it were spells and astrological tables, which gave minute instructions how, when, and in what circumstances it should be struck, if the country were invaded. These instructions had no resemblance to those governing the ringing of church bells in England in this year of 1942. The Yattara bell was not sounded as a warning, but as an occult offensive. The notes, provided the particularities of the tables were complied with, would operate to put the invaders to flight by deranging their astrological chart and so placing them in jeopardy. This belief in a magic reinforced by astrology was a characteristic of Arakan and more will be heard of it later on. In the exact centre of this top enclosure was the shrine. The original had been destroyed at the time of the Mongolian or Arakanese invasion of A.D. 957 and had been rebuilt during the period when the country was a feudatory of the Pagan kings of Burma. In Manrique's time it must therefore have resembled a small pagoda of the Pagan dynasty type, a structure with massive brick or stone walls enclosing a chamber and surmounted by a spire. In the chamber was the famous image, a bronze over ten feet high representing the Buddha dressed as a monk and seated on a throne, his legs folded under him, his left hand open on his lap, the right touching earth with the tips of the fingers, a symbolical gesture denoting active compassion for mankind. As mentioned further back, this image was removed in 1784 to Mandalay, where I have seen it on more than one occasion. An object of fervent worship by many Buddhist pilgrims, it has been plastered so thickly with gold-leaf that its antique beauty has been smothered. To look at it now you would never guess that it belonged to the first centuries of Indian colonization eastwards, a classical bronze perhaps eighteen hundred years old. Yet perhaps it is not the original. Who can be sure? The shrine was destroyed on several occasions and once deserted for a long period. But this is heresy. The orthodox Buddhist view is that it is one of five contemporary likenesses of the Master, two of these being in India and two in Paradise. Yet between the extremes of scepticism and belief there is much solid evidence. The archaeologist can bite on the fact that Sirigutta hill lies in the north-east corner of the site once occupied by the ancient city of Dhaññavati, whose walls are still traceable, an Indian city, built certainly not later than the first century A.D., perhaps much earlier. And the walls of the three courts of the Mahamuni, the reservoir, and the Hindu sculptures, have been declared by competent authorities to date from the period of that city.[1] We can, therefore, be certain that *a* Mahamuni image has sat on Sirigutta for a millennium and a half.

King Thiri-thu-dhamma would have found our archaeology very dry and stupid, compared with his own history of the origin of the great image. In his library, situated, as we have said, in the first court of the shrine, and near the west gate, he had a number of historical books in the form of palm-leaf manuscripts. The most ancient and notable of these was the *Sappadanapakarana*, which provided a detailed account of the casting of the Mahamuni. The number of persons in this country acquainted with the *Sappadanapakarana* will be very few, though for centuries it was one of the most widely read books in Further India. This would be insufficient reason to obtrude it here, were it not that to glance at some of its contents will give a better idea than any direct exposition of the religion of Arakan, an Apostolic Buddhism, yet tinged with myth and magic, though not nearly to the extent that these are found in Mahayana Buddhism. And the book illustrates vividly the extraordinary religious importance of the Mahamuni.

The manuscript begins by stating that Candrasuriya, king of Dhaññavati, the outer Indian state whose capital was built round Sirigutta hill, hearing that a new world teacher, a Buddha, was living in Central India, a Master who knew the truth which was salvation, desired to go and pay homage to him. Divining his intention, the Buddha called his beloved disciple Ananda and said: 'The king will have to pass through forests dangerous to travellers; wide rivers will impede his journey; he must cross a sea which is full of monsters. It will be an act of charity if we go to his dominion, so that he may pay homage without risking his life.'

In making this proposal the Blessed One not only planned to do a compassionate act but also to spread his gospel in what is now Arakan, for he had lived there in previous existences and relics of his former bodies were already in its soil.

The journey to Arakan was made by air, for the Buddha of legend always transported himself and his disciples in that manner. Landing on a hill named Selagiri, which commanded a view of the rice plain towards Dhaññavati, and the ranges about it, the Master pointed out to his disciples the various places in which his former lives had been passed. On the mount Veluvannapabbata he had been a boa-constrictor. On the mount Ghandagiri he had been

[1] For the whole matter see Dr. Forchhammer's *Papers on Subjects relating to the Archaeology of Burma.*

a rhinoceros. In a range called Salamaya he had lived as a gardener, on Selapabbata hill as a Brahmin, on the Rajapabbata hill as an elephant, and on Kasinapabbata as king of the peacocks. On all those mounts his relics would be found and enshrined in pagodas after his *paranivāna*.

This prophecy caused the earth to shake and the sea to boil. Candrasuriya in his palace was alarmed and asked his astrologers to explain the meaning of the signs. They replied that assuredly the Blessed One had arrived. A propitious hour being fixed, he set out to welcome his great visitor. A procession was formed—elephants, horses, chariots, foot-soldiers, with the queen at the head of the court ladies. On reaching the base of Selagiri hill, the king dismounted and approached the Blessed One on foot, bearing presents of flowers, perfumes, and parched rice.

When the ceremony of welcome was at an end, the Buddha preached a sermon, in which he instructed the king in the Five and Eight Precepts and admonished him on the Ten Kingly Duties, to wit, universal beneficence, daily prayer, the showing of mercy, the exaction of not more than a tenth, justice, punishment without anger, the support of his subjects as the earth supports them, the employment of prudent commanders, the taking of good counsel, and the avoidance of pride. This was the way of salvation, said he.

'Candrasuriya became transported with joy,' records the *Sappadanapakarana*, 'and addressed the Teacher thus: "Great King of Righteousness, have compassion, I beseech you, upon me and my subjects and condescend to visit my humble capital." The Blessed One consented.'

The Buddha's stay in Dhaññavati lasted a week. What he did day by day is recorded in the closest detail, and how he preached the law, urging mercy and charity. The history then continues thus: 'When the Blessed One began to make his preparations for departure, the King, who with his subjects had been converted to the new religion, made him this request: "Lord of the Three Worlds, when you go from us we shall have no-one to whom we may pay homage. Will you not leave us the shape of yourself?"'

To this request for a statue the Buddha gave his consent. Candrasuriya collected the necessary metals and, having deposited them in golden baskets overlaid with flowers and white cloth, sent them away to be smelted on a white elephant and under the shade of white parasols. The artist designated to make the wax model and the mould was no less than the Lord of Paradise, a personage who was one of the old gods and who, converted along with the king to Buddhism, now worshipped the Buddha. Yet the people long continued to call him by many grand names, such as Sakra, the Able One, Divapati, Lord of the Gods, Meghavahana, the Rider of the Clouds, and Swargapati, the Master of Heaven. He was a sculptor of supernatural power, as indeed are all great sculptors, for great works of art partake of Heaven and cannot be made except by those masters able to pass its gate and return. It was therefore natural that, for a work of such superlative importance as the statue of the Blessed One, an artist who was not only conversant with, but Lord of Heaven, should be selected.

Meanwhile the Buddha was invited to rest on Sirigutta under a banyan, in a pavilion decorated with carving, a pleasant retreat well provided with fans, where fruits abounded and music was played. Sirigutta, here explains the author of the *Sappadana-pakarana*, was so called because it was as white as fine silver and looked like a conch shell whose opening is towards the right, that rarest of shells which even to-day is worth its weight in gold. This comparison leads the author to even more unusual derivations. Was not Sirigutta once called Trikumbhanda because it reminded you in its form of three ogres standing abreast? Long ago, too, they named it Siharaja because on the summit was the carving of a lion-king roaring over his prey. Stranger still was the name Wakthazo, given because on its side was said to have been a relief depicting a sow suckling her young, possibly connected with the fact that the Buddha had lived there as a king-hog with five hundred consorts.

But we must leave these bypaths of mythological nomenclature and return to the statue. Within a week it was finished and delivered. The likeness was extraordinary. It is said that the Blessed One, anxious, as was his rule, to make even perfection more perfect, breathed upon the sculpture, when those who stood by declared in an enthusiasm without trace of flattery that there were now two Buddhas, an inestimable boon as they would be able to retain one of them in their city for ever. Candrasuriya embraced the feet of the Blessed One in a rapture so intense that he lost consciousness. On recovering sufficiently, he ordered the statue to be placed on a jewelled throne in a shrine surmounted by a carved spire which he had built on the top of Sirigutta hill.

When they were all assembled there, the Lord Omniscient thus addressed the image of himself: 'I shall pass into Nirvana in my eightieth year,' he said, 'but you, instinct with my essence, will live the five thousand years which I have prescribed for the duration of the Religion.'

With that, and when he had preached a final sermon, he called his disciples and took his departure, again by air.

For King Thiri-thu-dhamma this remarkable story was a statement of fact. The Buddha had died in 543 B.C. Altogether 2,173 years had elapsed since then, and for that immense period the image of the founder of the Religion had remained on Sirigutta, the oldest, most mysterious, the most holy object in the world. The relics detailed to the disciples on Selagiri had all been found and enshrined. Arakan was a sacred country; it was the heart of Buddhism; and he, as its king, was the most notable Buddhist ruler in existence. Grave indeed was his responsibility. He had not only to maintain the state as the homeland of the Arakanese race, but as the one place on earth where an authentic shape of the Tathagata was preserved, a possession of greater potency than the most precious relic. True, he had another possession beyond price, comparable even to the Mahamuni itself. He had a White Elephant, acquired by his grandfather in circumstances of splendid triumph. But though every care was lavished upon this creature, it would die one day. The country would be without a White Elephant, unless perchance another were found. But the Mahamuni would still be there, and would remain always as long as the frontiers were inviolate. His duty was to keep them inviolate. More, as the greatest Buddhist king it was his duty to extend them, so that all the world might learn of the Eightfold Path that led to enlightenment and salvation.

XVI

The Five Taslims

During the days which followed the royal audience, Manrique was occupied with practical affairs. His first duty was to relieve the anxiety of the Portuguese at Dianga by a letter announcing the success of his mission. With the letter he enclosed a sermon on the subject of gratitude. By God's grace they had been saved. They therefore owed God a debt. Let them pay that debt by living henceforth as better Christians. He does not suggest that this reformation need interfere with their slave raids; these he had already justified as war against the infidel. It is to their private lives that he refers. Let them free themselves 'from mortal sin and from those entanglements so prejudicial to your souls and to those of the unhappy women with whom you have contracted them.' Knowing the way the Portuguese of all classes lived at Goa, and under the eye of ecclesiastical authority, it is not to be supposed that at Dianga, in the midst of a vast paganism, much attention was paid to these admonitions.

This letter dispatched, a round of visits followed. The Admiral's brother-in-law, the courtier who had helped them so much and had been well rewarded for it, now advised them to pay their respects to all the members of the Privy Council. A present should, of course, be presented in each case, he reminded them, but it would be well worth their while, had they further requests in mind. Manrique had several further requests, and so made the calls and gave the presents as advised.

This careful observance of etiquette paved the way for a further royal audience, of which Manrique made skilful use. The King gave him his opportunity by asking whether it would be possible to induce the Viceroy of Goa to issue a formal order forbidding any Portuguese from entering the service of the Mughal.

Manrique: The present Viceroy and his predecessors have

issued such orders, which are in conformity with the wishes of our Sovereign, Philip IV of Spain and Portugal, who has declared that Your Majesty should always be supported against the Mughal in that the latter seeks to become absolute master of all India. But if Your Majesty desires to retain that support, the Portuguese in these dominions should be treated fairly.

Thiri-thu-dhamma: I have followed my father's and grandfather's policy in this respect. My relations with them have been very cordial.

Manrique: Your Majesty's treatment of them has been most fair, but your representative at Chittagong by falsely accusing them has not acted in a manner likely to improve relations.

Thiri-thu-dhamma: I have already taken disciplinary action in that regard.

At this news that the Viceroy of Chittagong was to be removed, Manrique was profoundly relieved, for that officer would never have forgiven him his mission. He expressed his gratitude by making the King the Indian salutation known as *taslim*, a profound bow, thrice repeated, when the ground is touched with the back of the right hand, which is afterwards lifted to the top of the head.

Manrique: Your Majesty's gracious declarations of friendship embolden me to ask further favours. There are nine families of Christian slaves resident near Mahamuni. May it please your Majesty to release them from bondage, with permission to serve the state in some paid capacity like the Portuguese at the capital.

Thiri-thu-dhamma: These men were captured during my father's reign from Mughal vessels on which they were acting as mariners.

Manrique: They have been in captivity thirteen years. If your Majesty will release them now, the whole Portuguese nation will be under a deep obligation.

Thiri-thu-dhamma: But service with the Mughal is precisely what I wish to penalize.

Manrique: Your Majesty's magnanimity will appear all the greater if you do not.

The King decided to make this concession. As we have seen and shall see again, it was of great importance for him to retain the loyalty of his Portuguese subjects. Manrique made a second *taslim*.

Manrique: Your Majesty has no objection, I trust, to my visiting the capital. The Portuguese there would be grievously disappointed were I to return without giving them spiritual comfort.

When the King intimated that there was no objection, the Friar made a third *taslim.*

Manrique: Your Majesty will think me importunate. But I have a last favour to ask. If the Portuguese and other Christians who are your Majesty's servants are to live contented, as it is to your Majesty's interest that they should, the provision of a church for them at the capital will be found expedient. Have I your Majesty's permission to build such a church?

This request Thiri-thu-dhamma might have refused. His predecessors had not encouraged a resident priest. There was always the danger that when foreigners had a recognized meeting-place they might use it for purposes less blameless than religion. Foreign mercenaries were particularly apt to conspire. What better place for conspiracy than a church? However, he had made up his mind to meet this friar. The report that the Portuguese at Dianga were plotting against him had been a great shock. Had it been true, the defences of his northern province would have been seriously weakened. The affair had brought home to him the necessity of improving his relations with the Portuguese. He could not suppose that his projected attack on Dianga had made them love him more. Clearly it was a moment for concessions. He sanctioned the building of a church. Manrique made a fourth *taslim.*

It would seem that this audience was of an informal or private character. The kings of the East, even on occasion the Son of Heaven himself, were wont to converse at their ease with Jesuits and friars. They did not use the same state with them as with lay envoys. Their cloth no doubt was their passport. Maybe, too, the kings were glad of an excuse for informality. On this present occasion we cannot suppose that Thiri-thu-dhamma was at his window-throne. He will have been seated on a dais among cushions and rugs. When the business was over and a secretary had been told to draft the necessary orders, betel was brought in on a gold tray studded with jewels. On the tray, which was shaped like a large *tazza,* was a variety of little vessels or boxes containing the nut, the lime, and the leaf. Thiri-thu-dhamma took up one of these, a box of heavy gold ornamented with sapphires and rubies, and presented it to Manrique, who performed a fifth *taslim.* His Majesty then rose and Manrique accompanied him as far as the door of the private apartments 'beyond which only eunuchs and women are allowed to pass'.

So ended a very satisfactory audience. The Friar had obtained all he asked for, with a gold betel box thrown in, a box which would do very well to contain the Eucharist on the altar of the new church to be built at Mrauk-u. In the course of the next few days he obtained from the secretariat written copies of the king's orders and the release of the Christian slaves. This cost him a few more tips and presents, but, as he remarks, you had to tip wherever you might be, and Arakanese officials were no worse than Portuguese in that matter. A day was then fixed for the journey to Mrauk-u. A police officer was detailed to accompany him thither.

XVII
The Dedication of the Church

From Mahamuni to Mrauk-u is only twenty miles in a straight line, but perhaps double that distance by the winding creeks through which the approach is made. Manrique and his party travelled in a galley provided by the police. The Japanese captain and some of his men insisted on accompanying them.

The slaves rowed hard all that day, and before nightfall, while still some distance from the city, galleys dressed with flags were seen rowing to meet them. 'As soon as our vessel came in sight of them, we were greeted with a salute of ordnance and a flourish of bugles,' says Manrique. The principal galley, which was flying the Royal Standard of Portugal with its device of the Five Wounds, contained the Captain-General of the mercenaries, Manuel Rodriquez Tigre. He and those with him made such a demonstration of respect and pleasure when receiving the Friar that he was obliged to remonstrate. The Captain replied, somewhat naively, that in Arakan, where the Buddhist monks were treated with the utmost veneration by the people, it would look bad if they received him with any less regard, particularly as word had gone round that he was an ecclesiastic of high rank.

This meeting took place ten or fifteen miles from the city. The night was spent at a village on the bank and next morning early they rowed on to Mrauk-u. The Portuguese, Eurasian, and native Christians did not live inside the walls but in a suburb called Daingri-pet on the western side. It was there that the party disembarked and was received by the main body of the Catholic community.

From Daingri-pet the palace was quite visible, for it was less than half a mile away and stood on a rise fifty feet above the creek. Its layout was similar to that of the Mahamuni. There were three enclosures which rose in tiers, each bounded by a thick stone wall. The circumference of the outermost square was 2,000 yards, the sides varying from a quarter to one-third of a mile. Its greatest width did not exceed 620 yards. The main audience hall and the private apartments were situated in the innermost square, which measured 218 yards from west to east, and 293 yards from north to south. To-day the walls remain, but the palace buildings have disappeared. They were of teakwood, lacquered and gilded, the roofs carved with figures and rising in spires. From Daingri-pet it must have been an imposing sight, though the Dutch artist whose impression of it in 1660 is given here has made it look rather more imposing, though less high, than it really was.

The measurements just given show that this palace-city was about one-third of the size of the Forbidden City at Peking. But as the territories which supported it were only a small fraction of those comprising China, it must be computed a great and surprising palace to find on the rain-drenched littoral of the Further Indian divide.

The map shows how curious was the city in which it was enclosed. The area surrounded by walls had a circumference of some twelve miles. But a considerable proportion of it was composed of rocky hills, artificial lakes, and tidal rivers. The walls did not run continuously round it, but were designed to fill in the gaps between the natural defences. Some of the lakes had sluice-gates which in emergency could be opened. It is on record that a Burmese invading army was overwhelmed in this way during the previous century. The principal fortifications were on the east side. The west was protected by a number of wide and deep creeks, more efficacious than moats; the north and south by a jungle of hills. But on the east, where there was an open plain, a chain of artificial lakes had been dug, which wound in and out, with blind alleys and false entrances. This maze of fortifications had been developed since the reign of Min Bin (1531–53) and owed something to Portuguese inspiration. The chief object was defence against a Burmese invasion.

On landing at the suburb of Daingri-pet, Manrique was conducted by his community to a house which they had prepared for him. The officer of police took leave of him there, sending him shortly afterwards a profusion of supplies, rice, salt, butter, cows, pigs, and fowls, treating him thereby in accordance with the rules prescribed for the reception of ambassadors. The Friar immedi-

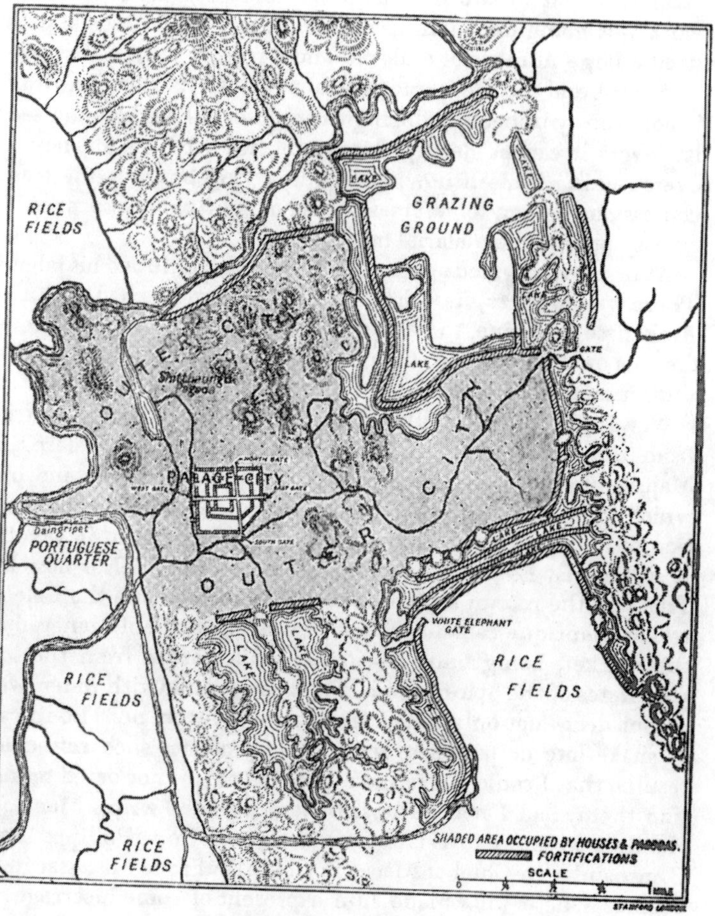

PLAN OF MRAUK-U

ately set about the business of selecting a site for the church. This was quickly done and its erection was put in hand at once. It was to be made of wood, as were all the buildings in the city, and as wood of the most excellent quality was easily obtainable, it was estimated that in two months it would be complete. While this work was going on, Manrique heard many confessions and baptized a large number of children and wives. It was the first week in August and the rain came on again with all its violence. Arakan is notoriously unhealthy during the monsoon. For those unused to its fevers it can be deadly. Manrique, tired by his journey and overstraining himself now by listening long hours to the frantic confessions of men for years deprived of spiritual reassurance, fell an easy prey to the malarial mosquito.

At first he struggled against the fever and continued his labours. There was no Portuguese doctor in the place and he had no faith in Arakanese medicine, so he had himself bled and took what remedies his own knowledge suggested, but grew weaker and weaker, until it seemed he was dying.

News of his grave condition reached the King, who had returned from the Mahamuni and was in residence at the palace. His Majesty immediately ordered the royal physician to attend him, which again was in accordance with the rules governing the reception of ambassadors. This man eventually cured him in October. It seems that he used a remedy, the secret of which is now lost. This was the root of a plant found only in Java and the Celebes, which Manrique calls lucerrage. It was not available generally in the market, being only procurable on an order from the local potentates of the Spice Islands. This root, groundwith water, was a potent drug, not only in the treatment of fevers but also in cases of snake-bite or poisoned arrows. 'It produces such miraculous results, that I could never have believed them, nor dared to mention them, had I not witnessed them myself,' writes Manrique. He then goes on to relate how a certain Dom Philippe Lobo, Commander-in-Chief at Macao in China, put in to Macassar in the Celebes whose king made him a present of some lucerrage. To demonstrate its extraordinary powers, the king arranged the following experiment. A condemned criminal was sent for and pricked with a poisoned dart. The wretch began foaming at the mouth and within a few minutes was writhing on the floor. He was given a drink of the lucerrage drug and in a short time was perfectly recovered. To prove that the experiment was no piece of play-acting, the criminal was again pricked and this time left to die.

Whatever may be the precise truth about this remarkable drug, of which other travellers make no mention, the Friar was convinced that the royal physician administered it to him and that it was the cause of his recovery.

By the time he was on his feet again the church was finished, and a day for its dedication fixed in the third week of October, when the monsoon was over. It was a great occasion. The interior was decorated with sprays of bamboo and palm and also with flowers made of silk which one of the Japanese Christians presented. The altar was covered with these flowers in gold vases studded with jewels which, somehow or other, had been borrowed from the royal treasury. (It is salutary to recall here how at Dianga Friar Manoel had refused the Hindus a loan of hangings for their festival.) The Mrauk-u treasury lent no less than twenty-four such gold vases, four of which were so massive that a man could scarcely lift them. Many silver vases were also lent, some being used as ornaments, some as incense burners, and some to hold Chinese incense sticks. In the middle of the altar was the gold betel box given by the King under a picture of the Virgin, with incense sticks of superior quality burning on each side. And the nave was completely covered with Indian and Persian carpets.

The flowers, the floating incense, the many colours, the air of mystery, became the talk of the Court, like all courts idle and attracted by novelties. Many grandees sauntered down to have a look. Manrique, engaged though he was with hearing confessions and conducting the Mass, was continually being called out to receive noblemen and answer their questions about the Virgin Mary. On the actual day of the dedication such a crowd of courtiers and their retainers appeared and tried to push their way through the door, that the Catholic congregation could not get in and it was found necessary to send for the police. The constables with difficulty turned away the Arakanese, the door was secured and Mass celebrated. Manrique preached a sermon, exhorting his congregation to worship the Virgin, whose support they sorely needed, living as they did among a people in the 'grip of the Devil'. There were fireworks that night.

XVIII
The Debate with the Royal Chaplain

When the dedication ceremonies were over, Manrique took an early opportunity of going to the palace to thank the King for sending his doctor. The most convenient way of getting there was by boat, for the streets during the monsoon were very muddy, while by creek you could get close to most places in the outer city. Mrauk-u had a distant resemblance to Venice. Indeed, a Jesuit called Farinha, who visited it ten years later, uses that comparison in a letter to Rome. Manrique puts it this way: 'A considerable river traverses the city, separating as it goes into many branches, so that most of the streets are waterways, navigable even by large vessels.' Where these creeks passed through the fortifications, there were water-gates, commanded by batteries. Most writers declared the city to be impregnable. But an impregnable city is like the Golden Age: there has never been one and never will be.

Going from Daingri-pet to the palace one saw the western section of the town. The houses stood on wooden posts, the roofs thatched with palm leaves and the walls made of bamboo matting. 'Much ingenuity', notes Manrique, 'is lavished on designing for them mats of the finest texture and of many colours, neatly and handsomely woven.' A house was thus a wooden framework fitted with mats, the same as are most houses to-day in that region, and not only in Burma, but in all the vast territories of the bamboo, stretching to Siam, the Islands, and southern China. 'But the princes and grandees', continues Manrique, 'have wooden walls to their palaces which are ornamented with carvings and gilt mouldings.'

On this occasion his boat landed him near the steps which led up to the west gate, in the outermost wall of the palace-city. He passed up through that gate with others who had permission to attend the royal levee and passing in turn through the second and third walls reached the topmost enclosure. There stood the palace proper in front of him, the hall of audience with its 'great wooden pillars of such length and symmetry that one is astonished that trees so lofty and straight can exist'.

It does not seem that the audience that day was held in this main hall, but in a lesser one inside. As at the Mahamuni palace, there was a window. When Thiri-thu-dhamma appeared at it, he noticed the Friar, who hastened to make the prostration used at that court, the *shi-ko*, and thanked the King for his kindness 'with all the most gracious phrases I could command'. He spoke in Hindústani, and Thiri-thu-dhamma replied in the same language with a smile: 'Father, I am very glad to see you well again,' and added: 'I was interested to hear of the festival you have been celebrating in the temple newly erected to your God.'

Manrique: And Your Majesty's God also. On the festival day and, indeed, every day since, I have prayed to Him for Your Majesty's health, both of body and spirit.

Manrique's meaning here was, of course, that God the Father, as Lord of Heaven and earth, was necessarily the King's Lord, whether he believed in Him or not. The King, however, did not take it in that sense. The Christian god was no doubt a genuine supernatural personage like the Hindu gods and had his position in one of the heavens. It was therefore gratifying to know that his good offices had been invoked. Such a personage, however, was necessarily subordinate to the Buddha, for all the gods worshipped the Buddha and themselves hoped one day to become Buddhas. The state of being a Buddha represented a state of mind when an apprehension of absolute truth was attained. Gods and men equally longed to reach that state, and it was possible for all gods and men to reach it if they followed the Excellent Law.

The discerning reader will perceive that the points of view of the Augustinian and the King were both very wide apart and very close together. They were very wide apart because their terminology was so different as to be irreconcilable; they were very close together because, as the writings of the Christian mystics show, union with God, the ultimate aim of Christianity, is a state of mind when an apprehension of absolute truth is obtained. While that apprehension lasts, and afterwards in so far as memory can preserve it, the mortal who has experienced it transcends mortality. Such transcendence when permanent was in Buddhist terminology styled being a Buddha, and the term, enlightenment, corresponded with the conception of union with God. God, therefore, for them was absolute reality, as it was for the Christian mystics. For Manrique, God was a personage. Hence the king's impression that he was just one more god.

But in the audience hall of a remote oriental palace in the seventeenth century, so nice an appreciation of their respective points of view was not likely to occur to a Buddhist king and an Augustinian friar.

The conversation which followed led nowhere. We must remember that Manrique's account of it was written twenty years later at a safe desk in the Papal city: he may not have been as bold and assertive as he pretends. What he does is to represent himself as expostulating with the king for his worship of the Mahamuni. Bowing in a temple before the image of a god was mere idol-worship. An idol could not be worth more than the material of which it was made. It was a demoniacal illusion to imagine that to adore it was to adore God. The King did not reply, as he might have done had the Buddhism of Arakan been as pure as the original doctrine preached by the Buddha, by saying that he was no more worshipping the image of the Buddha as such than did Manrique the picture of the Virgin on his altar. He did not say that because, mixed up with his apostolic conception of the Buddha-state, were magical beliefs in the potency of the Great Image, beliefs arising from the account given of its origin in his book, the *Sappadanapakarana*, and exemplified in the tradition that it was the palladium of the realm. He considered himself the greatest Buddhist king in the world precisely because he was its guardian. He could not give the Friar a strictly orthodox answer, and he did not choose to give him the explanation which would have disclosed his particular view. Rather, he did what many Oriental kings liked to do, when a foreign priest visited their court. He invited him to enter into a discussion with a Buddhist monk who was seated below him. The man was probably the Royal Chaplain.

The Chaplain, who was dressed in a yellow robe draped about him somewhat in the fashion of a toga, and whose head was shaved and feet were bare, a person, says Manrique, of venerable appearance, began in a tone of some asperity. He had always found it surprising, he said, that Catholic priests, judging from those he had met with, not only showed a deplorable lack of respect for the Blessed One, but also an ignorant intolerance of

Buddhism in general by declaring their faith to be the only one which led to salvation.

Manrique: If I did not know that to be true, why should I have come all this weary way to preach? Were there any other road except through Christ, our missionaries would only be wasting their time. It is because there is none other that they are here, for of all things we most desire to save men's souls.

The Chaplain: It is incredible that such a view could honestly be held by a person of intelligence. And as I will not accuse your Reverence of stupidity, I have no alternative but to attribute your so-called missionary zeal to some ulterior motive.[1]

At a look from the King the chaplain did not continue his strictures, but proceeded to sketch some of the doctrines of the Little Vehicle. A man's lot in his present existence was determined by his acts in previous existences. If he had behaved well, his present life was happy and earth somewhat like a paradise. And if he continued to act in accordance with the Way of Enlightenment, then the time came when at last he was fully enlightened and his happiness complete, for no evil could touch him. But if he did not follow the Way, but sought his pleasures outside it, then life by life he weighted himself with unhappiness until this world seemed to him a very hell.

Manrique: But what sense is there in a man being born over and over again?

The Chaplain: It is the only manner in which he can improve himself. Were he not given chance after chance, he could not see the result of wrong action or have opportunity, when he did perceive it, to take right action.

Manrique was unable to follow the monk's thought. It all seemed to him a rigmarole. He was never tactful in pressing the claims of Catholicism. There was nothing of Ricci or de Nobili about him. To admit the existence of any truth in a pagan creed was highly dangerous. That was the way heresies crept in. The Inquisition punished that very crime of tolerance, for crime it was. The Catholics in Arakan, as he had discovered from their confessions, were far too tolerant of Buddhism. Many of them, while still professing to be Christians, found some of its beliefs fatally attractive. Such people were no better than relapsed heretics. Had the arm of the Inquisition extended so far, they could

[1] The Jesuits had been expelled from Japan a few years before this because their motives were suspected of being political.

hardly have escaped the fire. Should he then listen further to this heathen monk? No, he would tell him flatly what he thought of his doctrines. 'Your exposition is meaningless,' he broke out, 'but one thing is perfectly clear: if you continue to believe your Buddha's false statements, you will go after death to the hell where he lives.'

The Chaplain was on the point of making a tart reply, when the King motioned to him to be silent. 'Father,' he said to the Friar, 'it has been a pleasure to hear you argue, but you are still weak after your fever and ought not to overtire yourself. When you are stronger I will get you to have a debate with the Arch-Abbot of the Order, the Shitthaung Hpongri. He is an ecclesiastic of greater scholarship than your present opponent.'

Saying this with an inimitable dignity and politeness, he made the sign that the audience was at an end. The curtain was drawn across and hid him from view.

XIX

The White Elephant

If it was not easy for Manrique to grasp the theological situation in Arakan, it was hardly more possible for him to know what was really happening in politics. There, the three chief personalities were, as we shall see in the last chapters of this book, the Chief Queen, Nat Shin Me, the Mistress of Paradise, and the two rival councillors, Lat Rone and Kuthala. His narrative gives no hint that he was aware of this. But, like any modern visitor to a new country, he tried to find out what he could. After the audience just described, he was conducted on a tour of the palace-city. He saw some curious things and the mention of them here will serve to throw more light upon the Court, on the position of Arakan *vis-à-vis* the kingdoms farther east, and generally upon the history of the preceding half-century.

What they showed him was the Burmese loot. Thirty-one years before, in 1599, Arakan had inflicted a great defeat upon Burma. This occurred during the reign of Thiri-thu-dhamma's grandfather, the great Razagri (1593–1612). The Burmese then had their capital at Pegu. Under their king, Bayin-naung, who died in 1581, so remarkable had been the successes of their arms that their military supremacy was undisputed in that part of the world. In 1564 Ayuthia, the capital of Siam, had been sacked by them and a great booty, including four White Elephants, was carried to Pegu. Faria y Sousa, whom we have quoted earlier in this volume in Captain John Stevens's bold seventeenth-century translation, gives the picture of Bayin-naung's triumphal entry into Pegu. 'Braginoco,' he says, for so he renders the king's style, as if he were a paynim knight from Ariosto, 'Braginoco entered the city in triumph, many wagons going before loaded with idols and inestimable booty. He came at last in a chariot with the conquered queens laden with jewels at his feet, and drawn by the captive princes and lords; before him marched two thousand elephants richly adorned, and after him his victorious troops. He built a palace as big as an ordinary city. The least part of its beauty was carving and gilding; for the roofs of some apartments were covered with plates of solid gold. Some rooms were set with statues of kings and queens of massy gold, set with rich stones, as big as the life. He was carried on a litter of gold upon many men's shoulders, the reverence paid him more like a god than a prince.'

Faria y Sousa published his book in Lisbon in 1666, and Stevens's translation, published by Brome, at the Sign of the Gun, London, appeared in 1695. But the London public had had some first-hand information relating to Pegu as early as 1625, five years before Manrique's visit to Arakan. This was contained in a collection of voyages edited by Samuel Purchas, called *Hakluytus Posthumus* or *Purchas His Pilgrimes*. The book included, among other narratives, that of Ralph Fitch, a Londoner, who visited Pegu in 1586. Bayin-naung had been dead five years, and Nanda-bayin was on the throne. Fitch describes the new city of Pegu, and how he was shown the Siamese loot, including one of the White Elephants: the other three may have died. You had to pay half a ducat to get in to see the beast. If you were lucky, you might get a glimpse of him feeding from silver and gold platters. For his bath in the river he went under a canopy of cloth of gold held by eight men, with a band playing light music in front. 'When he is washed and cometh out of the river, there is a Gentleman which doth wash his feet in a silver basin,' added Fitch. As for the other loot, he was shown a number of the Siamese golden and bronze images, and, though this was of Burmese not Siamese workmanship, a huge statue of Bayin-naung's predecessor, Tabin-shwe-ti, 'a king in golde with a crowne of golde on his head full of great rubies and saphires'. This may mean the statue had a treasure of jewels inside it.

When Razagri invaded Burma thirteen years later in 1599, he carried away to Mrauk-u the Siamese loot, the most important items of which were the White Elephant and a pair of ruby earrings of fabulous value. The gold statue of Tabin-shwe-ti was also taken, along with other images, some of them from Ayuthia. And among the captives was a princess, Nanda-bayin's own daughter.

Thirty-one years pass and another European views this loot. Manrique is conducted into a building, the rooms of which were panelled with scented timbers, such as sandalwood and eaglewood, the latter an aromatic wood with a sweet cloying fragrance, which clings always to it in a damp hot climate, but in the drier colder air of England evaporates, as I have found, so that a walking-stick which once could scent its corner on a close tropic night is now odourless. Passing through these perfumed chambers he came to a pavilion known as the 'House of Gold', the walls of which were plated with gold. Along the ceiling was a golden creeper, like a melon or a marrow plant, with many gourds or pumpkins moulded in the same metal, like the vine which at that date was in the Great Mughal's audience hall, though that was more in the Chinese style, the stalk being of agate, the leaves of emeralds and the grapes of garnets. 'In this chamber were seven idols of gold, each the size and shape of a man, the metal being thicker than two finger breadths,' writes Manrique. They were covered with precious stones of great size. In the courtyard was the statue of Tabin-shwe-ti. There was a hole in it, for it had been cut open to get at the jewels which it contained. In a further room Manrique was shown a golden casket standing on a golden table, carved with devices and studded with gems. This contained the ear-rings. 'I must confess', says he, 'that I have seen very many rich and valuable things in other parts of the East, but when they opened that casket for me and I saw the Chauk-na-gat (the ear-rings) I was thunderstruck, finding that I could scarcely look on them owing to the intense brilliancy they emitted. They are each made of a ruby, like a pyramid or obelisk, as long as the little finger, the base being the size of a bantam's egg.' In addition to these jewels, which were part of the regalia, he saw a great quantity of golden flasks and ewers, all part of the Burmese loot, as he was informed.

He was then taken to visit the White Elephant, and saw him again on several occasions. The creature's origin and history interested him so much that he devotes no less than three chapters to the subject. These give a legendary history, some account of the Arakanese invasion of Pegu, and of the triumphal return of Razagri with the White Elephant 'which in his eyes was of greater value than all the kingdoms of the world'. And he goes on: 'I myself saw in Arakan the adornment and service of this elephant. Speaking as an eyewitness I can say that when he went out, even on an ordinary occasion, as in springtime to take his bath, he was conducted there under a white canopy embroidered with the insignia of royalty, and to the sound of music. Following him were servants with golden water-heaters, ewers, scrapers, and other golden utensils of the bath.' On days of festival he wore a coat of crimson velvet, edged with gold and embroidered with pearls. A gold pectoral studded with diamonds and rubies clasped the coat in front, while a heavy gold chain was used as a girth. His tusks were banded with gold, in which precious stones of many colours were set.

Was this elephant one of the four which the Burmese King Bayin-naung took away from the King of Siam in 1563? That it was the same elephant which Ralph Fitch saw in Pegu in 1586 is certain. But was that elephant certainly one of the four? I think we can assume that it was. Supposing that in 1563 its age was fifteen years, in 1640 it would have been eighty-two. For elephants that is a ripe, but by no means an unusual, age. What an extraordinary life the animal had had, the petted darling for nearly a century of the kings of three kingdoms!

Why did these kings go to such enormous expense in keeping a White Elephant? Why did they regard it as the most valuable of their possessions? Why did they make war on each other on account of it? Manrique's long account affords no answer to these questions. He thought the White Elephant was a god or a devil. But it was not, it was a symbol, a symbol of royalty. Further India derived its ideas of royalty from Hinduism. Just as Christianity has been harnessed to supply rites and ceremonials to make kingship more august, so it was with Hinduism. The Buddhist kings of Further India were obliged to use Hindu rites, for Buddhism did not provide any. In Apostolic Buddhism there was no place for rulers; governments were regarded as one of the Five Evils. For that reason there was a Hindu element in all Buddhist courts. A corps of Brahmins was maintained to supervise the coronation, the royal funeral, and, for instance, the royal ploughing ceremony. The Brahmins had charge of the White Elephant. They were the repositories of an ancient tradition which had to do with the glorification of absolute monarchy.

The Emperor of China was considered, as Son of Heaven, to be Lord of the World, and similarly in India from the most ancient times there existed the tradition that the Emperor of India was Universal Emperor. In historical times emperors, like Asoka in the third century B.C. and Harsha in the seventh century A.D., had ruled over the vast spaces of Hindustan. But long before them there were legendary monarchs, supposed to have been Cakravartin or Universal Emperors. In the old Burmese history, called the *Glass Palace Chronicle*, there occurs this sentence: 'Not even the Universal Monarch, King Mandhata, sovereign ruler of the Four Great Islands and the two thousand lesser isles surrounding them, and of the Two Limbos of the world of spirits, was free from rise and fall, separations and the breach of death.' The Buddhist writer does not deny the existence of Universal Monarchs, but claims that even they, incomparably great though they were, had to submit to the vicissitudes of fortune, determined by the balance of their good and evil actions in past existences, and must pass from death to death until at last they reached the perfect enlightenment which was the Buddha-state.

That there was or had been or might be again such a being as a Universal Monarch was the tradition of Hinduism and was accepted by Buddhism subject to the limitations here cited. Any king might aspire to become a Universal Monarch. It was the dreaming hope of every king. India had now fallen to the Mohammedan conqueror. But there were kings, great kings, in Further India, Buddhist kings watched over by Brahmin priests and astrologers. Now that the Mughal had come and strangled the classical land, one of these kings might be fated to become Lord of the World, a conception which since the coming of the Blessed One had taken a greater significance, for the Universal Monarch would be the instrument by which the peace and happiness of the Excellent Law would be extended to the whole world. In such a dispensation, the Universal Monarch would appear as a Buddhist figure of the highest conceivable rank; maybe, it would turn out that he was Maitreya, the Saviour long foretold. To become a Universal Monarch was therefore a hallowed ambition, far transcending mere governance of the whole world. It was a dream, incomparably lovely, and though no monarchs since the times of such personages as King Mandhata had fully realized it, at any time it might again become a reality.

How could a king tell whether he might hope for such a glorious destiny? How could mankind tell that he was so destined? We are here in the realms of Hindu-Buddhist fantasy. The answer was that a Universal Monarch-to-be would have possession of the Seven Jems. And these Jems, what were they? All seven were great rarities, for sure. One of them was the Golden Wheel. This wheel, of course, was the Wheel of the Law, an impression of which was on the foot of every Buddha. But the Golden Wheel itself?

Ah, we cannot know. But we can well imagine. Were we able to interrogate an old court Brahmin, he would tell us that this was the identical wheel which King Mandhata had received from Paradise, or was the wheel which the first Buddha, Kakusandha, had caused Vishnu to make for him, or was the wheel which was thrown up by the sea dragon on the shore of Suvanabhumi enveloped in flames—or all three of these wheels. Another of the Jems was the Divine Guardian of the Treasury. What manner of guardian this was I cannot tell. But, since we are in the realm of fantasy, why should it not have been the very guardian ghost that once I saw rising from the topmost enclosure of the palace-city, where had stood the Golden Room of the Kings?[1] But pass to the next Jems, the Horse, the Jewel Maiden, and the Jewels that Wrought Miracles. As to these last, assuredly King Thiri-thudhamma possessed them, for if his ear-rings were impotent to give sight to the blind or transport a man to heaven, no jewels, even of the imagination, could have accomplished it. The sixth Jem was a General who had never been, nor ever would be, defeated, perhaps the most difficult of all the Jems to acquire.

And now the last Jem. It clarifies my whole argument. This Jem was the White Elephant. The reader is thus fully documented. He will perceive precisely why Bayin-naung invaded Siam in 1563 and why Razagri invaded Burma in 1599. Each was the most powerful monarch their countries had produced. Each was a devout Buddhist. Each allowed himself to dream that perhaps he was destined to be that Universal Sovereign who, it had long been foretold, would come as a Saviour, a new Buddha, and restore the Golden Age. But an essential step was to secure a White Elephant. On his triumphal return to Arakan, Razagri immediately struck medallions, on which, preceding all his styles, he inscribed the greater style *Hsin Hpyu Shin*, Lord of the White Elephant. As long as the animal lived, his successors, including Thiri-thudhamma, retained this glorious title, always hoping it might be vouchsafed to them to realize its implications. These medallions or coins have been dug up in the palace-city. I have a few of them before me as I write. The title continued to be used till 1652, after which date it may be assumed the White Elephant died, though Dutch envoys in 1660 said they saw it.

Much more might be written about the White Elephant. For instance, to give it a more Buddhist complexion, there was stated

[1] See my *Trials in Burma* (1938 ed.), p. 25.

to lodge in it the soul of a future Buddha, not the next Saviour, but one to come in the remote future, when the soul, through countless migrations, had worked its way upwards to enlightenment. This belief was founded on the fact recorded in the Buddhist classics that the last Buddha had in previous incarnations been a White Elephant.

Finally, the White Elephant was not strictly speaking white at all, but an albino with pink and yellow eyes, a pale-brick shade of skin, white-edged ears and white-tipped trunk, five white hind toe-nails, and russet hair.

XX

The Tooth

In general, it is a fault of composition to interrupt a narrative with a separate relation. But this book is concerned not only to describe the experiences of Friar Manrique but to build up a picture of society both in Portuguese Asia and in some of those kingdoms with which it had dealings. Incidents have been chosen, not only to bring out contrasts, but to suggest that what appear to be differences may in fact be similarities. Thus, in the last chapter we showed that at the back of the minds of the Buddhist kings of the Bay was always the dream that they might be the divine instruments of saving the world. But that was also what Goa stood for. Xavier, who was the embodiment of Catholic Portugal, dreamed of rescuing Asia from certain damnation and bringing it under the jurisdiction of St. Peter's, thereby unifying the world under one spiritual government.

The story which follows perfectly illustrates that *mal entendu.* In 1560, three years before Bayin-naung, King of Burma, invaded Siam to procure a White Elephant, Dom Constantino de Bragança, Viceroy of Goa, led an expedition against Jafna, a Buddhist kingdom on the north coast of Ceylon. Its rightful heir had fled some months before from his usurping brother, and coming to Goa had turned Catholic, taking on baptism the name of Affonso. Possibly he calculated, as have many others, that apostasy would serve his cause. Certain it is that he gained Dom Constantino's ear, and when he alleged that converts, made by Francis Xavier during a visit to Ceylon some twelve years previously, were being persecuted by his brother, easily persuaded him to head the expedition. It will be recalled that after the death of Xavier in 1552 there was a religious revival in Goa. This Jafna expedition was one of the results of that revival.

The Viceroy landed near Jafna with a force of 1,220 men and

VIEW OF MRAUK-U
from the Portuguese quarter of Daingri-pet
(*From Schouten, 'Voyages'*; 1676)

ROYAL PROCESSION IN THE CITY
OF MRAUK-U
(*From Schouten, 'Voyages'*; 1676)

forced the king, who opposed him with 2,000, to fall back into the city, whither he pursued him. In the main street the Portuguese came under the fire of a battery, and Luis de Melo, the most redoubtable of their captains, was struck by a ball. Jao Pessoa, snatching up the standard of the Five Wounds, which had fallen from his hand, and shouting 'Santiago', made a rush at the guns. Though the king attacked down a side-street and killed some of the invaders, the battery was taken; that night he fled the city.

The sack began. Among the treasures found was an object unlike any the Portuguese had seen before. When looting a Buddhist shrine, they came on a tooth set in gold and in a jewelled casket. Priests were guarding it, and they resisted so fiercely and appeared so grief-stricken when it was taken from them, that the Portuguese were convinced it was something rare and strange. Inquiries were made and it was reported that the object was a relic of the Buddha, his tooth, that it was, in fact, the famous Kandy Tooth, which had been temporarily sent down from Kandy, a city on the hills in the centre of the island, where its proper temple was situated.

The Kandy Tooth was one of the most famous of Buddhist relics. If it ranked below the Mahamuni as a sacred object, it ranked above any other Buddhist antiquity. It had been associated with Kandy for over a thousand years, from the time when Ceylon had become a Buddhist centre with the decline of both the Vehicles in India. There is nothing in Europe to-day comparable to it in importance, if we judge of a thing's importance by its value in popular estimation. It would be incorrect to compare it with one of our masterpieces of painting, for it was much rarer and its power more phenomenal. Nothing we possess is at all like it. To the inhabitants of Further India and of the isles it was instinct with the sacred spirit of the Blessed One, was a symbol of salvation, meant enlightenment and peace. And it meant that its possessor was himself on the threshold of the final enlightenment. The modern world is not moved by such thoughts and so has not attributed to any object such virtues. To conceive of how the Tooth was valued is therefore hardly within our competence.

The Portuguese of the sixteenth century, however, could understand, for they attributed occult virtues to objects. They had the body of St. Francis Xavier; they had their fragments of the True Cross, of the Nails, and of the Blood. So, as they carried home to Goa the Tooth, they saw it as a potent idol of the Indies. The expedition against Jafna had been something of a crusade, and had fittingly been crowned by the capture of the most devilish relic in all heathendom.

Rumour was soon busy in the capitals of the bay. Bayin-naung heard at his seat in Pegu. The Feringis had got the Tooth: it was news that touched him closely. Since his accession in 1550 he had made a number of offerings to its shrine at Kandy. He had sent craftsmen to beautify the building, had given vessels for the altar. Moreover, he had bought a piece of land near by and settled slaves whose duty it was to tend the lights. In 1555 he had made a signal gift. A broom was made from his hair and his chief queen's and forwarded to the slaves with orders to use it for sweeping the precincts. Such a presentation may seem eccentric to us. At that time and place it was not held eccentric, but an act of the most adoring respect. So, the news that the Tooth had fallen into the hands of the Portuguese, notoriously the most disreputable of pirates and pagans, was a shock to him. Goa was two thousand miles away. An expedition there was out of the question. What was he to do? Was there anything to be done?

On occasions of misfortune kings seek counsel, nor are such kings as Bayin-naung without shrewd counsellors. Such a one now came forward. The rape of the Tooth, he submitted, was not altogether as deplorable as it appeared. As long as the sacred relic remained in the hands of its traditional guardian, the King of Kandy, His Burmanic Majesty could not hope to do more than offer gifts. But now that Kandy had lost it, having foolishly run the risk of lending it to Jafna, his guardianship was at an end, and it was open to anyone to succeed to his title, a very glorious title with many implications. There were more ways of getting possession than by going to war. It was true that His Majesty had offered to buy one or two of the King of Siam's White Elephants and had been refused. But the present case was very different. The Portuguese were pagans. A holy thing like the Tooth could have no value for them as such; and though they might demand a stiff price, knowing the estimation in which it was held by all followers of the Eightfold Path, yet sell it they would for a good offer. When the sale had gone through, His Majesty could style himself Master of the Tooth, a title to which later he might be able to add that of Master of the White Elephant, should his projected invasion of Siam prove successful. With these two titles he would be the greatest king in the world. Nor would they be empty titles, for he could not have gained them without the warrant of his past good deeds. And since his accumulated merit was great enough to win him such styles, assuredly he must be the coming Saviour, for whom the whole world watched and prayed.

In reply to this flattering submission, Bayin-naung asked how much he should offer. The minister suggested a sum which at modern rates of exchange represented about £60,000, say, the price of a good Titian. But in 1560 the purchasing power of £60,000 was considerably greater than would be a million to-day. The offer was therefore a very handsome one. There happened to be a Portuguese ship in port which was about to leave for Goa. Her captain was requested to convey the proposition to the Viceroy.

Dom Constantino de Bragança, the three years of whose office were half over and who, by a diligent sale of places and pardons, was accumulating enough to let him live at home in a style befitting his name, received with pleased surprise the news of this substantial addition to his savings, for he regarded the Tooth as his exclusive property and had no intention of sharing the sale proceeds with the Treasury. The sum offered seemed so exceedingly big that he accepted at once, a mistake, says Faria y Sousa, who gives it as his opinion that had he held out for a larger price he would certainly have got it.

However, in the long run it made no difference, for a most unfortunate complication soon arose. The Archbishop, a grandee named Dom Gaspar de Leão Pereira, called at the viceregal palace. He was something of a fanatic. The Inquisition, which had been introduced into Goa the previous year, had been warmly welcomed by him. Forbidding in appearance at any time, his features that morning were particularly severe. Received as he mounted the steps with a fanfare, he was ushered in through the rooms we know with every sign of courtesy and respect.

Face to face with Dom Constantino, he announced the object of his visit. News had reached him, he said, of the Burmese king's offer. Had His Excellency reflected what that offer implied, or rather, what would be implied should he accept it? The Viceroy answered that he had given the matter the consideration which it was his practice to give to all affairs of consequence and believed that its implications were tolerably clear to him.

'May I know what you conceive them to be?' inquired Dom Gaspar.

'Certainly,' replied Dom Constantino. 'They are very simple. The King of Burma offers me a thousand times more than I calculate the casket and its contents are worth. A chance of such a kind does not occur twice. I have accepted the offer, and who in his senses would have refused it? King Bayin-naung presumably was deluded by Satan. All the more reason why we should take advantage of him.'

To this the Archbishop drily returned that he feared the Viceroy had overlooked the main point. 'The tooth in the casket is an idol,' he said. 'Is it Your Excellency's intention to trade in idols? Not only is it an idol, but it is one of their most important, and so is probably the habitation of a devil. If Your Excellency sells this abomination, you will be encouraging the very evils from which the Holy Father seeks to deliver these countries.' And he continued with a hint of menace: 'The Church would find it difficult to condone such an error. I have not yet consulted the Grand Inquisitor, but am sure his views will not differ from mine.'

Threatened with the total loss of a vast fortune, the Viceroy began to talk of his treasury, explaining that the late war against Jafna had been expensive and that he was loath to call on His Majesty for a subsidy when he had in his hands what would supply the deficiency. Though the so-called Tooth was an idol, it was also loot, come by in the usual way on the sack of a town, and as loot its value might properly be used to defray the expenses of the expedition in which it had been taken, an expedition, he reminded the Archbishop, which had had for object the protection of Christian converts from disabilities imposed on them by the pagan King of Jafna.

In this plea Dom Constantino's staff hastened to support him. They had calculated that some of their number would be deputed to escort the Tooth to Burma, there to collect the purchase money. It was indisputable that Bayin-naung was rich, and they had eagerly been looking forward to the handsome presents he would give them, and also planned to show the Tooth at stopping-places *en route* to those prepared to pay substantially for the privilege.

But their submissions and the Viceroy's arguments did not move Dom Gaspar. He insisted that a joint meeting of the council and the ecclesiastical court be held to decide the matter. The Viceroy was obliged to agree to this demand and an early date was fixed for the session.

When they were assembled, the Archbishop opened the proceedings with a sermon on the text '*Da mihi animas, cetera tolle tibi*'. It was a long sermon. In the course of it he spoke of the Golden Calf, of the abominable sin of idolatry, and of how Moses destroyed the Calf, golden though it was. Before he was done, several members of the council were won over, men who, seeing little profit to themselves in the transaction, thought it good policy to secure their reputation for orthodoxy at a moment when the newly arrived Inquisition was showing a vigilant interest in that subject. In the debate which followed the sermon, these people supported the Archbishop. But the Viceroy still held out, advancing fresh arguments in favour of closing with the offer.

Waiting his moment, the Archbishop suddenly called him a Freemason. Now, the Inquisition had always been hard on Freemasons, many of whom had died at the stake, and to be called one by an archbishop, even though you were Viceroy of the Indies, was highly alarming. Such prestige had the Inquisition that the viceregal bodyguard would not have dared to resist its Familiars and prevent the arrest of the head of the government. Dom Constantino crumpled under the threat and agreed to do whatever the assembly decided. On a vote being taken, it was resolved that not only should the King of Burma's offer be rejected, but that the Tooth itself should be destroyed.

On the date fixed for the performance of this act, a great crowd, both Portuguese and Indian, assembled in the square in front of the cathedral. The Archbishop stood at the top of the steps. Beside him were a mortar and a brazier. The Viceroy, who was present with his whole staff, handed him the Tooth, which he placed in the mortar, and with a heavy pestle ground it to powder. The powder was then thrown into the brazier. When the fire had died down, the ashes were carefully collected and consigned to the sea. This elaborate public destruction of the Tooth proclaimed to the world that even a great sum of money could not soften Portuguese hatred of idolatry. But it also showed that their estimate of the Tooth's power only differed from Bayin-naung's in that, while he considered it a good, they were convinced it was bad, potency. The Archbishop, we cannot doubt, set out to destroy a devil, a difficult feat to accomplish, as will appear in the sequel. Yet the act was, perhaps, the most disinterested ever performed by the Portuguese in India.

Fourteen years now passed by. Bayin-naung sacked Ayudhya, returned to Pegu with the White Elephants, and knew himself to be the most glorious king in Further India. But actually he was not yet at the summit of his glory. His astrologers informed him that further good fortune, of an extraordinary kind, was coming to him from Ceylon. He was destined to marry the daughter of the King of Colombo, a Buddhist kingdom adjacent to Jafna. Yet it was not the marriage in itself which was to be so lucky, but a circumstance attendant upon it, which they were unable to describe with greater precision. They strongly advised him to take the first step and send a mission to Colombo to demand the daughter, and make her queen, for there was a vacancy, one of his four queens being dead. The rest would then follow of its own motion. Bayin-naung accordingly sent a deputation, the members being both monks and laymen.

When the envoys arrived at Colombo and made known to its king that their great master desired to marry his daughter, a complication arose: he had no daughter. Making the envoys an evasive reply, he summoned his council and asked for advice. No need to say how undesirable it would be to disappoint Bayin-naung. But as he had no daughter . . . ?

In reply his ministers submitted that there was a lady at court who might be represented as his daughter. It seems that the Chancellor's daughter, a young person of charming and innocent character, had moved the childless king's heart, so that he treated her as if he were her father. This girl, they suggested, should be sent.

The king objected that to send her would be dangerous. Were it discovered she was no princess, she would be executed. He was too fond of her to run that risk, and too prudent to put himself in so false a position.

At this his chief minister suggested that if a dowry were sent with her which should particularly appeal to the Burmese king, he would be unlikely to bother unduly about her pedigree.

What sort of a dowry, inquired the king. The sack of Ayudhya had given Bayin-naung everything which was rare and curious in Further India. What was there in Colombo to merit his special attention?

The chief minister smiled. He had learned in a private conversation with the envoys, he said, that the Burmese astrologers, who had predicted their master's marriage to a princess of Colombo, had added that the alliance would be accompanied by a circumstance of singular good fortune. His submission was that they should supply that circumstance. His Majesty would recall that

King Bayin-naung had offered the Feringis of Goa after the affair of Jafna a sum equal to three times the revenue of the kingdom of Colombo for the Kandy Tooth, which, it was alleged, they had taken from Jafna. His disappointment, his grief, when he learnt that the pagans, rather than sell it to him, had ground it to powder, was notorious; indeed, it was said that, even in the midst of his subsequent enormous triumphs, when he entered Pegu borne aloft like a deity, the four White Elephants treading before him, he was not entirely happy, and that with the years this dissatisfaction had increased, as if he had begun to doubt, the Tooth being lost to him, whether he was indeed the Saviour he had believed himself to be.

'But what can we do for him?' inquired the King of Colombo 'I have no Tooth. There is no Tooth here.'

'Your Majesty also has no daughter,' replied the chief minister. 'And just as a daughter can be provided, so may a Tooth.'

The king, who had great respect for his minister's perspicacity, intimated that he left the matter wholly in his hands.

A few days later the Burmese envoys were invited to view the treasures of the palace-city. They were shown the war elephants, a selection of the jewels, the regalia, the state robes, and the magical banners. Finally, when night had fallen, they were led up to a golden shrine, where perfumes were burning and silver lamps, before which the chief minister and his colleagues prostrated themselves with more than usual rapture and devotion. The Burmese, who had hastened to follow their hosts' example, inquired whether the shrine were of particular sanctity. The minister drew their attention to a golden casket on the altar. With proper ceremony this was unlocked for their inspection. It contained a box, inside which was another. When this was opened, a third appeared, and so on until six boxes were opened. In the seventh box was disclosed a tooth. 'This is the Kandy Tooth,' said the minister.

On the Burmese expressing astonishment at seeing it safe and undamaged, certain explanations followed. We cannot say precisely of what these consisted, but it seems they took one of two forms. Some accounts state the envoys were told that the King of Jafna, before evacuating his capital, buried the Tooth, and that it was only a monkey's tooth which the Portuguese carried to Goa, the genuine one coming later into the custody of the King of Colombo in a manner unspecified. Other accounts relate that the

Portuguese got the authentic Tooth, but that at the moment they were about to destroy it, a spirit from Paradise substituted a porcelain replica and carried the original to Colombo. Either of these explanations would have convinced the Burmese, and so it is of no importance which was given them.

Nothing further was said on that occasion, for the chief minister was too clever a man to show his hand so soon. The envoys retired dazzled and thoughtful. They remembered the prophecy. Could it be that they were fated to bring it to pass? They must attempt to do so. No service they could render their king would be, they knew, so richly rewarded as the bringing back of the Kandy Tooth.

At the earliest opportunity they sought an interview with the chief minister and begged him to sell the Tooth to their master. Any price he liked to name they guaranteed would be paid. But they pleaded in vain. The minister knew very well how to increase the impressiveness of what he proposed to do. He said the Tooth was not for sale.

But the envoys did not despair. They had by this time been told that the King of Colombo would send his daughter and, while completing the arrangements for her transfer, continued to press for the sale of the Tooth. Eventually, after interminable conversations, the chief minister revealed that His Majesty had from the beginning resolved to include the Tooth in his daughter's dowry, and would have told them so, had it not been that he desired King Bayin-naung to have the happy surprise of learning the fact from his bride, who might thus, as her father hoped, more particularly commend herself. He therefore charged them to keep the secret, which they readily promised to do, though immediately, as the minister had foreseen, they sent a messenger in a swift galley to apprise their sovereign of his extraordinary good fortune.

The bride's preparations being shortly complete, the envoys set sail with her to Burma. It was arranged that the Tooth was to follow later, partly for astrological reasons and partly because a sacred object requires its own particular escort and must be welcomed on arrival with its own appropriate ceremonies.

Bayin-naung's arrangements for the reception of the supposed princess were splendid, his respect for her having been enormously increased by the news of the supposed Tooth. She was received by a brilliant gathering and, embarked on a golden barge, was rowed by Amazons up the Pegu river to the moated capital, where the king awaited her. But her reception was eclipsed by that accorded to the Tooth. On that occasion Bayin-naung descended the river in the royal barge, followed by his courtiers in gala canoes. The casket of the Tooth was landed after he had taken a ceremonial bath. An immense procession of river-boats was then formed. The casket was placed under a spire on a raft attached by scarlet ropes to the royal barge, which became the centre of a great web of craft, all similarly connected one to the other. As the flotilla started north on its fifty-mile journey, musicians posted on the bows of the royal barge began to play and dancers to pose, while the many who lined the bank prostrated themselves and adored the tooth. At the Pegu anchorage the rest of the Court was there to welcome it. In excited devotion a company of princes waded into the water and bore the casket ashore. The road to the city was paved with silk, bright clothes which the grandees stripped off in their ardour. In this guise they paraded to the crocodile moat and into the carved and gilded palace.

After ceremonies which lasted for days, the spurious relic, now in a more precious casket studded with the rubies and emeralds of Burma, was walled up in the Dhammazedi pagoda. It seemed to King Bayin-naung that night that he had at last reached the summit of greatness. The acquisition of the Tooth was the seal on his other achievements, the guarantee that he would become a Buddha, if not in his present incarnation, certainly in the next. He had succeeded where his predecessors had failed. He had procured the real Tooth when Anawrahta, the famous king of the Pagan dynasty, had only been able to obtain a replica of it, and the forever victorious paladin, King Alaungsithu, whose tremendous title was composed of no less than sixty-eight letters, had sought it erroneously in China for years.

The reader of this unusual comedy will want to know more precisely why Bayin-naung was so certain he had the genuine Tooth. Since, as related here, its proper habitat was Kandy, and since he was so well aware of this that for years he had enriched its shrine and kept it dusted with his own hair, how was it he believed that the Portuguese took it at Jafna, and later saw nothing incredible in the King of Colombo's story? It has been suggested that the Tooth was at Jafna on loan, say, on exhibition at some festival. But afterwards why should a celestial being take it to Colombo and not to Kandy? Or, in the alternative already given, what were the circumstances which enabled the King of Colombo to acquire it, for he was disposing of it as if it were his own property? Clearly our information is incomplete at this point. We shall never know what convincing explanation was given to Bayin-naung. But convinced he was that the King of Colombo had become the owner. One is only surprised he did not inquire at Kandy. But perhaps he did, and what he heard there did not shake his belief.

The strange thing is that hardly was the tooth in the Dhammazedi when a letter was received from the King of Kandy expressing surprise at the elaborate rituals which his brother of Burma had seen fit to perform over the tooth of a mere monkey. The Tooth, the writer declared, was where it had always been, to wit, in the Temple of the Tooth at Kandy. It had never been out of the place, never been to Jafna, the Portuguese had never had it nor had the King of Colombo.

But Bayin-naung was unmoved. He had had, as we have said, his weighty reasons for holding his Tooth to be authentic. And he had equally weighty reasons for refusing now to admit he had been deceived. Accordingly, he dismissed the bearers of the letter with the reply that it would ill become one destined to be a Buddha to enter into a controversy with wilful sceptics.

Whether there was any real Buddha tooth must be extremely doubtful. But the priests of Kandy insist to this day that their Tooth is a true relic, and I myself saw it in 1931, at the Temple of the Tooth, one day when it was being shown to some distinguished Burmese visitors.

XXI
The Grand Dowager

The Arakanese invasion of Burma in 1599 during the reign of Bayin-naung's successor, Nandabayin, ruined that country for the time being. It broke up into petty states. All Bayin-naung's glory passed to Razagri. Possessing the White Elephant and the Mahamuni he had a right to call himself the champion of Buddhism. Arakan, not Burma, became the centre of the Buddhist world. It is true that the Arakanese did not get the Tooth. They overlooked it in the sack of Pegu and it remained in the country, to be enshrined a few years later in the Kaung-hmu-daw pagoda at Sagaing. But as it was a spurious relic, we must suppose that was no matter.

Burma's recovery was slow, but by 1610 Bayin-naung's grandson, Anauk-petlun, had again united the greater part of the country. He was most anxious to get back the White Elephant, and in 1616 proposed to the Viceroy of Goa a joint attack on Mrauk-u, declaring that if he secured the animal the Portuguese could take the rest of the loot. But the proposal came to nothing. Arakan was too strong. Yet the Government of Arakan had reason to take note of Burma's returning strength, since this coincided with the growing power of the Mughal. This latter threat in part explains Manrique's good reception. As we shall see, Thiri-thu-dhamma hoped by an arrangement with Goa not only to ward off that threat, but to be strong enough himself to threaten both countries.

The friar's visits to the sights in Mrauk-u, which have allowed us this informative digression into current history, were made despite his preoccupations as a religious. The church had been consecrated on the 20th of October 1630. During November and December he was busy organizing and instructing the congregation. One of his problems concerned the local people who had been converted by previous missionaries. Living often with Buddhist women and scattered among the Buddhist population, they had become careless. For peace's sake, and out of easy good-fellowship, they would attend Buddhist festivals, give charity to Buddhist monks, and show respect to Buddhist shrines. To know how to stop this was not easy. When he returned to Dianga, as he must do very shortly, these people would forget his exhortations. He had frightened them now with threats of excommunication and by detailing what that meant in the life to come. They were contrite for the moment, but would their contrition last? He had enough experience of native converts to know that it would not. Something more was required. If he could oblige them to leave their present houses and come to live in Daingri-pet among the Portuguese and Eurasian Catholics, then the vicinity of the Church, the influence of their co-religionists, and the absence of pagan distractions would keep them more straitly in the fold.

But this course, he was aware, could only be taken with the concurrence of the Government. For him to call in without sanction and seem to concentrate all the Catholics in one place would arouse suspicions. He would be credited with other motives. It might be said that some sort of a rising was contemplated. Like all kings who employ foreign mercenaries to protect them, Thiri-thu-dhamma was obliged to be careful. Well armed as his Portuguese guardsmen were, and with their superior knowledge of artillery, there was always a possibility that they might attempt a *coup d'état*, if not on their own motion, then at the instigation of some rebel prince or disgruntled minister. The captains knew well they were under close observation. They would strongly object, for the sake of a few local converts, to being brought under suspicion. Manrique was therefore careful not to mention his project to the Captain-General, Manoel Tigre. If the men were to be moved, it would have to be done in some roundabout way. The King must be induced to give his consent. But the real reason would not seem to him a sufficient reason. A reason which he would deem sufficient must be discovered.

'In the midst of these perplexities,' writes Manrique, 'I remembered the friendliness of the Japanese captain, Leon Donno.' When the problem was put to him, the *Samurai* was able to make a practical suggestion. It may be recalled that along with the White Elephant, the Arakanese carried back from Burma King Nandabayin's daughter. Razagri married her. On his death thirteen years later in 1612 she became Queen-Dowager. She was not the mother of Thiri-thu-dhamma's father, Min Kha Maung, but as Queen-Dowager her position was that of first lady at Court. On Thiri-thu-dhamma's accession in 1622 she became Grand Dowager. By 1630 she was probably about fifty-five years of age. Her name was the Lady Htwe Naung. Now, it so happened that the Japanese captain's wife was Burmese, and that before her marriage to him she had been the Grand Dowager's lady-in-waiting. In virtue of that appointment, she still had the entrée to Court, and had remained on close terms with her former mistress. What therefore Captain Donno proposed was this: he would ask his wife to mention to the Grand Dowager the Friar's predicament. It was quite possible that the old lady would be sympathetic, for in her youth at Pegu she had been somewhat attracted by the Catholic faith and was known to have encouraged the priests who ministered to the Portuguese mercenaries in the employ of her father. That, of course, was long ago, went on the captain, but his wife had informed him that Her Majesty had not forgotten and sometimes referred to what the priests had told her. In any event, it was worth trying to obtain her ear, for if she chose to exert herself her influence could be very great.

This bit of backstairs diplomacy appealed to the Friar. As we have seen, he had a way with women. Three days later Captain Donno called to say that his wife had found an opportunity of raising the question with the Dowager. As she had hoped, Her Majesty had shown interest. Indeed, she had been very gracious, saying she would mention the matter to the King, and advising his reverence thereafter to seek a favourable opportunity of petitioning him. But he should not ask for the Christians directly. That would complicate what might otherwise be effected without difficulty. No, he should take advantage of the existing pagoda-slave system. No doubt his Reverence was aware that when a pagoda was dedicated, slaves were dedicated along with it to act as servants, gardeners, and watchmen. She understood that a church had been recently dedicated. The appropriate course would therefore be to ask for a grant of slaves. She would suggest that his Reverence should make a point of stating that he was not petitioning for Arakanese, but only for foreign slaves. When permission was given, he could get inserted into the grant what names he desired. Twenty was a very usual number, but with the wives and families, and whatever relations or alleged relations he might add, no doubt that number could be increased ten times, when perhaps the greater part of the converts he had in mind would be provided for. The later stages of the negotiation could be greatly smoothed by tips, but she was sure his Reverence hardly required such a hint.

Such was the substance of the Grand Dowager's message. It is extremely characteristic of a Burmese woman of the world. Indeed, anyone acquainted with the Mongolian courts of Further India and of the Far East will declare it to be precisely what a woman of character and position would send.

When he had repeated it, the Japanese captain added: 'I think your Reverence would now be well advised to seek audience with Her Majesty and thank her in person for her kind interest.'

Manrique agreed. But there was a difficulty. What he calls the 'curiosities' he had brought with him, and his stock of fine Indian cottons and Chinese silks, were exhausted, for he had had to make more presents than was anticipated. Clearly he could not appear empty-handed. However, by taking some of the richer Catholics partially into his confidence, he secured enough to buy an adequate gift. Sending this ahead, 'to light the way for him', as he says, he was shown without delay into the presence.

Her Majesty was seated on a dais eight inches high, on which was a splendid silk Persian carpet and cushions of purple velvet embroidered with seed pearls. Six ladies-in-waiting were kneeling by her, some holding betel-boxes and others fans. At the side of the hall stood twenty gentlemen, of ancient and venerable appearance, dressed in long coats of purple damask. After Manrique had made the dowager the *shi-ko*, which she acknowledged with a slight lowering of the head, two of these gentlemen came forward and conducted him in courtly manner to a second dais, lower in height than the first, which was furnished with a good carpet, though of ordinary make, and with two plain velvet cushions.

On receiving permission to speak, the Friar in his best manner —and we should remember that the Portuguese had elaborate manners—protested the extraordinary obligation under which Her Majesty had placed him by her great condescension. He would never forget it and hoped that he would always know how to repay it, as, he was sure, would the Christians whose good fortune it was to live under so munificent a protection as Her Majesty's. He continued in this strain for some little time, improving the occasion after his wont by dwelling, though with more tact, it would seem, than usual, upon the excellencies of the Catholic Church. His manner, and perhaps his appearance, certainly his words, impressed her. She became less stiff, laid aside her grand air, and began to speak of her girlhood in Pegu, how the good Fathers used to come to see her and how they told her of the Blessed Virgin. As she chatted on, her own memories began to move her. 'I often went to the Catholic Church at Pegu,' she told him. 'I even learnt to say the Ave Maria, but alas! can remember little of it now.' Becoming more emotional, she said with a sigh: 'Those happy days came to an end. There was the invasion. I was carried away. My home was destroyed. My father was killed. I have never seen dear Burma since. I was married here, but my lord died young. It was another tragedy, for I had got to love him.' Her tears were flowing now as she continued: 'Even then my misfortunes were not ended. Both my sons were foully murdered. Little wonder I have forgotten it, the Ave Maria which used to comfort me so much.'

No longer able to restrain her grief, she broke down utterly and was supported to an inner apartment in a state of collapse.

Manrique, who had come to pay a state call and do a little business, found that he had intruded upon a woman's heart. He felt himself at a loss, nor was sure that the event was favourable to his plans. Should he retire at once or await her permission? In this uncertainty one of the lords-in-waiting came up to him. In the low tone one should use on such an occasion, and with the well-bred desire to put the Friar at his ease, he said: 'Father, do not let yourself be upset because the Mistress of Life has left so abruptly. No-one who had suffered such misfortunes could recall them without giving way to tears.'

At this moment a lady of high rank accompanied by two maids came out of the room to which the Dowager had retired. Going up to the Friar, she apologized on behalf of Her Majesty, who had desired her to say how much she regretted not having been able to take a cheerful leave of him, but he might go in confidence that, God aiding, she would have opportunity of giving him the help he desired. Manrique thanked her for so gracious a message and expressed deep concern for Her Majesty's grief. But in grief there was One to whom all could turn. 'If Her Majesty addresses herself to the Sainted Mother, great will be the consolation which she will obtain.'

The lady withdrew and the ten ancient lords-in-waiting, attended by ushers carrying silver wands, conducted him softly to the outer door.

XXII

Toys for the Princes

The Grand Dowager was as good as her word. A few days later she sent Manrique a present and a message. The royal footmen carried in hens, rice, butter, fruits, and, what the Friar afterwards had made into curtains for the church, two pieces of muslin ninety yards long and three feet wide. The message was to the effect that she had spoken of him warmly to the King, though without specifically mentioning his business, as she did not think it prudent to do so. She advised him to seek audience without delay.

Next morning he went up to the palace. It had been announced that His Majesty intended to view a pair of young elephants which his hunters had brought in from the western border. It would be an informal occasion when with tact it should be possible to get speech with him. Two of the royal children would be present, boys aged about four and seven. This suggested to Manrique a little stratagem. He would bring toys for the children. If he succeeded in pleasing them, it would be a good way of introducing his requests.

On reaching the palace he took his station among some noblemen and waited for the King to pass by on his way to the courtyard where the elephants were kept. Presently the royal procession appeared. Thiri-thu-dhamma noticed him and in a good-humoured way said in Hindustani: 'Ah, Father, you have come to see the elephant show?' To which Manrique replied like a courtier: 'When I come to the palace, it is to see your Majesty, a spectacle better worth than any show, especially when I see Your Majesty looking so well. God has Your Majesty in His keeping.' To which the king replied piously: 'All we receive of good is from Him,' adding in a cheerful tone: 'It is He who has sent me the elephants. Let us go on and see them.' We must suppose the Friar used a term translatable as God or Buddha, and that His Majesty presumed he was referring to the latter.

At this invitation Manrique joined the procession. They walked on till they reached a gallery opening on the courtyard. There a seat had been prepared for the king. The rest sat down slightly below him.

The younger of the King's two sons had been carried in the arms of a member of the household. This gentleman now selected a place next to Manrique and put his charge beside him on a cushion. Presently, the Friar took out of his sleeve the toy he had brought, a Chinese novelty, the Chinese being noted for their ingenious toys. It was contained in a black and gold lacquer box. When the child was shown the box, he wanted it opened. The Friar, with an indulgent smile, slipped back the lid, when out popped a dog, fluffy and white, which moved its paws about in a playful manner. The little prince was wild with delight, snatched the toy and ran to show his father. The King laughed heartily and made the dog wave its paws. Beside him was standing the elder boy. 'Oh, let me do it!' he cried excitedly and took the toy and began playing with it. This upset the younger child, who tried to get it back and, when his brother would not let him, he burst into tears. To stop his screams the King had to intervene and tell the other to hand it over. This made him cry and he sobbed to the Friar: 'Haven't you another toy dog for me?'

Manrique had not another toy dog, but he had come provided with a second present. From his capacious sleeve he drew out a sheath of green velvet. This did not contain a toy, because he had judged the elder prince too old for a plaything, but two daggers, the crystal handles ornamented with gold and small rubies, a piece of Ceylon work 'more showy than costly', as he says. But their rather tawdry charm was just what delighted the boy. He took his own dagger from his belt—it was a valuable one in good taste, the hilt gold with a great pearl atop, and the sheath gold, too, and set with sapphires—and sticking the two Ceylon daggers in its place, gave it to Manrique as a return present. This show of fine manners was much applauded by the courtiers. The King, too, was pleased, and his son, going to him, knelt and holding up the daggers on the palms of his hands displayed them for him to see.

'You have got two daggers for the one you gave the Father,' smiled the king, and calling the other child who was playing with the toy dog, said: 'And you have given the Father nothing. I shall have to do it for you.'

The young elephants were now led into the courtyard. The King got up and walked across. Sugar-cane was brought and he had it thrown to them. They took it up in their trunks and stuffed their mouths in a glad greedy way. The king discussed their points as if they had been horses. Presently, when the cane was finished, they wanted a drink. There was a pond or basin nearby, and into it they stuck their trunks, and growing excited squirted themselves, and squirted the courtiers who came too close.

When they had been led back to their stable, Thiri-thu-dhamma took his seat again in the gallery and asked Manrique if there were elephants in Portugal. A conversation ensued, the King making a number of inquiries about the naval resources of the government at Goa, for his mind was running on the practicability of an alliance. Manrique's replies were encouraging. The King's manner grew more condescending.

It was the propitious moment for the Friar to make his request. 'Lord of Life,' said he, 'thanks to God's mercy and Your Majesty's great kindness our church has been built. But as Your Majesty is aware, a shrine must be kept up, there must be slaves to look after it, keep it fresh and clean, that God may dwell in it. Our church is not provided with such servants. May it please Your Majesty to appoint me some. God will reward you, God will have you ever in his keeping, you will be fortunate and ever greater if you grant this boon.'

The request seemed a small one to the King. It was very natural, quite in keeping with precedent. He had no idea there was anything behind it. Nor did he associate it with any undesirable coming together of the Catholics. He gave his assent at once, and calling for one of his ministers directed that a formal deed of grant be drawn up for as many slaves as might be required. 'The slaves are my son's return gift to your Reverence,' he declared genially, as Manrique made him a profound salutation. Shortly afterwards he intimated that he wished to retire. They all accompanied him in procession to the door of the private apartments, where the queen resided and his secondary consorts. At the door the Amazon guard awaited him. The courtiers knelt as he passed within.

The reader will have noticed that Captain Tibao has disappeared from the story. In all probability he returned to Dianga as soon as the object of the political mission was achieved. Manrique's reason for staying on was purely ecclesiastical, the building of the church, the confession and instruction of the Catholic community, and their collection in one place. The King, however, seems to have taken a fancy to him. He sends his physician when he is ill, receives him afterwards in a pleasant manner and allows him to dispute with a high ecclesiastic in his presence, and, at the instance of the Grand Dowager, lets him join the inner circle of the Court on a private occasion. It is quite certain that Captain Tibao would never have been treated with such informality. The Portuguese residents at Mrauk-u were, we know, not allowed into the palace-city. We can ascribe Manrique's great success partly, as I have said, to the plain fact that the King liked him. It was also due to his being a priest. Oriental kings of that date had a great interest in religion as a subject. The good reception of the Augustinians, the Jesuits, and other priests at the various courts of Asia must often be ascribed to this. But, as has been suggested, Thiri-thudhamma had a further reason for his conversations with Manrique. He was feeling his way towards an agreement with Goa and was glad of an opportunity of getting some information. Manrique does not appear to have been aware of the motives at the back of the King's questions. His mind at the time was wholly occupied with the affairs of his church. Nor does he seem to have made any attempt on his side to find out what Sir Thomas Roe calls 'the pace of the Court' in his account of his embassy in 1615 to the Mughal Jehangir. Behind that door which led into the private apartments curious things were afoot. Manrique had no clear picture of the Court parties, of their aims and intrigues, of the men who led them. Nor was he aware either of the secret dread or the extraordinary ambition which haunted the monarch who was so pleasant to him.

He left for Dianga in January 1631, the length of his stay in Arakan having been six months. Since in January the sea is calm and the weather fine, it was not necessary to take the land route. He embarked in a galley at the city wharf, rowed down the Kaladan river, and passing through the present Akyab harbour, turned north into the outer sea and was back in his vicarage at Dianga within a few days.

XXIII

The Taking of Hugli

Manrique spent the whole of 1631 and the year following at Dianga busied with his duties as vicar. He had been given permission by Thiri-thu-dhamma to build a church at Angaracale, the neighbouring fishing village, and to collect and settle round it the Indian Christians who up to that time had lived in various parts of the province of Chittagong.

During 1632 Hugli was the scene of terrible events, Hugli where he had spent such a happy time in 1628–9, 'appreciating the sweet association' of the friars at the Augustinian monastery. In 1628 the Mughal Emperor Jehangir had died. The Portuguese had been able to remain on excellent terms with this easygoing monarch. But his successor, Shah Jehan, was a strict Moslem and, so, prejudiced against all Christians. He was prejudiced in particular against the inhabitants of Hugli because at a time when he was fighting against his brother in the struggle for the imperial throne, some of their captains had played him false. Moreover, on his accession the city had not sent the customary present and congratulations.

Hugli, as we have seen, represented a private trading venture outside Portuguese Asia. About three hundred Portuguese men lived there. Their wives or mistresses were in some cases European, but mostly Eurasian or Indian. The rest of the population, perhaps ten thousand all told, were Indian traders, shopkeepers, sailors, and slaves, the slaves being in a majority. All were Catholics. Large custom dues were paid to the Mughal, the town otherwise being quite self-governing. It was not fortified, though the inhabitants were well armed. The goods it supplied to the Court, and the revenue it paid, made it an asset to the Government. Under Jehangir its leading men had been given grants of land and many privileges and exemptions. The utmost prosperity and comfort prevailed.

The Taking of Hugli

Useful though it was in general to the Indian Government, some of its activities were a source of annoyance. Thus, it used to sell a quantity of gunpowder and arms to the Portuguese mercenaries of Dianga, who harried Bengal in the name of the King of Arakan. And these ruffians were able to find a good market there for such of their captives as they did not keep for themselves or send to Mrauk-u. The slave raids, always an irritation, had been growing worse. The seizure in 1629 of the high Mughal officer's wife, whom Manrique had rescued from death and afterwards converted, was said to have infuriated Shah Jehan.

The plain fact was, however, that the authorities of Hugli were not actually in league with the pirates of Dianga. But they had been indiscreet, and their indiscretions gave Shah Jehan an excuse to satisfy his private and religious animosity. In May 1632, four years after his accession, he ordered the Viceroy of Bengal to march on Hugli, loot and burn it, in the name of the Prophet and in the interests of the state.

As is often said, there are no secrets in the East. Copies of Shah Jehan's dispatch were seen by Jesuit Fathers both at the capital and at Dacca, the Viceroy's headquarters. An urgent warning was sent to Hugli. But the city council refused to believe that danger threatened. It seemed incredible that the Emperor should proceed so drastically without giving them opportunity to show cause. After all, what had they done? Nothing which could not easily be adjusted by negotiation. Accordingly they took no steps either to make representations or to put themselves in a better posture for defence. It is curious that two Fathers, previously resident at Hugli, who were either astrologers or natural psychics, had some years earlier made a detailed prophecy of the destruction of the settlement and the great tribulations which its inhabitants would suffer. But these prophecies, though well known to everybody, were not connected with the warnings now received and no alarm whatever was felt.

The Viceroy of Bengal was Qasim Khan. Not only was he a man of the highest birth, and a poet of reputation, but was extremely well connected at Court, his father being Grand Huntsman and his wife the sister of Nur Jehan, the Dowager Empress and one of the most remarkable Indian women who ever lived. On receiving his Emperor's commands he hesitated to put them into effect. It was true that the Portuguese of Hugli had no walls to protect them, nor any artillery; there were only three hundred of them, and their Indian soldiers did not exceed fifteen hundred. But the

Portuguese as a race still enjoyed a prodigious reputation, in spite of the decline in their resources since 1580 when Portugal was annexed by Spain. Numerous attacks during the previous hundred and thirty years had been made by Indian kings and, later, by the Mughal, against their possessions, but none of them had been successful. Those who lived at Dianga were the terror of Bengal and no adequate defence against their raids had been devised. It was not a light matter to attack such people. If they had no fortifications or artillery, they had excellent firearms, their courage was fanatical, they would inflict great loss before they were overwhelmed by numbers. Furthermore, the open market they maintained had enabled some Indians to enrich themselves, so that it would be impossible to count on local sympathy to the Mughal. These were the considerations which made the Viceroy hesitate; and it also occurred to him as possible that the Emperor would change his mind and cancel his orders, for on reflection he might shrink from destroying a trade which paid such a good revenue. But a renegade captain, named Martim de Mello, who had a grudge against the Hugli authorities, persuaded him to act at once by recounting to him in detail the enormous loot which he might expect to get from the sack of the Augustinian monastery and of the Jesuit House which was also at the place. De Mello was able to convince him there was little danger. The Hugli Portuguese had become effeminate, he said. They were rich and most of them had many concubines. At the mere sight of the host which His Excellency could assemble they would surrender. And there was no ground to fear that King Thiri-thu-dhamma of Arakan would take the opportunity of attacking in the east when the Mughal army was away to the west, because the monsoon would prevent his fleet from putting out. Moreover, he had no engagement to assist the Portuguese of Hugli.

These arguments prevailed. Qasim Khan assembled an army of 150,000 men, with artillery and river boats, giving the command to Inayatullah Khan, his son, assisted by Bahadur Khan, a Pathan general of great experience. That he should have held it prudent to make such elaborate preparations to overcome the allegedly debauched Europeans at Hugli suggests the extremely poor quality of the Mughal forces even at their heyday in the early seventeenth century, and prepares us to understand how a hundred and twenty-five years later Clive with a mere handful defeated the then Viceroy of Bengal at Plassey.

On 26 June the Mughal army supported by a fleet was within three miles of the city. What followed is recorded in a long letter written by John Cabral, S.J., dated 12 November 1633 and addressed to the head of the Jesuit House at Cochin. Cabral was an eyewitness of what he relates. He has an excellent style, was clear-headed, and well informed. Manrique also describes what took place, but since his account is founded only on what he heard at Dianga, the other's narrative is much to be preferred.

The apparition of the Mughal army was a great shock to the Portuguese. At first there was the utmost confusion, but by nightfall the commandant, Manoel de Azevedo, had restored order and began to barricade the streets. Muskets—there were plenty of them and of good quality—were distributed and captains were appointed.

Next morning a council was held and it was resolved to try diplomacy. Father Cabral was sent to ascertain the Mughal general's intentions and whether terms could not be arranged. He was received by Inayatullah Khan, who pretended that he had come merely to inquire into certain complaints which had been made against the town's administration. On being asked to specify what these were, he said that raiding galleys from Dianga were frequently helped by forces sent from Hugli, and referred particularly to the case of the great lady who had been kidnapped. Cabral pointed out that these charges of complicity were false and declared he could prove it. The Mughal replied that the best way to prove the opposite would be to search the town for kidnapped Indians. If such were found—and he believed they would be found—collusion with the pirates of Dianga would be established.

There were, of course, many such kidnapped persons in Hugli, but they had been bought from the Dianga raiders in what was then regarded as a legitimate manner. They had, moreover, all been converted to Catholicism. Cabral was accordingly instructed to inform the Mughals that such a search would be resisted; nor could it be agreed, search or no, to give up any of the slaves, for as Christians they could not be abandoned.

Negotiations having broken down, the assault was launched on 2 July at dawn. It came from every side, both by land and water, and resulted in the fall of the suburbs. But Manoel de Azevedo had not spread his main defences too wide. The well-entrenched core of the position held. Very heavy casualties were inflicted on the Mughals by the accurate musketry fire. It was said they lost six hundred men, while no more than six Portuguese and fifteen Indians were killed. But this was only the first day of a siege which was to last nearly three months.

'The Moors were greatly disconcerted at their losses', writes Cabral, still using in the seventeenth century the old-fashioned word which dated from the Ibero-Moorish wars. Some of them urged Inayatullah to give up the enterprise. 'If the Portuguese get the better of it,' they declared, 'the whole of Bengal, or, at least, all the adjacent country, will rise with them.' This statement of Cabral's lets us know how insecure was the Mughal administration, and suggests that had Portugal remained independent and by prudent finance found resources to support her settlements in Asia, she might have founded a territorial empire. A remark of Manrique's suggests the same. One day, after looking over the defences of Mrauk-u, he came to the conclusion that they 'would have been of little use had the Portuguese prosecuted their conquests with the same earnest vigour with which they had initiated them. When Portugal was merged in Spain, the empire became unwieldy and sufficient ships could not be spared to go east. Lacking this support the colonies not only ceased to grow but were unable to withstand the attacks of their enemies, Asiatic as well as European.' As will be clear from the narrative of the siege of Hugli, the Portuguese spirit was as high as ever. Their way of life may have been luxurious and disreputable, but it was not their morals which lost them their empire. That was lost in Madrid and Lisbon, just as the indignities and defeats recently suffered in Asia by their successors, the French and English, have been due far less to the ineptitudes and follies of those on the spot than to lack of support from Paris and London.

Whatever Inayatullah Khan may have thought—he was a weak youth—his general, Bahadur Khan, would not hear of retreat. The assault on Hugli continued, though it was pressed with more prudence. The Mughals also sought to split opinion in the Portuguese camp and by trickery to effect an entrance into the town. They were so far successful with their promises of an honourable settlement that the Prior of the Augustinian monastery was deputed to effect it. His parley, however, only resulted in their demanding that four leading men should be sent to negotiate. Four captains accordingly went to Bahadur Khan's tent, when the original demand for the slaves was reiterated. Thinking to satisfy him, about ninety slaves were surrendered. The Mughals laughed. 'People of that kind, they said, were not so scarce. Let them send their black women, their clever cooks, their dancing girls, their confectioners, their seamstresses, and so on.' When the Portuguese refused, the Mughals pretended to waive this point and declared they would settle the matter finally if more leading men came to talk it over. Six were sent, with Cabral and the Prior. The Mughals then raised their price. Half the goods and money of the inhabitants of Hugli were to be given up. Aghast at what they now realized was but a methodical plan to ruin and possess them, the envoys asked for permission to return. For reply they were placed under guard in a tent. 'Next day we were all of us put in irons', says Cabral, and to frighten them still more an elephant was led in, one of those trained to execute criminals by tossing them in the air and pulling them limb from limb. As the terms had to be conveyed to de Azevedo, Cabral was sent back to inform him.

When the Jesuit made his report, adding that he feared even surrender of half their wealth would not save them, the Portuguese saw clearly at last where the negotiations were leading them. They had swallowed enough indignities and now resolved to fight it out, though enormously outnumbered, and surrounded by a hundred and twenty pieces of cannon.

For a month and a half the Mughals made every effort to break in, but failed. They occupied both the Augustinian monastery, which was burnt to the ground, and the Jesuit House, but they could not take the main defences, though they pounded them with their guns and sought to breach them with mines.

If the Mughals kept on, their victory was only a question of time. But the Portuguese had one card in reserve. In spite of the cannonade they had a sufficient number of undamaged ships on the river to enable them to evacuate Hugli and sail down to some spot near the mouth of the Ganges, out of reach of the Viceroy's army. Once on an island among the Sundarban creeks, they were safe, for the Mughals had neither the ships nor the skill to take such a position. This, of course meant abandoning all their possessions except cash. But it was becoming evident that only such a drastic course could save their lives.

The Mughals, tutored by the traitorous Martim de Mello, perceived that the Portuguese would attempt to escape and took measures to anticipate and prevent it by a pontoon bridge at one point and, where the river was narrow, by a great iron chain.

Fireships also were kept in readiness, and trenches to shelter musketeers and archers were dug on both banks.

On 24 September the defenders embarked secretly by night on some fourteen barges and a number of cargo boats, which had an armament of light cannon on swivels, pieces little more deadly than a blunderbuss. The survivors of the siege numbered about 150 Portuguese men, both of pure and mixed descent, perhaps 100 women of similar blood, with slaves and Indian soldiers to the number of 3,000. Many of the Indians had managed to escape.

Owing to some miscalculation the boats were overtaken by dawn before they could weigh anchor. Then began an evacuation which ranks with the most remarkable in history. When the Mughals realized that the garrison had embarked, they streamed into the town with a great show of valour 'so as to be able to boast they had taken it by storm', says Cabral with bitter scorn. In the river were about 500 Mughal boats of various sizes. On land the enemy numbered, it is said, 100,000 men, many of whom were posted in the trenches which stretched down the banks for twenty-five miles. All the cannon were now trained on the river, which was shallow on account of a poor monsoon. And the wind was contrary. It was a desperate situation.

The attack on the Portuguese ships began by the launching of a fire-raft of sixteen boats laden with firewood, pitch, and gunpowder. But a company of Portuguese managed to board the raft and kill the men on it before they could set it on fire, and afterwards used it to breach the pontoon. Night fell before this was accomplished. It seems that the Mughals were so busy looting the town that they did not press the attack at this stage.

But de Azevedo failed to get his flotilla through the pontoon in the darkness and on the following morning the battle began in earnest. 'The fury of the attack,' says Cabral, 'surpassed imagination.' The sun was darkened by the cannon smoke; bullets and arrows fell like rain. Many deeds of notable valour were observed. A boat, manned by three Portuguese and a negro, was set upon by several enemy boats. 'One of the Portuguese had had both legs shot through by a swivel. His comrades had put him on the prow, whence he kept fighting the whole fleet with two blunderbusses, which a native woman loaded for him.' He got away, 'saving the lives and honour of several white women whom he had on board'. One woman was captured at this time, a famous beauty, Lucrezia

Tavares, who had been the mistress of Sebastian Tibao, son of the Tibao who was the pirate king of Sandwip island in 1615, and so probably a cousin of the Tibao who had accompanied Manrique to Arakan. Another woman had a narrow escape. She was the wife of one Pedro da Coutto, and was on board the ship carrying the treasure of the Jesuit House, which consisted, not counting the gold and silver plate, of cash to the value of 190,000 pieces of eight. This ship was fired and then boarded by the Mughals. But the lady, rather than fall into their hands, jumped into the river with an infant in her arms and held on to the end of a cable. So desperate was she, that when it seemed they must take her she ordered one of her servants to set her on fire. But she was rescued in time by another boat.

In this frantic manner, losing several barges, they fought their way down the river. They had got past the pontoon and the chain, but now near the village of Betor, situated on the site of the present Calcutta Botanical Gardens, and so twenty-five miles from Hugli, they came to the last obstacle, a narrow blocked by another chain where the navigable passage was close by the shore. The Mughals were waiting here in force with more cannon. This was the fiercest moment of the long-drawn-out battle. However, the flotilla got through, or what was left of it, and reached the island of Saugar, sixty miles on at the mouth, that island where annually was held the festival at which the devotees offered themselves to the sharks. As no-one dared live there permanently on account of the raids of the Dianga Portuguese, the refugees from Hugli found it deserted and decided to build themselves a settlement. Good water abounded, and a quantity of old fruit trees. Of buildings there were the temples, to which once a year the pilgrims came. Strategically it was very strong, as it could not be attacked by a land army. From the point of view of trade it was not badly situated, being within easy sailing distance of Hijli, the place across the river near which Manrique had been wrecked on the way to Hugli. Accordingly de Azevedo decided to convert the main temple into a fortress. The slaves were immediately set to work.

On reflection, however, it struck the captain that it would be just as well to make sure that King Thiri-thu-dhamma had no objection. Saugar Island was about 250 miles west of Dianga and so outside the King's dominions, but as his galleys ranged as far in their raids, and had depopulated it, it was within his sphere of operations. The prudence of, at least, acquainting him with the new situation was obvious. Father Cabral was accordingly asked to go to Mrauk-u and lay the matter before him.

But in point of fact Thiri-thu-dhamma had heard of the Mughal attack on Hugli. We have seen that he was feeling his way towards a treaty with Goa. It now occurred to him that were he to send his Dianga fleet to the rescue of Hugli, he would put the whole Portuguese nation under an obligation, thereby facilitating the negotiations which he contemplated. What he wanted was to drive the Mughals right out of Bengal with the assistance of the Goanese fleet and artillery, a stroke which would not only greatly increase his importance but also anticipate what he believed must otherwise develop, a Mughal invasion of Chittagong. Indeed, he calculated that a sudden onslaught upon the Mughal forces investing Hugli would be a brilliant first move in this general plan. The relief of the town, the destruction of the Viceroy's fleet, and the dispersal of his army, taken unawares in the rear, would enable him to represent as so feasible a full-dress attack on Dacca, the Bengal capital, that Goa would join without hesitation. He had, therefore, unknown to the Portuguese at Hugli, ordered his galleys at Dianga to sail. But delayed by the weather they had sailed too late. By the time they reached Hugli the place had fallen and the Mughal fleet was returning to Dacca laden with spoil. This they interrupted and burnt, getting back much of the Hugli loot. Then learning that the survivors were on Saugar Island, they hastened downstream to look for them there.

Before Cabral was due to leave for Mrauk-u, twenty-seven Dianga galleys, 'all so swift and warlike', as he says, 'that they alone would have sufficed to give us victory', anchored in the island road. Their commander was Manoel Palmeiro, and he had with him all the Portuguese mercenaries of Dianga. He told de Azevedo that no less than 300 more ships were mustering and that he was most anxious to avenge their great losses and sufferings. But reflection showed that a naval raid on Dacca was not feasible. That would have to be postponed till greater military forces were available. Meanwhile Cabral was right to go to Mrauk-u. He would put a galley at his disposal, give him introductions and an assistant.

The monsoon was now over. Cabral first went to Dianga. Manrique was there but the two men did not meet. After a stay of a week with a fellow Jesuit, Father Antonio Farinha, he left for Mrauk-u, reaching it in four days by the open-sea route.

Thiri-thu-dhamma, says Cabral, 'received us with expressions of sorrow at the fall of Hugli and of joy at an embassy which he and his people equally longed for'. Though the Jesuit was no envoy of Goa nor Hugli, strictly speaking, a part of Portuguese Asia, the king proceeded to take him into his confidence, saying that his intention was to invade the Mughal Empire and wrest from it the whole of eastern Bengal, carrying his arms as far as Kuch Bihar, which was three hundred miles from his Chittagong frontier. In this enterprise he was seeking an alliance with the Viceroy of Goa, who, now that the Mughals had treacherously attacked and robbed his nationals at Hugli, would no doubt be ready and anxious for revenge. Cabral, he hinted, should on his return do his utmost to bring about such an alliance. Meanwhile the Portuguese might fortify Saugar Island, which would give his fleet a useful base of operations.

What are we to make of this? The Mughals were no match for the Arakanese on the rivers and the seaboard, but Thiri-thu-dhamma's project was a military conquest of Bengal, not a mere extension of his raids. The potential military power of the Mughal Empire was enormous. It is true that the levies of the Viceroy of Bengal had had difficulty in taking Hugli and had been unable to prevent the escape of a great part of its garrison. But Thiri-thu-dhamma had no army of importance. His proposed Portuguese allies could not have sent him more than a few hundred Europeans. A sudden swoop on Dacca by his galleys might succeed. The armed men they carried might be able to overcome the Viceroy's troops. But he would not be fighting merely against Bengal. The attack would be on the Mughal Empire. Shah Jehan would inevitably muster the Imperial army, which was said to number 700,000 men, a fantastic figure for those days. How could Thiri-thu-dhamma have entertained so foolhardy an ambition?

We already know the curious answer. King Thiri-thu-dhamma was the guardian of the Mahamuni and Lord of the White Elephant. As such he was the greatest Buddhist king in the Bay, greater than the kings of Ceylon, greater than the King of Burma or Siam. But he was more than that. He had the attributes—or some of them—of a Universal Monarch. He might be the long-foretold Saviour of the World, the Buddha who would unite the whole world, give it peace, happiness and, ultimately, salvation. He could not know that he certainly was that Saviour until he had been successful in his great crusade. His grandfather, Razagri, who had taken Pegu and become possessed of the White Elephant, had dreamed that same dream, as before him had Bayin-naung, King of Burma, but neither of them had been able to realize it, no doubt because of some sin in a former life not yet expiated. This also explained why his father, Min-kha-Maung, after a short reign of ten years, had died without achieving anything. It might be that he also would be held back by a past fault from the supreme bliss, the incomparable glory, to which his two unique possessions entitled him to aspire. But there was nothing to prove this to be likely. It could not indeed be proved except by his failure after the attempt. It behoved him, therefore, to try. The first step in his long climb to universal glory must be the defeat in battle of an emperor who, on paper at least, had much of the appearance of a Universal Monarch, though without the appurtenances. After the conquest of Bengal would come the conquest of all India. India was the birthplace of the Buddha, and at Gaya in Bengal was the bodhi tree under which he had reached the state of Enlightenment. What could be more fitting than that from the throne of India he should declare the new dispensation? Having done so, all the kings of the world would come and do reverence to him, when he would crown them again and, after admonishing them to follow the noble Eightfold Path, dismiss them to rule their states in charity and love.

Such was the vision of this strange Buddhist king. To begin to put it into effect the right course was to obtain the assistance of the white foreigners of Goa, whose skill as mariners, musketeers, and gunners exceeded that of the Mughal's best troops. He did not know that they had a parallel ambition, quite as fantastic as his own. He did not know that the Pope had given to Portugal all Asia, designing by that grant to bring at last its kings to the Holy City, where he would admonish them in the beatitudes of the Sermon on the Mount, and afterwards send them back to rule as partners in the Christian world-state, which it had always been the Catholic Church's dream to see established. He did not know all this. Had he been informed, it would have seemed to him without meaning, for the Portuguese were heathens, they had no knowledge of the Eightfold Path, which was the way to salvation, for only by following it could rebirth into illusion be ended and the state of Enlightenment be attained.

In this singular way Goa and Mrauk-u came together, both in the world of reality and in the place of dreams.

But, as we shall see in later chapters, when the narrative of this book begins to enter its more curious phase, King Thiri-thudhamma was afflicted by harassing doubts. There was a prophecy that he would die soon after his coronation, whenever that might take place. There were aspects, moreover, in his horoscope which caused him disquiet. These indications of an adverse fate had to be balanced against the fact of his possession of the Mahamuni and the White Elephant. Difficult and uncertain is the reading of the future. Yet for a king there were expedients, ways of fortifying oneself against evil, of circumventing bad aspects.

Before Cabral left Mrauk-u, he made a discovery. Four years earlier he had been in Tibet and become dimly aware that its inhabitants were not Hindus, but had a religion of their own. It was not clear to him what that religion was, but now in Mrauk-u he noticed that the images resembled those he had seen in Tibet and that the monks wore a similar kind of yellow robe. Further similarities also struck him, and he concluded that the religion of Arakan was identical with that of Tibet. As we know, both were and are Buddhist countries, but the Buddhism of Tibet is a variety of the Mahayana, and that of Arakan is Hinayana. The differences between the two schools are very great in practice, particularly between the practices of the lamas and the monks in Arakan, and it was not very observant of Cabral to find there was no difference. Yet we must give him the credit for being the first European to connect the two, and to realize that besides Hinduism and Mohammedanism there was a third great religion in Asia. We shall not meet him again in this narrative and may state here that the clarity and grasp characterizing his letter generally—he was only just over thirty at the time—was in fact indicative of excellent abilities, for he eventually became rector of the Professed House of the Jesuits at Goa, that palatial building beside the Bom Jesus where Mandelslo dined and found the canary so good.

XXIV

Friar Manrique is Appointed Attaché

Cabral left Mrauk-u probably in January 1633. Manrique was still at Dianga and remained there until October or November of that year, when he received two letters which obliged him again to set out for the Arakanese capital. The first was from a certain Gaspar de Mesquita, who announced that he had just arrived at Mrauk-u, having been sent there by Dom Miguel de Noronha, Viceroy of Goa, to conclude a treaty with King Thiri-thu-dhamma. The letter went on to request him to come to Mrauk-u, since he knew the King so well and the grandees of the Court, and assist the writer in his negotiations. His other letter was from Friar Gaspar de Amorin, the head of the Augustinian Order in Asia, and amounted to a grant of leave from his duties at Dianga, so that he could comply with the ambassador's request.

That Manrique should have been asked to join the ambassador's staff shows that the able manner in which he had conducted the special mission to Mrauk-u in 1630 had been reported to Goa and had made an impression. Almost three years had elapsed since then. He was wholly immersed in his duties as vicar of Dianga and had no wish to exchange the mission field again for diplomacy. But the letter from the Father Provincial left him no option. After giving careful instructions how the arrangements he had made for the neophytes and Christians lately collected at Angaracale were to be carried on in his absence, he sailed to Mrauk-u in the galley which had brought the letters.

As the King had sounded him on his last visit about the possibility of such a treaty, it is likely that Manrique had passed on the information to his headquarters at Goa. The sending of de Mesquita can, therefore, have been no great surprise, even if news of what transpired during Cabral's visit did not reach him. That he understood tolerably well Thiri-thu-dhamma's extraordinary ambitions will become clearer as the narrative proceeds.

The negotiations lasted five months—until March 1634. They did not go smoothly. Manrique has little to say about them in detail except that they failed to bring about an alliance against the Great Mughal. It seems that Thiri-thu-dhamma pressed de Mesquita to promise more help than his instructions permitted him to promise. The probability is that when the Portuguese realized that Thiri-thu-dhamma had vast dreams of conquest, far transcending the capture of Dacca and the throwing back of the Mughal from eastern Bengal, he saw that it would be madness for Goa to be entangled and extricated himself as fast as he could.

The King, says Manrique, was profoundly disappointed. He had failed in the very first move towards his grand goal. Without the aid of the Portuguese fleet he could not start on the emprise of which he dreamed. Could it be that he was not fated to become Lord of the World? But there were ways of compelling fate. If he had had a diplomatic setback, if his fleet and army were not potent enough, there were other potencies, there were occult powers, there was magic, medicines. . . .

Yet his disappointment was bitter. At the end of the negotiations, when de Mesquita had sailed away, Manrique petitioned for leave to return to Dianga.

'What do you want to go for?' asked the King roughly.

'As a member of the ambassador's staff I ask for my passports like the rest,' replied the Friar.

'You did not come on his ships,' retorted the King. 'I see no reason for you to go. Have I not granted you a church with slaves and everything else you wanted? You shall stay.'

Manrique was somewhat alarmed. He thought that perhaps the King blamed him for the breakdown of the negotiations.But there was nothing he could do. Offend His Majesty he dare not. To escape or attempt to escape would jeopardize the existence of the Christian community for which he had worked so hard. His only course was to obey with the best grace possible. 'I therefore continued assiduously to attend at the palace,' he says. 'This convinced the King that I was satisfied to stay, and he made me certain concessions', including the offer of a monthly stipend and rations. But he could not get permission to leave. The King had his reasons. The Friar now knew too much about Arakan. It was not certain that he could be trusted outside the realm, while inside it he was useful for keeping the Christians contented and quiet. This was quite a normal view. No oriental king liked foreigners to leave his kingdom when they had become well acquainted with its secrets.

XXV

Friar Manrique takes the Yellow Robe

Shortly after the events described in the last chapter, certainly before the onset of the monsoon in this year 1634, a Buddhist monk came to Manrique's door. The Friar asked him his business, and the man whispered he had a matter for his private ear. Manrique led him aside and he produced a bamboo tube, taking a letter from it written on palm-leaf. 'Read this', he said, handing it over.

The Friar was astonished to see that the language was Latin. The contents were equally surprising. The writer was a Portuguese, Ignatius Gomez by name, a native of Estremoz in eastern Portugal. He had come out to Goa and in 1608, twenty-six years previously, had taken ship thence on a trading venture to Burma. While off the Arakanese coast they were caught in a cyclone and driven on shore. The waves were so fierce and the coast so rocky that only seventeen out of the ninety-two on board reached land alive. These were immediately arrested by the local authorities on the ground that they were pirates, a reasonable ground enough, for in 1608 Gonzales Tibao was King of Sandwip and his galleys scoured the coasts in search of slaves and plunder. When the shipwrecked men came before the magistrates at Mrauk-u, so certainly did they appear to be Sandwip pirates that without even the formality of an inquiry they were exiled to a region situated in the mountains some days' march behind the capital.

Before being sent there, they were hamstrung so that they could not escape. They had lived ever since in the mountains, had married local women and brought up families. But no priest had visited them; their marriages had not been consecrated; their children had not been baptized; and they themselves or as many of them as survived had not been to confession all those years.

The letter did not complain of their lot as prisoners, but as persons outside the Catholic pale and fold. Gomez in moving sentences expresses the horror he felt in this predicament. He begs Manrique to come to his spiritual aid. It was rumoured in the mountains, he says, that a 'priest in a black robe with wide sleeves had arrived at the capital'. And he goes on: 'To whatever brotherhood you belong, I beseech you, by the divine wounds of Christ our Redeemer, to come here and relieve my soul!' After a life of captivity far from home, death would not bring him release and happiness but an eternity in hell's fire. And his wife and children, though he had taught them the faith and they tried to practise it, for lack of baptism were also condemned. 'Should you fail to come,' he exclaims, 'I swear before God's throne that our perdition will lie at your door!'

The letter then introduces the bearer. He is the brother of Gomez's unmarried wife. And 'I well understand', it concludes, 'the great risks you will run in coming hither, but the monk is competent to guide you, and if you follow his advice you can reach us and return in safety.'

The reading of this letter was a shock for Manrique. What answer could he give? He knew it was forbidden for anyone under the severest penalties even to get into communication with prisoners of this kind. To go to them would jeopardize not only his life but the future of his little community. Not to go would sear his conscience. 'What have you decided?' asked the monk who had been watching his perplexity. 'Give me time to consider,' he replied.

The monk said he had business in Mrauk-u which would detain him a week. At the end of that time he would come again. The difficulties of the journey were not insuperable. And he knew a means by which they might be obviated. With this hint he withdrew.

Manrique at once sent for a native Christian and, pretending that he wished to know about the mountain prison so that he could ask the King to grant him the Christians there, obtained a good deal more information. It was a place of exile, said the man, for any Europeans suspected of piracy or espionage. The prisoners lived scattered among the hill tribes who inhabited what in effect was a piece of arable land surrounded by the mountains of the Burma divide. The approach to it was by certain valleys, strongly guarded by police-posts. No-one except monks of the Order was allowed to pass by the guards unless he had a passport sealed by the King. The penalty for improper entry was death for the perpetrators, their families, and abettors. A European could not possibly hope to slip in. He would be detected at once, whether disguised or not.

This seemed to settle the matter. Putting aside personal risks, no good to anyone could come of an attempt. When, therefore, the monk called again, Manrique asked him in a jocular way whether he was joking. Somewhat offended, he replied: 'If Catholic priests are in the habit of cracking jokes when the unfortunate demand their aid, Buddhist monks are not.'

Manrique was disconcerted by this reply. He knew well that Gomez's letter was no joking matter. The dilemma had deeply exercised him. His life was dedicated to the saving of souls. He was ready to face martyrdom, if need be. 'You misunderstand me,' he replied. 'I am not joking, but I am appalled by the difficulties.'

'I am surprised to hear you say that,' retorted the monk. 'My brother-in-law, Gomez, has told me time and again that Catholic priests take account of difficulties only to overcome them. Having travelled ten thousand miles over the ocean, nothing can deflect them when a soul is to be saved.'

'But we are only human,' urged Manrique. 'We cannot do the impossible.'

'It is not impossible if you follow my advice,' said the monk.

Manrique: What then do you advise?

The Monk: Two things are necessary, secrecy and dispatch. Dispatch is the main part of secrecy, for an enterprise, be it never so secret, will be betrayed by lack of dispatch. Yet dispatch cannot be achieved by ordinary means.

Manrique: I do not understand you.

The Monk: I have a proposal to make which, if put into effect, will enable us to go straight to the place, but I do not know whether you will entertain it.

Manrique: Tell me what it is.

The Monk: If you discard your black habit, scapulary, and hood, and don the yellow robe, then as two monks of the order we can enter without passports.

Manrique did not reply. To abandon the dress of an Augustinian and take that of a pagan priest was abhorrent to him.

The Monk: I see that you are upset. I shall call again in two days, when you can tell me your mind.

Saying this, he took leave.

'He had judged me rightly,' records Manrique, 'for I was indeed in a state of indecision, sailing hither and thither on a sea of doubts.' But before the two days were up, he had made up his mind to go. The monk returned as he had said. When Manrique informed him he was ready to start at once, he exclaimed: 'What my brother-in-law told me about the Christian faith must be true!'

'Believe me, brother,' said Manrique earnestly, 'only through it is salvation possible.'

'*Amé*!' cried he, a word which in such a context expresses astonishment and half-amused protest, like our exclamation 'Good gracious!' And changing the subject, he said: 'I will come for you after dark,' and took his departure.

Night fell and when all Manrique's household had retired, the monksilently entered the building, which was in complete darkness. Together they groped their way to a room used by the Friar for meditation. There, by the light of one candle, the monk shaved Manrique's head, for all Buddhist monks have the head shaven. This was followed by the change into the yellow robe, which is in two pieces, one part falling from the waist like a skirt and the other draped over the left shoulder, though this can also be used as a cape or hood. Manrique does not state whether he wore a beard. If he did, it will also have come off, for hair does not grow on Arakanese faces.

Manrique with the olive complexion of southern Europe and his high nose cannot have looked like a local monk, for the Arakanese countenance is Mongolian in cast and dark in complexion, with flat nose and the ear-lobes pierced and long. Indeed, the disguise was but partial and could only deceive at a distance. Moreover, his knowledge of the language was limited. In short, he had little chance of getting past the police-posts unless his companion had prepared some further deception. It is interesting here to recall de Nobili to mind. But the Jesuit dressed himself as a Brahmin priest for profoundly different reasons.

The monk had a boat waiting on the river near by. 'Brother,' said he, 'we can now safely start. You are at least half a Buddhist monk.' Manrique, as if to emphasize that he was wholly an Augustinian, knelt before a crucifix and recited the *Viam Pacis*. Then they went quickly to the boat, the monk carrying for him a basket in which were packed vestments and wine for the Mass.

Friar Manrique takes the Yellow Robe

The boat was larger than Manrique had expected. There were eight rowers and a steersman, and four novices were in attendance. The middle part was covered with matting, arched over to form a cabin. Seated under this they could not be seen.

Rowing when the tide was in their favour and tying up at the bank during the ebb, it was not until late the following day that they reached the vicinity of the first police-post. As night was falling, they disembarked. The monk had explained that, when he came out of the mountains, his brother, also a monk, was with him, and that he had left him in Mrauk-u. Manrique would have to impersonate the brother. The guards would be told he had fever and not to bother him. 'Sit under the tree there,' he now said, 'while I go and talk to them. Pull your robe over your head as if you were cold and sick.'

Manrique did as he was bid and saw the monk approach the guards. They got up from their seats and received him with all the respect due to his cloth. After a quarter of an hour two clerks were sent to count the novices and crew who were waiting on the bank. Manrique was much alarmed when afterwards they came over towards him. To give himself heart he repeated under his breath a passage from one of St. Augustine's sermons. But the clerks were not suspicious. With a sympathetic salutation they asked what ailed him, to which he replied in a faint voice, his head covered and bowed, that he was ill of the fever. Satisfied, they returned and reported to the guards. The monk was then handed a passport and allowed to proceed.

But this was not the only post. Next day two hours before sunset they reached the inner gate, as it was called, where the scrutiny of passengers was more rigorous, said the monk. The boat would be left here and they would walk the rest of the way.

On landing, the first thing the monk did was to give a present of twelve pounds of pepper. This created so excellent an impression on the officer in charge that he waived the usual inspection of goods and passengers, and gave the party leave to proceed at once. But the monk thought it would be safer not to appear in a hurry and told the novices to prepare dinner. While this was being done, he entertained the officer and his lieutenants with the latest news of the capital, Manrique as before sitting apart as if ill.

When dinner was announced, the monk asked the officers to join him. They accepted with alacrity, for life in their outpost was extremely dull. Moreover, and this was the more cogent reason, the monk declared his intention of reciting certain magical formulas to give the food a prophylactic potency, such as the food of paradise possesses.

When they were seated—Manrique still keeping aloof—the monk directed the novices to bring from the boat a jar which contained some gallons of liquor. This he served liberally and soon the meal, under his encouragement, became a drinking-bout. When the officers were drunk, he distributed drinks to the clerks and finally to the guards, and continued this lavish hospitality until everyone attached to the post was either asleep or in a state of uncritical hilarity.

He then left the table, and signed to Manrique and the novices to take up their bundles and follow him. As they passed the guard-house itself, the constables on duty appeared at the door. They too had had their share of liquor, and with wide smiles, bows, and incoherent pleasantries, sped the party on its way.

Here began the climb into the mountains, called in the text the mountains of Maum. But the track was too rocky and steep to attempt in the dark, and after walking a mile or so they halted for the night, climbing trees to be safe from wild animals. The habitat of the prisoners was some fifty miles in, and as Manrique was obliged to go barefoot, for Buddhist monks never wear shoes, the pace was slow. His feet soon became lacerated; unlike St. Francis Xavier he had never been accustomed to tramp unshod on his missionary tours; by the fourth day he could walk no more and the novices had to carry him on an improvised litter.

By this time they had reached the plain inside the mountains. It was inhabited by some non-Arakanese Mongolian tribe, probably Mro or Chin. Primitive though these people were, they were farmers, nor did they offer any incivility to the party. The monk now sent ahead a messenger to Ignatius Gomez to inform him of their approach and to ask that four men be sent to help to carry Manrique's litter. This was at dawn on the fifth day. The messenger reached Gomez's house by ten o'clock in the morning. The Portuguese immediately sent eight servants, and himself with two companions followed, though slowly as their heel tendons were cut.

The servants took over the litter, but it was not until five o'clock in the afternoon that Gomez hobbled up to meet them. As soon as he perceived Manrique in the litter, recognizing him instantly in spite of his disguise, he was overcome with emotion and the tears poured down his cheeks, while he uttered a fervent thanksgiving to God. Then, with his two friends, he began to kiss the Friar's hands. For his part, Manrique felt that he ought to get out of the litter and embrace them, but attempting to do so, collapsed on the ground, so swollen and painful were his feet. At this Gomez, still weeping with happiness, tenderly lifted him back into the litter. Wending very slowly their way through the late afternoon and beguiling the time with talk of God and the Holy Virgin, of sin and salvation, Manrique quoting from St. Gregory and the Fathers, Gomez thirstily listening to the comforting words, lack of which for so many years had turned his life into a misery, they reached the house when the sun had set.

Here, in the midst of the remote jungle, says Manrique, he was received with all the courtesies of Portugal, being carried to a bed, served with food, and his feet bathed with a herb lotion which alleviated the pain. It seems that the house was situated in or beside a village and that Gomez was the only Portuguese there, the others being planted in villages some distance away. The prisoners lived a life resembling that of Russian exiles to Siberia, or of political prisoners in China sent to the provinces beyond the Great Wall. But there was no hope of release. Never could they aspire to see Portugal again. They had to make the best of things, with a local wife and half-caste children. But the thought of death —without absolution, without consolation—that was the shadow which haunted their days. Now the friar would absolve them and give them heart for the long years they must go on alone.

Three days after his arrival, as soon as he could stand, Manrique celebrated the Mass in a hut in Gomez's compound before a rough altar on which was a wooden cross. The whole family attended, the wife, four sons and a daughter, a widowed sister-in-law with her children, eleven persons, who all knelt before the altar and kissed the ground, murmuring a Latin prayer which Gomez had taught them. Manrique was deeply touched by their rustic earnestness. In due course, after instructing them, he baptized these catechumens. 'They wept unrestrainedly,' he said, 'no doubt for their past sins, now washed away, so that I was myself ashamed at thinking how few were the tears I had shed for sins committed and but little expiated.' Gomez's confession and marriage followed.

The old mother-in-law lived in the house. She was a Buddhist, had always resisted the attempts by her son-in-law to wean her from that faith. She had, however, no antipathy to Christianity and found Manrique an interesting distraction. As a priest he had her respect, and during the days that followed she often came to his room with a present of eggs and fruit. He took what was curiosity and the desire for a chat to be an inclination for the true faith, and began to urge her 'to abandon the false tenets of her sect'. Further misled by the old woman's polite nods and smiles he thought he was going to convert her. But when he pressed the point and asked her direct questions, she answered very vaguely. She had not, of course, really listened to his arguments. She had no need of his consolations. Her own beliefs were too real to her. When Manrique called at her house one day and with her daughter's help made a strong effort to bring her round, declaring how the devil kept her deceived and blinded, she described cheerfully how that very night a vision had been vouchsafed to her, how she had seen the Buddha smile and promise her Paradise. 'I am seventy-two years of age and near my end', she declared, and suddenly throwing off her half-complaisance desired that he trouble himself about her no more.

Manrique was much dashed by this failure. 'As I saw no human means of softening the hardness of that soul, I left her alone and sought how to spend my time where I could procure more fruit.'

Accordingly next day he moved to another village twelve miles away where the other Portuguese prisoners awaited him. There, in a house in which they were accustomed on Sundays and saints' days to assemble and recite litanies and other prayers, he celebrated Mass at the altar, its wooden cross under a cotton canopy, and an earthenware lamp burning before it. Five Portuguese, two Eurasians and their households, numbering thirty-six persons, were baptized, confessed, consoled, and absolved. Thereafter he returned to Gomez's house and stayed three weeks more, preaching, instructing, admonishing, advising, and providing for a future in which there was little hope of their seeing another priest.

In spite of their earnest prayers to continue with them longer, their tears, protestations, arguments, reproaches, he now resolved to return, for he dared not make a greater stay. The monk, who during these Catholic exercises had betaken himself to his monastery, now reappeared. It would not be possible, he said, to leave by the way they had come, for it was the rule that a seal should be stamped on the arm of everyone leaving the region, and as that formality would entail a close inspection, Manrique's disguise would certainly be penetrated. But there was another route. It involved a long detour. Instead of nine days, it would take fourteen. No police-posts lay in that direction. It was not an easy journey, but it was safe. Indeed, no other way of getting back existed, except through a jungle so notorious for tigers that to venture into it without a guard of at least twelve men with firearms would be suicide.

So it was settled. They started on their fourteen-days' walk. The direction was eastward of the route they had taken to the mountains and came out on the sea coast below the mouth of the Kaladan river. At a village there they purchased a boat and by winding inner creeks entered the Kaladan and reached Mrauk-u on the third day after dark. Choosing the back streets and obscurest shadows, they made their way to the church, which Manrique immediately entered and, robed as he was, knelt at the altar to give thanks. Afterwards, on the steps, the monk bade him farewell, saying he desired at once to find the brother he had left in the city. Before dawn both of them must be on their way back to the mountains.

It will be agreed that this monk showed a great example of Buddhist charity and tolerance in exposing his life in order that the consolations of a religion hostile to his own might be brought to a suffering human creature. Nor was his high character unappreciated by Manrique, for whom it remained a mystery how agents of the devil could also be good men. 'I never heard of him again,' he writes, 'nor of any of those who formed part of our band, nor of the exiled Christians in the mountains.' And concludes: 'May God in His infinite mercy have kept them steadfast in His sacred service. And may He grant to the heathen a true knowledge of His sacred faith, to their salvation.'

XXVI

The Elixir

Manrique had been away six weeks. No doubt before his departure he had instructed the faithful how to explain his absence. It was now May 1634, and the monsoon was near its breaking. He took an early opportunity of letting himself be seen at Court.

There very queer things were going on and he heard some rumour of them. We have already given indications of Thiri-thu-dhamma's state of mind. Readers may have begun to ask themselves whether he were not mad. If they have not already put this question, they will certainly put it now.

It seems that during the fine season a Mohammedan had visited Mrauk-u, a man who declared that he had made the pilgrimage to Mecca and who passed himself off as a doctor and the possessor of occult secrets. He effected a number of cures and acquired the reputation of a master of magic. News of what he claimed to be able to do reached the King's ears and he was summoned to Court. What transpired at their first meeting we do not know, but by the time Manrique was back from the mountains, the Doctor, as we shall call him, for we may be quite sure that the Arakanese referred to him by their term *Saragri*, was well established in the King's confidence. Then, or perhaps after the break of the rains, Thiri-thu-dhamma will have spoken to him of his situation as he conceived it. We already know its elements. On the credit side was the Mahamuni and the White Elephant, 'huge cloudy symbols of a high romance', which pointed to world conquest and world salvation. But the possession of these Jems was not sufficient alone to carry him there, or else Razagri or his father Minkha Maung would have preceded him. Rather they were pointers, showing what might be done, what could lawfully be done. Yet, to succeed in the world of appearances right action must be taken. The Jems of themselves would not bring him to glory. But his people were not numerous, his army was small, and though his navy was superior to that of other kings, great conquests were won by great land battles or the threat thereof. Perhaps, had he succeeded in making an alliance with Goa, their combined land and sea forces would have sufficed, so superior in modern armaments were the Europeans. But that had not materialized and now it rested with him to take the right action. Besides the smallness of his forces there was another matter which deeply worried him, the prophecy, impossible to discount, which declared he would die soon after his coronation, certainly before he could achieve the tremendous deeds which were foreshadowed. This prophecy had easily been forestalled for the time being. He had postponed his coronation for twelve years. But he could not do so indefinitely. To dispense altogether with the coronation ceremony would suggest that it was without importance, that it conferred no occult potency, no measure of divinity, an absurd supposition, for all kings were crowned so that they might acquire such added power. It was essential to be crowned, not only to obtain this heightened force and for the plainer reason that his subjects would respect him the less were he not and would begin to plan rebellion or usurpation, but also because, before he could set out to become King of the World, he must first be crowned King of Arakan. How would distant peoples accept him as their king if he came the unconsecrated king of his own? No, he must be crowned. Yet, how to meet the prophecy? And if he escaped the prophecy, how, in the realm of appearances, to conquer the world?

Whether Thiri-thu-dhamma so expressed himself directly to the Doctor, or whether the latter had the information conveyed to him, or gathered it from hints, or whether his experience suggested that ideas of the kind were in the wind, we cannot know but we do know that at a certain stage he told the King that he possessed a secret which would enable him to conquer the world.

It would be a mistake to suppose that Thiri-thu-dhamma received this intelligence with amazement. All Asian kings were on the lookout for sages who could tell them the great secrets, the secret of immortality, of invisibility, of invulnerability, of invincibility. Such sages were known to exist. They existed in China. Had not Genghis Khan in 1219 sent for the alchemist Ch'ang Ch'un, sent a messenger with a golden tablet in the form of a tiger's head to Teng Chou near Peking to bring the Master three thousand miles to where he sat on the Oxus, that he might hear from him the secret of immortality? If there were sages in China, they were to be found also in Persia, for the Mohammedans of these regions yielded nothing to the Chinese in their knowledge of arcane lore. We may be sure that the Doctor had first convinced Thiri-thu-dhamma that he was that rarity, an authentic sage, and therefore that when he announced his knowledge of the hidden way by which the king might obtain his desires, he was believed without amazement, but with joy and excitement.

Manrique gives the terms of the Doctor's offer. 'I can make your Majesty invisible and invincible so that not only will you be safe from the death prophesied to follow your coronation, but you will obtain possession of the vast empire of the Mughal and of the kingdoms of Burma and Siam.' To become Lord of India and Further India was to be as great a monarch as the Emperor of China. In 1634 the Ming dynasty was tottering and like to fall—it fell ten years later to a bandit and then to a barbarian. The Doctor may well have promised China to Thiri-thu-dhamma. Indeed, Manrique hints that he boasted himself able to give everything which imagination could conjure. The colloquy will have resembled that in *La Vie très horrifique du Grand Gargantua*, published exactly a hundred years before, where King Picrochole is incited by the Duke of Menuail, Count Spadassin, and Captain Merdaille to emulate Alexander, Master of the Universe.

But after a while the King, calming himself somewhat, asked for particulars. By what means would the Doctor make him invisible and invincible, invulnerable alike to hurt by men or spirits?

'By means of an elixir,' reported the Doctor. This was the answer for which the King had hoped. It was well known that a medicine of the proper constituents, if taken internally or applied as an ointment, would give a man supernatural powers. Tattooing with magical squares might also effect this, but an elixir was more certain, more suited to royalty, far rarer. The King was pleased it was to be an elixir.

'But,' said the Doctor, 'the elixir I propose is not easy to compound. The ingredients are difficult to get.'

The King had not thought their procurement would be easy. An elixir capable of giving him victory over the Great Mughal would certainly have to be composed of rarities. He would have been disillusioned, have doubted, had the Doctor suggested it was simple to make, and now assured him that whatever ingredients he required would be supplied.

'The elixir must be made of hearts,' said the Doctor, 'two thousand hearts of white doves. . . .'

The King promised him white doves could be found to that number.

'Four thousand hearts of white cows. . . .'

This was more difficult. But no doubt there were four thousand white cows in the country.

'And six thousand human hearts,' concluded the ruffian.

It is clear enough from Manrique's account that Thiri-thu-dhamma was taken aback at this last item. That he should have been so was natural. After all, he was a Buddhist king. The noble Eightfold Path of compassion was his creed. In accordance with it he yearned to lift the intolerable burden of woe from the shoulders of humanity. How, then, could he begin his work of mercy by demanding six thousand human hearts? Many a man before and since has been confronted with this same problem of whether to do evil that good may come, and though his religion, be he Christian or Buddhist, warns him that an evil deed will bring forth evil fruit, his dreams delude him and he disregards the warning. We may well believe, however, that Thiri-thu-dhamma hesitated some time before resolving to murder six thousand of his subjects. On those occasions when we have seen him at close quarters, his mild tolerance in the face of Manrique's bigotry, the amiability with which he sent his doctor when the Friar was ill, his unsuspicious readiness to grant requests, his happy familiarity when playing with his children, all showed him to have been kind and easy-going. So, to account for his present atrocious resolution we must suppose that, duped by his paranoiac vision, and in deadly fear of the alternative fate predicted for him, his reason deserted him, till he was as deluded, though more criminal, than the unfortunates who gave themselves to the sharks in order to ensure their salvation. Doubtless the Doctor employed every trick of chicanery to overcome his scruples. Such men's whole trade is specious argumentation. Once they know their victim believes them to possess the power they claim and is desperately anxious to have it exerted in his favour, they have a fund of cunning expedients and a dark power of suggestion.

The reader may wonder why the Doctor demanded a holocaust before he would deliver his supposed elixir. Surely a simpler prescription would have served his fraudulent purpose equally well? If his object were to enmesh the King, enrich himself, and decamp, as presumably it was, why was he not content with doves' and cows' hearts? Here we are on difficult ground, but may presume that he was psychologist enough to know that the king would consent, and that the higher and more fantastic his demand, the greater afterwards would be his reputation. Moreover, it will be safe to assume that he took up the profession of alchemist because he enjoyed the power it gave; and the more evilly he could exercise it, the greater his enjoyment. To induce a king to immolate six thousand persons had therefore a double attraction, the forcing of his will upon a great personage and the delight he took in the contemplation of death. He also was a paranoiac and, so, akin to Thiri-thu-dhamma. The psycho-analyst will show in what they differed. As laymen we may think that they represented opposites, for there can be a paranoia of good as well as of evil. The King's object was to become master of the world so that he might be its saviour, the Doctor's to become master of kings so that he might destroy the world. But as to accomplish the first Thiri-thu-dhamma had to involve himself in the second, the difference between the opposites disappears and in an absolute sense they are seen to be identical. In short, paranoia of any form is demoniacal nor is Manrique so old-fashioned as at first sight appears when he declares in this connection that both the King and the Doctor were devils.

The matter having been decided on, Thiri-thu-dhamma issued instructions to the police to seize six thousand persons, kill them, and deliver their hearts to the alchemist. Put thus, the statement seems almost incredible. Despotic though an Asian king was at that date, had he the power to give such an order? Surely his commands went out through the proper channel, the minister concerned being made aware of them, probably after consultation, when he caused them to be written and resubmitted for the royal seal? That certainly was the way ordinary business was done. There are numerous references throughout Manrique's narrative to quite an elaborate secretarial procedure. But the King possessed a secret police who were subject directly to him. His orders to them did not go through any minister. In this case, moreover, when instructing the Chief of Police to procure the hearts, he enjoined the strictest secrecy. As far as possible the victims should not be seized before witnesses. Houses should be entered at night and sleeping persons kidnapped; or victims should be arrested in back streets and byways; or if a number of people were collected together for some purpose, all should be taken. After their apprehension, they were to be conveyed to a lonely spot among the jungle-clad hills surrounding the city and there dispatched. Should any police officer be detected at this work and complaint be laid against him in the courts, he would not be protected by pleading the King's orders, nor escape the legal penalty, which was impalement.

The proscription began in this way, the police taking the greatest care to do their work unostentatiously, and selecting widows, orphans, labourers in from the villages, slaves, in short, anyone whose disappearance would arouse the minimum of comment But as six thousand were required, these sources were soon exhausted, and they began kidnapping residents in the poorer quarters. Though they themselves succeeded in keeping out of sight, the result of their activities could not be hid. It began to be whispered that people were disappearing. Rumour became a certainty as more were reported missing. The citizens were distraught with horror. Stories circulated of a place in the mountains, where the kidnapped were murdered and buried in trenches. It became known that the Doctor was there. Witnesses declared they had peeped through the trees and seen him stirring cauldrons that simmered on fires. At night he was heard reciting incantations and yelling as he invoked evil spirits. Some people were so terrified that they barricaded themselves in their houses, not daring to go out even in broad daylight. Others became savagely enraged and began to plan a mass rising and the overthrow of the government. A few policemen were caught in the act, dragged to the courts, sentenced, and impaled. But their colleagues continued the round-up, transferring their activities to the neighbouring villages when feeling grew too hot in the city.

In this way, in the course of a few weeks, the six thousand hearts were procured and the elixir concocted. Then one evening the outraged people were startled to hear discharge after discharge from the heavy cannon on the palace walls. At nightfall the state buildings in the high central circumvallation were seen outlined with illuminations.

According to Schouten, the Dutchman who visited Mrauk-u some thirty years later, there was 'a vast esplanade in front of the fortress', an open space outside its east gate. Into this the populace now ventured to crowd, looking up at the lights and wondering what they portended. Presently rockets shot into the sky, there was a display of fireworks, and the royal orchestras, in pavilions high on the walls, played loudly gay airs from the national operas. This free entertainment continued all night and reassured the people. The operatic passages chosen were interpreted as meaning that the time of trouble was over. As dawn was breaking, the crowds dispersed to their houses, certain they could now rest in peace and safety.

In the course of the day it was officially proclaimed that the coronation would take place when the monsoon was over. Flags were hoisted on the palace roof, when a tall elephant emerged from the south gate. On a golden tray inside the howdah was placed the Royal proclamation. In front of the howdah sat the Chief Justice, in a silvery coat spangled with gold. The driver was in red damask and his driving-prong was of gold. Thirty-two war-elephants in silk caparisons lumbered behind, great bells jangling at their necks and standards flying from their saddles. They were led by a drum-major. Six hundred cavalry of the Guard went prancing with them. Massed bands completed the cortège. Every now and then a halt was made. From a platform the Chief Justice read out the proclamation.

XXVII

Prelude to the Coronation

Needless to say, Manrique found this compounding of the elixir one of the most shocking things he had ever come across. In some pages of comment, interspersed with quotations from St. Thomas Aquinas and the Vulgate, he deplores that the King should have fallen under the influence of such an irresponsible adviser as the Doctor. Again, as in the case of the sharks, he emphasizes the paramountcy of reason. Here, without knowing it, he is in agreement with the early Buddhist texts. Both Catholicism and early Buddhism have an equal distrust of the subliminal contents of the mind. The King's surrender to this uprush of paranoiac fantasies and his neglect to guide his actions by the sane dictates of an intellect ready to weigh with propriety the problems confronting him, was a sure indication that he would not long maintain his throne, a point which Manrique makes, in his laborious manner, by saying that the cries of the unfortunate victims of the King's experiment would one day rise, in the form of a revolution, and overwhelm him. As we shall see, this revolution took place, though not in the form in which he envisaged it.

A few days after the coronation was announced, it occurred to him that now was an opportunity to renew his application for leave to depart. He anticipated finding the King in a good humour and in this he was not mistaken, for on his presenting himself at audience he perceived His Majesty to be graciously inclined. Having imbibed the elixir, and being relieved in consequence of all anxiety, and confident that after his crowning he could begin his great career, he was dispensing favours with prodigality. When his turn came to speak, Manrique submitted that, as he had not been to confession for a long time, it was essential he return to Dianga for the purpose. But unexpectedly the King refused permission. Laughing, he rallied him on his want of courtly tact.

'Come, come, Father,' he said, 'you do not mean to tell me you want to leave Mrauk-u just when every person of any standing in the kingdom will be hastening to it to attend my coronation!' And without giving him a chance to reply, turned the conversation to another topic. Manrique dared say no more, and gave up all idea of leaving before the coronation.

When this came, it took the form of a great national festival which lasted three months, and was attended not only by the grandees of the court, but by all the notabilities in the kingdom. The capital was crowded, too, with visitors from the towns and villages, and a large number of foreign merchants from the countries of the Bay, Siam, Burma, India, and the Spice Islands, took the opportunity of what was expected to be a lively market and arrived in ships laden with every sort of merchandise, food, medicines, scented woods, minerals, silks, carpets, metal-work, and porcelain. The goods were allowed in duty-free. The main streets became a vast bazaar, where in addition to the articles mentioned it was possible to buy a wide variety of precious stones, with such rarities as ambergris, musk, and quicksilver, as well as lac, cinnabar, opium, and incense. It should be borne in mind that Mrauk-u, though less substantially built, was comparable in size and wealth to such Western cities as Amsterdam and London. Schouten, writing, as I have said, a little later, declares it the richest city in that part of Asia, exceeding in its resources both Pegu and Ayudhya, the capital of Siam. The fact is, of course, that before the coming of power-driven machinery cities were not large by modern standards, except in China where the extraordinary talent of their inhabitants enabled them to put on the market luxury goods without parallel anywhere else and hence enormously in demand throughout the world. In general, a capital city was no more than what we should now call a country town. That term applies very fittingly to Mrauk-u, whose wealth depended principally on the extensive regions of rice-land which surrounded it. With a rainfall of between 200 and 300 inches a year the crop never failed, while in adjacent India poor monsoons followed by famines periodically occurred. Thus in Arakan wealth increased from generation to generation. The export of rice to undernourished India brought in a steady flow of those commodities which were lacking on the spot. Moreover, the dynasty of Mrauk-u had maintained itself successfully against all foreign or domestic rivals for two hundred and ten years. The few wars were short and ended in victory. No civil strife had ruined the peasantry. Little wonder, then, that it was a rich and prosperous country. What state in Europe could boast of two centuries of peace, uniformly good harvests, a tolerant religion, and a slave population to do some of the hard work? And the administration was not inefficient. Though corrupt in the manner of the age, it administered a code of law. Person and property were reasonably safe. These facts throw into relief Thiri-thu-dhamma's truly extraordinary aberration in compounding the elixir. We may be sure that the bulk of the population had no interest in grandiose schemes of conquest and so were little inclined to excuse the sacrifice. The King's proscription shocked them as profoundly as it shocked Manrique. It was wholly contrary to every teaching of the Buddhist Church. No doubt, they believed that the elixir was authentic, that the King had acquired powers by drinking it. But some of them, if not sceptical, were certainly angry. Manrique explicitly states that the King's action split society in the capital into two parties, one of which, consisting both of nobles and commonalty, was in favour of an immediate rebellion. He hints further at an already existing subversive movement among the aristocracy, who, he opines, were not displeased that the King should alienate his people, though he does not mention who these conspirators were. We shall meet them further on.

The spectacular festivities which the King now arranged as a prelude to his coronation were calculated to win back popular regard. They began with what was called the Coronation of the Twelve Kings. The kingdom of Arakan was divided into twelve provinces, each under a governor. Thiri-thu-dhamma directed that these governors should be crowned as subordinate kings. In the ordinary way the governors received insignia of office and paid homage in the course of a coronation. Now this ceremony was to take the form of an actual coronation, as if Arakan were an empire and Thiri-thu-dhamma the suzerain of many kingdoms. It is impossible not to see here an anticipation by analogy of what he hoped to become. As suzerain of India and Further India and beyond, one day twelve real kings would come and receive their crowns from him.

Manrique gives a very full account of the coronation of the first king, the governor of Urritaung, the town near the present Akyab where he had met the Admiral. It took place in one of the halls of the palace, 'a vast room covered from floor to ceiling in magnificent brocaded cloths and tapestry, the floor spread with rich carpets'. In one wall was a window under a canopy of white satin, spangled with golden stars and fringed with seed-pearls. The window itself was curtained across on the inner side with a golden net. Six steps led up to it. The princes, nobles, military officers, and officials took their seats on the carpets, a place being reserved for the Portuguese captains. Presently the drum-major struck a great drum hanging from silver chains. At the signal everyone made a *shi-ko* towards the window. The golden net was drawn aside and Thiri-thu-dhamma, in a green robe, wearing a pearl necklace and holding a fan decorated with emeralds in clusters shaped like turtle scales, was disclosed seated on a silver chair, as it were framed in the window at the top of the steps. He was being fanned by two of his ladies with peacock fans. A number of ecclesiastical personages in yellow damask and horned tiaras stood about him, probably members of the Board of Astrology and Rites, Court Brahmins recruited from India who were in charge of all state ceremonial.

The proceedings opened with a concert and a ballet. Classical songs were sung, and twenty-four dancers dressed in green and white, with high crowns like Siamese dancers, some carrying musical instruments, danced in two lines which intermingled, separated, ebbing and flowing gracefully, a dance which is reminiscent both of the Burmese *yein* and the Balinese *redjang*.

After an hour of this, twelve girls, mere children, entered, bearing golden crowns in their hands, which in turn they laid below the throne, each child being conducted thereto by insignia-bearers dressed in scarlet. They were followed by twelve more little girls with sceptres, which were placed beside the crowns. The genuflexions, prostrations, and posturings which accompanied these acts were carried out to music and as if part of a ballet.

The coronation proper of the Governor of Urritaung now commenced. He was a well-built young man, a relative of the King's, and came forward in his court robe of red velvet, preceded by a company of attendants, graceful youths, in blue and white damask, with head-dresses of the same. As soon as the governor—his name was Prince Toon-htan—was within sight of the King, he made the *shi-ko*, got up, advanced a few paces, repeated the prostration, and lay prone until two old Court Brahmins conducted him to the foot of the throne steps. At this point a statuette of the Buddha was placed on the throne, the King vacating it for the purpose, and Prince Toon-htan touched the ground with his forehead seven times before the image, swearing by it to be loyal and true.

Thiri-thu-dhamma now reoccupied the throne and a Court Brahmin stepped forward and in a ritual apostrophe hailed him as Lord of the White Elephant, rightful heir to the throne of Burma, Lord of Bengal, Lord of Sea and Land, and of Life, and declared that by divine grace he would become Lord of the World.

Then a crown from among those at his feet was handed to him, and causing Toon-htan to mount the steps, which he did by crawling, the King laid it on his head and gave him a sceptre. At that, the golden net was drawn across: the ceremony was at an end.

When the audience broke up, Manrique found himself carried along in a cheerful crowd of courtiers to the enclosure outside the hall, where a hundred elephants of the Household were drawn up in two lines and behind them many more belonging to lords who had ridden them to the levee. There was a buzz of conversation; sound of gongs and flutes filled the air; and troupes of dancing girls and acrobats postured or leaped, sang or made fun. It was a gay scene. The Arakanese did not seem tired by the audience, which must have been very long, for the sun was declining. But Manrique felt quite exhausted and wanted to get home. He was not to escape so easily. When Prince Toon-htan was about to climb into the howdah of his elephant, Manrique and the Captain-General of the Portuguese stepped forward to take leave of him. 'Father,' said he to the Friar, with the utmost cordiality, 'I am giving a dinner-party to-night at my house. You know my sentiments towards the Portuguese. We have always been on the best of terms. Join my party, you and the Captain. I will take no refusal. I positively insist.'

'I was much put out at finding myself in this predicament,' writes Manrique. But to decline the invitation was impossible. It would have offended a man on whose good offices the Christian community was dependent. Accordingly he accepted with a fine Portuguese flourish, mentally resolving that on arrival at the Prince's house he would slip away.

Two magnificent state elephants were then led up, one for him and one for the Captain. But feeling it would be unbecoming for him as a priest to parade alone through the town on an elephant suited to a royal personage, he took a seat along with his companion.

The Prince moved off. The crowd was very thick in the palace courtyards. There were shouting and songs, more music and dancing. The confusion was so great that the elephants, though as always they took care with their feet, could not help knocking over and injuring quite a number of people. As they passed through the outer gate into the esplanade, there came a formid able blast from the ordnance on the wall, so startling and sudden that it defeated its object as a mark of respect.

In the esplanade a halt was made to allow a procession to form. Elements of the Household Cavalry joined them here. A squadron of Mohammedan horsemen galloped up, big fellows from northern India, in green uniforms, carrying gilded bows, carved quivers, and curving scimitars. Their horses were caparisoned in silk trappings. Another squadron appeared, composed of Burmese from Pegu, their uniform of purple satin, in their belts long swords, the scabbards of embossed silver, and on their left arms small oval bucklers. The horses were semi-armoured, their caparisons studded with iron plaques. The third squadron was of Upper Burmans from Ava or beyond, a heavier cavalry in corselets and steel helms. Their weapon was a short spear, like a javelin, which carried a flag. The caparison of their horses was multicoloured.

More elephants now poured into the great square, until there were a hundred of them in two lines, all war-elephants, endorsed with towers and carrying short swords in their trunks, which glistened in the red light of the setting sun, as they whirled them.

And this was not all. For now the nobles who attended the levee had mounted their elephants in the upper courtyard and came swarming out, two hundred of them or more.

When all were in their proper stations, the procession started, the cavalry in front, the war-elephants second, the nobility third, and the Prince last with his personal attendants, the forty handsome youths who had accompanied him to the palace. Manrique and the Captain rode among the nobility. It was a splendid train, immensely long. There is no animal which better graces a parade than an elephant, with its stately walk and lofty mien. Here were four hundred elephants, each decked till it was a pageant in itself, an ambling treasury of colour and magnificence. The howdahs were so various. Each nobleman strove to make his the most notable. Some were gilt, some lacquered, they were carved with reliefs of monsters, serpents, flying spirits; their canopies were of all shades, and embroidered or woven, tapestried, of appliqué work, their fringes strings of pearls. And the elephants themselves differed in character. The eyes of the war-elephants had a red glimmer, while the beasts that bore the lords were smug or bland. Yet fierce or mellow, they were equally disciplined. Manrique was much struck by their demeanour. It seems that between the elephants, as they came on two by two, were musicians. With them were several troupes of dancers, the girls who had performed in the palace and others. Richly and gaily dressed, with garlands of flowers on their heads, they danced and sang, like bright birds gliding in and out among the ranks. passing even beneath the trunks of the war-elephants, tapping them with their fans, and crying out their names, resounding names which they wove into their recitative, the Victorious, the Master of Thunder, the Van Lord. And the great beasts, says Manrique, were as tame as dogs, minded their step and tucked in their trunks, an expression of indulgence on their antediluvian masks.

In this gaiety they paraded through the city, passing by quarters where were assembled princesses and noblemen of high rank, who bowed to them and to whose courtesies they responded, all save Manrique, who concealed himself behind the Captain and was screened by the howdah curtain, for he had had enough that day of bowing and scraping, and was wearied out, and longing for bed.

It was lighting-up time when they reached the Prince's palace. On entering the large courtyard, where linkmen held torches, they were met by Prince Minawtata, a close relative of His Majesty's, who had been sent there to represent him. This nobleman, with pleasant ease of manner, assisted Toon-htan to alight and there followed many salutations and mutual compliments. This was the moment when Manrique and the Captain designed to slip away. But Toon-htan noticed them and beckoned them to follow as he led the party into the building, its pointed roof adorned with carved figures of men and animals entwined in foliage. A hall was reached, richly carpeted and well lit with lamps burning aromatic oils. On the walls were silk hangings, and from the galleries came the sound of voices singing to harps.

The dinner which followed was an interminable affair, longer even than Manrique had feared. The two Princes sat together along with the Admiral whom we met at Urritaung. The other guests each had his own table, a low one as he was seated on the carpet. On it were placed five or six porcelain dishes. The food was brought in on trays by a hundred servitors, and was very copious and highly spiced, consisting of every kind of fish and fowl, domestic animal and wild game, with mountains of rice, many relishes, and much fruit. For some of the dishes an acquired taste was necessary, such as shredded rat, fried snake, and fricasseed bat, all of which Manrique firmly declined to sample. There does not seem to have been heavy drinking, an omission which northern Europeans would have found inexcusable.

When the sweets were cleared away, dancers came in. These were not of the decorous sort who had danced the classic ballet up at the palace, but girls trained to please a bachelor party. Dressed in diaphanous silks or lawns, which did not hide any detail of their persons, they postured so brazenly that Manrique was obliged to shut his eyes.

The feast went on till dawn, when 'we went home', says he, 'very weary and peevish'.

These festivities continued for six more days, and for each of the remaining eleven governors there were similar festivities lasting seven days. For three months the city was given over to jollity. It must be confessed that the King was doing his best to induce his subjects to forget the proscription. But, as we shall see, though they all enjoyed the spectacles, some of them did not forget.

XXVIII

The Coronation

It was now January 1635. In England and China events were hastening towards the death of kings, but neither Charles I nor the Emperor Ch'ung Chen had an inkling of their fate. Thiri-thudhamma knew he was threatened, but believed he had taken measures to avert all danger, believed that in his victory over death a new and glorious span of life would be his. He had drunk of the waters of immortality. He was embattled against men and spirits and their malice. So with a light heart he took the step, which he had hesitated to take for twelve years, and fixed January the 23rd for his crowning, selecting that day after consultation with the Board of Astrology, a body which, if its science had given it a hint of what was to be, would have been hard put to it to discover an auspicious date.

The ceremony took place in the main pillared hall of the palace, not in the subsidiary hall where the governors were crowned, nor in any of those minor though sumptuous throne-rooms to which on different occasions we have accompanied Manrique. It was a beautiful clear morning. While yet scarcely light, there came a roaring salute from the cannon on the palace walls. An outburst of music followed from bands stationed in the principal streets and squares. Drums thudded on the battlements, bamboo clappers in the monasteries, and the sweet sound of triangular gongs throbbed from the boats moving in the canals. These sounds were the signal that the princes and official nobility should hasten to take their places in the Hall of Audience. They had been up dressing, scenting and powdering themselves, long before dawn. Now they called for their elephants. These, in new caparisons, waited in the courtyards among the shrubs in blossom and the flower-pots, swinging their trunks and flapping their ears, solemn, important, yet roguish, their docility so little in keeping with their formidable

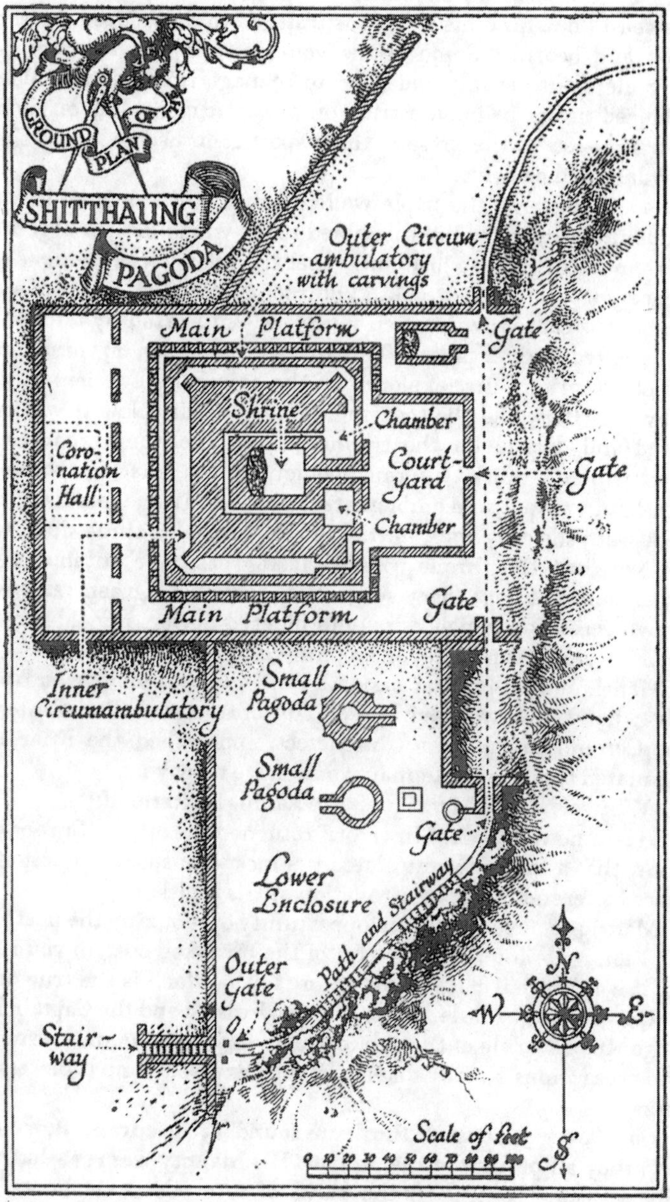

GROUND PLAN OF THE
SHITTHAUNG PAGODA
Outer Circum-
ambulatory
with carvings
Main Platform
Gate
Shrine
Chamber
Coro-
nation
Hall
Court-
yard
Gate
Chamber
Main Platform
Gate
Inner
Circumambulatory
Small
Pagoda
Small
Pagoda
Gate
Lower
Enclosure
Path and Stairway
Outer
Gate
Stair-
way
N
W
E
S
Scale of feet
0 10 20 30 40 50 60 70 80 90 100

bulk as to appear an affectation. The grandees issued out, each dressed to outshine his rival, his train of youths picked for their looks and bearing. Some of the younger princes were proud of their elephantmanship and liked to manage their mounts alone, balanced prong in hand astride on a scarlet cloth. But on such a state occasion as the present these sportsmen had to loll in their howdahs and be driven.

As they entered the triple-walled fortress the sun rose, its rays suddenly bringing to life the gilded roofs, which flashed as if they were made of gold, so brilliantly that travellers often thought the palace was plated with gold. The roof of the Hall of Audience, which was carved with much fancy, was supported by a forest of gilt and red lacquer pillars. This was the hall, open on three sides, which Manrique first explored on the occasion when he saw the ruby ear-rings, the choicest item of the regalia. Now it was carpeted and decked for the coronation, all the appurtenances of royalty being there; insignia, golden vessels, magical banners, whisks of yak-tail, and emblematic standards. In the middle of the back wall, the only wall, for the hall was open on three sides, was the window, the throne-window facing east, the entablature a stylization of a legendary serpent. A curtain of green satin was drawn across, on which were embroidered flowers in gold thread, their centres being rubies or sapphires or emeralds.

Manrique had his seat beside a Portuguese captain who had a silver hand, his own having been cut off in a duel. The Master of the Ceremonies, noticing this defect, approached the Friar and intimated that the gentleman would have to leave.

'Why so?' asked Manrique. 'He has his invitation.'

'Then he was invited in error,' returned the other. 'Surely you know that a man thus mutilated is a most inauspicious guest at so sacred a ceremony as the coronation of His Majesty?'

Manrique never let slip an opportunity of rebuking the heathen. 'If I am ignorant', he retorted, 'of the mistaken custom you refer to, it is because it has no part in my faith, which is the true one.'

However, the Master of Ceremonies insisted and the Captain had to go. It was a rule of the palace; and Thiri-thu-dhamma, after all the precautions already taken, must be exposed to no unnecessary risks.

Soon after this episode the drum sounded, the curtain flew open, and they all prostrated themselves. His Majesty was revealed on a silver throne resting on the backs of four silver elephants. He wore a long velvet coat the colour of the sky, embroidered with pearls and other gems. On his head was a white fillet and in his ears glowed the famous ruby ear-rings which his grandfather had taken from the King of Pegu, each of them as large as a bantam's egg. On the steps of the throne were the so-called twelve kings, arranged in two rows, each with his crown and sceptre. Behind it were two ladies-in-waiting in fabulous gowns who took turns to fan. It was a well-calculated tableau. But etiquette forbade the guests to look at it. They had to remain face downwards and in dead silence.

The ceremony began by an announcement made by some ecclesiastic, perhaps the Royal Chaplain. He was on a dais to one side and declared that the placing of the crown upon the King's head would not take place in the hall but in the Shitthaung Pagoda, situated half a mile outside the palace-city. There the Shitthaung Hpongri, the head of the Order, would crown and bless him. After this declaration he pronounced a panegyric. It is unlikely that Manrique understood Court Arakanese, a style of speaking most elaborate and ornate, sufficiently well to follow very precisely what was said. But what he did catch was the main point. The chaplain was comparing the King to a saint or saviour. His Majesty was destined to become a Buddha. When he obtained omniscience he would be Lord of the World. All the kings of the earth would come bearing presents. Like the twelve kings now on their knees, these others would kneel and surrender their crowns, until he saw fit to crown them again. Then as a saviour his light would shine over the world. For all mankind would dawn the new age, when suffering, injustice, the oppression of the strong, would come to an end, and compassion reign.

The Chaplain was an orator and expressed himself with extraordinary felicity and grace. Manrique listened to him with onctempt, but could not help noticing the King's earnest attention. He sat motionless, never seemed to wink an eye, though the discourse lasted a full hour; seemed fallen into trance, as if to hear expounded his dearest dream in such a wealth of words had rapt him away already to paradise.

When the Chaplain ceased, the curtain was drawn across the window, signifying that that part of the ceremony was at an end.

The second part was the procession to the Shitthaung or Eighty Thousand Pagoda, so called, perhaps, on account of the very large number of images it contained. It had been built a hundred years before by the Indian workmen, whom King Min Bin brought back with him from eastern Bengal after the termination of the victorious campaign which gave Chittagong to Arakan. While all trace of the palace buildings in the triple enceinte have disappeared, the Shitthaung stands to-day, somewhat damaged by a bombardment to which it was subjected by the British in 1825, but retaining its principal features intact. It is a very curious structure, as I have seen for myself. In the first place, it is more a fortress than a pagoda, and was undoubtedly used as a place to which members of the Order could retire, were the city attacked. The second curious thing about it is the sculptures, which are partly Brahminic. That the pagoda, in the precincts of which was the arch-abbot's residence, should contain representations of the gods of India is a mystery which has not altogether been cleared up. It is hardly an explanation to say that the Hindu architects put them there. They could not have done so without Min Bin's permission. Why did he give that permission? It is true that the majority of the sculptures are Buddhist or represent, in friezes, scenes of court and village life in Arakan. But quite a number are not and show such gods as Vishnu with Brahmins adoring him. We cannot suppose the building was erected in the first place as a temple for resident Hindus, for why in that case should there be Buddhist sculptures? Does the explanation rest on the fact that, according to Buddhist theory, the gods and goddesses of India were converted by the Buddha, thereafter becoming spirits who ministered to him? Unfortunately, the sculptures can hardly bear that interpretation. Vishnu is shown as if he were a god in his own right. The arch-abbot may have viewed him and his fellows as harmless celestial personages and for that reason have seen no need to deface them, yet King Min Bin's attitude must have been more than passive, and we are obliged to conclude that, during his campaigns in Bengal, he either acquired a taste for Hindu iconography or, with the idea of pleasing his new Hindu subjects in Chittagong, admitted a few of their gods into his new shrine, an act not out of keeping with the extraordinary tolerance and charity of Buddhism.

To this massive and curious, rather than beautiful, edifice King Thiri-thu-dhamma now set out. The grandees had adjourned to a saloon adjoining the great hall, and it was into this apartment that the king entered, borne in a palanquin by eight youths in green velvet. A procession was formed, consisting of the twelve kings and their attendants, the whole crowd of grandees, a body of household officials, officers of the army, and a contingent of eighty monks, all on foot, the King bringing up the rear and surrounded by a hundred pages. The route taken was by the east gate of the palace and then northwards the half-mile to the pagoda. The way, according to immemorial custom, had been made into a Spirit Road. It was carpeted throughout its length with sheets of coloured cotton and at intervals roofed and walled with the same. Absolute silence was preserved by everybody, a great contrast to the disorderly, even riotous, procession of Prince Toon-htan from the palace to his house.

The Shitthaung Pagoda stands some forty-six feet above the level of the road. To reach its platform you must first climb a flight of steps sixteen feet high, which leads to the main gate, called the Wheel of the Law. The arch-abbot was waiting to receive His Majesty at the foot of the steps, supported by two thousand monks of the Order. On seeing him, Thiri-thu-dhamma alighted from the palanquin and made the salutation which consists in raising the hands, joined as if praying, up to the face and bending the head. The arch-abbot's response was a faint inclination. This was in accordance with Buddhist practice, a contrast to the Christian, for no king in Europe would have treated the head of an order with such deference, or any ecclesiastic.

Manrique had walked with the rest in the procession, and it was now intimated to him, to the Portuguese captains, and to the Moslem officers of the guard, that they could proceed no further. Only Buddhists might enter the precincts and witness the crowning. The Friar here goes out of his way to declare that the pagoda-guardians, who told him of the existence of this rule, did so with an affable politeness and consideration, which contrasted agreeably with the bad manners of underlings 'in certain places in Europe, where, taking no account of a man's position or quality, they hustle and harry him'.

Owing to this rule, we have no information about what occurred inside the Shitthaung. But we can follow Thiri-thu-dhamma a certain distance. He walked up the steps between two stone walls. At the top was the gate, the Wheel of the Law, so called because on the underside of the stone architrave the Wheel was incised. Also carved on it was a conch shell with the opening to the right, from which issued a lotus, the design signifying that Buddhism had grown out of Hinduism, a Brahmin rather than a Buddhist view. This architrave now lies on the ground, though the pillars of the gate are undisturbed.

The gate leads into a large enclosure thirty feet below the main courtyard of the pagoda, which looms above, a square low building topped by a solid dome sixty feet high, shaped somewhat like a bell. To reach the upper courtyard the procession will have followed a footpath, interspersed with steps, which is cut into the slope of the hill, on a spur of which the pagoda stands.

The pagoda itself is unfitted for any ceremony. As the ground plan here given shows, it has not an interior in the ordinary sense of the word, but consists of an outer and inner gallery driven through stone and brickwork of enormous thickness, and occasionally enlarged into chambers not more than twenty feet square. The shrine in the centre is also a very small room. These galleries contain the sculptures and in their mazelike way are a sort of circumambulatory.

The crowning either took place in an improvised wooden pavilion in the courtyard or on the western terrace, where, judging by the ruins still to be seen, there was a hall of tolerable dimensions. What ritual was employed we cannot tell, but it may safely be assumed that the arch-abbot preached a sermon and that before the assembled Order Thiri-thu-dhamma promised to defend the faith.

Manrique waited for two hours outside. At the end of that time the King emerged, girt with the Sword of Victory, and wearing on his head the tapering Crown of Victory, whose jewels, large and brilliant though they were, his ruby ear-rings totally eclipsed. The day now lost its formality. The gate into the lower enclosure was opened and Manrique entered to admire it, for he found it beautiful. Here all the princes and lords assembled. The King mounted a very tall elephant, which awaited him thereabouts, and sitting under a white parasol passed forth in procession with the grandees, all of whom were on foot. A number of war-elephants and cavalry of the guard led the way. This time they took a detour through the outer city. Great crowds lined the streets; there were triumphal arches at intervals, and masquerades. As they came to the houses of the aristocracy, ladies, young and old, appeared on the verandas, more particularly so when they re-entered the palace-city, where the princesses and ladies-in-waiting made a gallant show in their silks and jewels. 'These', says Manrique with feeling, 'though of a yellowish-brown complexion gave no less motive to praise their divine Creator than those of our Europe with their white skins and ruby cheeks.'

On reaching the state apartments, the King dismounted and took up his station in a hall hung with gold brocade. Manrique was allowed in and saw there a person whom till then he had never seen: the Queen entered with her ladies. This was the famous Nat Shin Mé, the Mistress of Paradise. We have hinted at her existence before and of the part she was destined to play in the curious drama we are describing. Manrique does not seem to have understood her importance. On the present occasion he had no more than a distant vision of a very smartly dressed woman. He saw the King take her by the hand, conduct her to a window overlooking a courtyard crowded with people, where both of them threw down a quantity of silver money specially minted for the purpose.

That was the last act of the long-drawn-out festivities.

XXIX

Friar Manrique is taken for a Slaver

We cannot feel that Manrique's character will have moved the reader to sympathy or admiration. The fact is that he was a very plain man. Probably not born with much intellect or originality, his education in a novitiate and his long years in cloister and vicarage had moulded him into an ecclesiastical type. His mind no longer moved freely, if it had ever been characterized by freedom of movement. Yet he had excellent qualities. He was brave and resolute. He was perfectly honest and very painstaking. His address was agreeable, both men and women liked him; he was loyal, kind, without malice and without pride. As a diplomatist he had much acuteness. His observations are exact, he had an eye for detail, and though his *Travels* show a complete absence of literary talent their matter is so unusual that, edited with circumspection, they make singular reading and will suffice to preserve his name.

Allowing all this—that he was a decent sturdy Latin, with a love of the sane, the reasonable, the ordered, and a hatred of what was extreme or eccentric, a man with no interest in the pseudo mystical, in excesses of the spirit, in enthusiasm run wild—granting him these qualities and that he took a simple pleasure in seeing happy faces, and in his heart loathed cruelty, the fact remains that he was a bigot.

Now, to be a bigot, whether religious, political, in the arts, in the sciences, in any activity, is a sin against the intellect, a degradation of the mind, a crime that leads to other crimes, a wickedness that brings its punishment. Examples of Manrique's bigotry are scattered through this narrative. It clouded his intellect when he had to do with Buddhism and made him appear more stupid than he really was, made him ridiculous, robbed him of dignity. Had it done no more than this, though tiresome it would not have been criminal. But it did do more, because it led him to defend what was indefensible, to excuse the slave raids made by the mercenaries at Dianga. The horror of these raids. the cruelties connected with them, their negation of everything that was Christian and humane, have been described at length, as have the reasons why Manrique condoned them, why he shut his heart to pity, forgot compassion, arguing falsely that any excess was justified against the followers of Mohammed and that the kidnapped persons were fortunate, in a long view, because their capture enabled him to convert them. This was a preposterous view to take of what was a nefarious business. It made him the abettor of a gang of murdering kidnappers. That was the crime to which bigotry had brought him. But he was totally unaware that his condonation was criminal. We may be sure that he made no mention of it in confession. When he spoke of sins committed and his unworthiness, he was not thinking of his palliation of the slave raids. Yet his heart should have prompted him. He saw the wretches arrive, with his own eyes he witnessed their despairing tears. He saw them dragged in chains to perpetual slavery. But bigotry made him dumb. He never raised his voice against what his whole religion told him was an atrocity. He did not even admonish the slavers, except in such minor matters as their morals. Bigotry it was that dulled his sensibility. He had no feeling for the unhappy victims. How different a character was St. Francis Xavier's! He worked among the slaves, the downtrodden, the wronged. He loved them with a truly burning enthusiasm. Never did he give face or countenance to their oppressors. Never would he have excused the slavers of Dianga. His heart would have told him that they were evil men, and he would have listened to his heart, not to a specious argument.

A criminal act, unrepented, is always followed by some punishment, even though this be no more than a coarsening of the individual, of which he may not even be aware. But sometimes the punishment is more objective. In Manrique's case it took this form. Fate ordained that he, the condoner of slavers, should himself be mistaken for a slaver by the very persons who so long had suffered by the raids; that he should fall into their power and that they should punish him.

His departure from Mrauk-u followed the coronation. When he went to give the King the present which was customary on such an occasion, he was accompanied by a captain, Delemos by name, who was recently from Dianga. He had arranged with this man to assist him in his application for leave. The present having been accepted, he made his petition. The King hesitated, when Captain Delemos remarked casually that the Catholics in Dianga were saying their vicar was a prisoner and seemed much disheartened at his continued absence. This remark somewhat ruffled Thiri-thu-dhamma, but Manrique was quick to turn it into a compliment. 'Lord of Life,' said he, 'the Catholics of Dianga think of me as the prisoner of your Majesty's generosity, and, indeed, your Majesty's condescension has been so overwhelming that not only has it made me your slave and prisoner but also all the Catholics in the realm.'

This piece of flattery caused Thiri-thu-dhamma to laugh—like most of his race he laughed easily—and he granted Manrique permission to go. In due course passports were issued by the department concerned. As it was early February the sea was quite smooth and the passage was quickly effected.

On arrival at Dianga he found letters from the Provincial of the Order and from the Viceroy of Goa. The first directed him to go to Banja in Orissa in connection with missionary work. At the same time by the Viceroy's letter he was asked to negotiate a trade arrangement with the Governor of Hijli, a town not far from Banja and near which he had been wrecked on his first coming to Bengal.

The acting vicar of Dianga having arranged for a galley, he left the place secretly at night, for it was prudent not to advertise one's departure over the frontier. The route taken was first by Sandwip, the old pirate stronghold, and thence across the mouths of the Ganges delta, till somewhat eastward of the Hugli river the galley entered the Sundarban creeks. Though it was the dry weather these regions were nothing but swamp, with crocodiles on the banks and rhinoceros further in. Presently they came out into the Hugli main stream not far from Hijli. Crossing it they entered a fresh network of creeks which wound in the direction of Banja.

On the eleventh day of the journey the oarsmen, who had been rowing hard since dawn, tied up the galley to a tree and went ashore to bathe and breakfast. Manrique also disembarked, as did his party, consisting of a Portuguese named Trigueros and three Indian Christian youths. A lookout man was posted at the top of a tree, for they had to be careful. As they were on a Dianga galley and the Bengal river patrols were, not unnaturally, very suspicious of any vessel from that port, it was necessary to avoid them. That was the reason they had chosen to thread their way through the more unfrequented creeks of the Sundarbans.

The rice was not yet cooked when the look-out man shouted that two patrol vessels were approaching at speed. The rowers immediately bolted into the wood. Manrique and his companions saw no alternative but to follow their example. They caught up their firearms, but had no time to fetch anything from the galley. As they seem to have been bathing, Manrique had left his friar's habit on board. The patrol boats seized the galley and landed some archers. These, coming up with the Portuguese, who soon had become bogged in the swampy ground, called on them to surrender. The Portuguese answered by covering them with their muskets. 'It is useless to try and escape,' shouted the archers, who were much afraid of the muskets. 'You can never hope to get through these swamps. You will all die of starvation or be eaten by tigers.'

'To this advice,' says Manrique, 'we replied that God in His infinite mercy would deliver us from whatever dangers might beset us.'

Seeing them so resolute, the archers retired and boarded the patrol boats, which departed with the galley in tow. Manrique and his four companions were thus stranded in the midst of swamps which extended for miles in every direction. The country was wholly uninhabited. They determined, however, to seek a way on to the cultivated land further in, where they might hope to meet villagers ready to assist them. But this was more difficult than they expected. The sun blazed on them; they grew weak with hunger; their legs were covered with leeches; at last they could go no further. Night found them in this plight. As darkness fell they climbed a tree, fearing tigers, for tracks had been seen. Having few clothes to protect them, they were terribly bitten by the mosquitoes.

The night seemed interminable, for they could not sleep. When the light returned, they considered what to do, debating their chances of getting out of the swamps. These appeared to be extremely meagre. To go on seemed useless. The archers were right. They would die of hunger or be killed by tigers. The only chance was to return to the creek, where the land was less swampy, and make their way along the bank till they saw a boat. Perhaps, too, they might find the rice which the oarsmen had been cooking for their breakfast, unless these men had crept back and eaten it.

A long weary march brought them an hour before sunset to the place where they had landed the previous day. There they found the rice and made a good meal, enough being over to last for some days with care. They were somewhat comforted and passed the night more comfortably than the last, for they were able to light a fire, the smoke of which kept the mosquitoes at bay.

All next day they walked along the creek-side through a low jungle, sometimes marshy, without seeing a boat. At nightfall they came to a place with two large trees on open ground. Here a very miserable night was spent. The creek at this point was shallow and, as on the further side was another open piece of ground, at dawn they decided to cross and explore it. Two of the Indian youths went ahead, one a slave of Trigueros's, and the other a recent convert of Manrique's. As crocodiles might be lying in wait, a volley was fired to frighten any such, and the two youths also carried muskets. But they had only gone a few steps into the creek when with a splash and a rush a huge crocodile suddenly broke water and struck down the slave with a blow of his tail. It was done so quickly there was no time to fire. The man disappeared, never to be seen again, the only trace of him being a red stain on the surface. The other youth in his terror dropped his gun and scrambled ashore. They were all profoundly shaken by this mishap.

Yet there was nothing to be done but continue their march. 'We spent two days and a half in this way,' says Manrique, 'our eyes fixed on the spectacle of death, which in our hopeless state seemed ever to draw closer.' At noon on the third day they were sitting in a state of the deepest despondency on the bank, when the convert cried: 'God has not deserted us! Look, there is a canoe!'

The canoe, which contained two men, was heading for the spot where they sat. To avoid alarming its occupants and so causing them to paddle away, Manrique, Trigueros and one of the Indian youths hid behind a bush, leaving the other to explain the situation. As the canoe drew in, he hailed the men, begging them for the love of God to take him into the boat. This they did, after a few questions. When he was on board, his companions showed themselves. The apparition of two armed Portuguese, who could be no other than raiders from Dianga, so terrified the boatmen that they caught up their paddles. 'Stop!' cried Manrique. 'If you move we fire!' Quite cowed they came weeping ashore and threw themselves at his feet. 'If we must go as slaves,' they besought him, 'at least do not sell us to the Arakanese.'

Manrique replied by telling them the story which he and Trigueros had prepared to account for their predicament. 'We are not connected in any way with Dianga or Arakan,' he said, 'but are Portuguese merchants of these parts. On our way to Banja we were attacked by Arakanese pirates who seized our cargo boat. We have been stranded here for days and if you take us to Banja you will be well rewarded.'

The boatmen, very much relieved, salaamed. 'We are entirely at your orders,' they said. 'But as you may see for yourselves, sirs, this tiny canoe is incapable of carrying us all to Banja. About three miles from here are a few huts where some companions of ours are collecting lac. A ship to load it is expected in a few days. We will take your Honours to the huts, where you can wait in safety.'

This was splendid news for starving desperate men. All four of them managed to fit into the canoe and soon reached the camp of the lac workers. When the situation was explained to them, poor as they were, they immediately cooked a large curry. The sight of this food, says Manrique, was like a view of Heaven's courts.

That night they slept in a hut on some boards and, to keep at bay the mosquitoes, covered themselves with cloths which they managed to borrow. They thought it prudent, however, to take turns and watch, being careful not to let this be seen, for though the lac workers seemed favourably disposed to them, it was risky to place absolute trust in them.

Early next morning, with many salaams and smiles, one of the men told them that he and another were going to a neighbouring village to buy a goat for their breakfast. The rest would be absent collecting lac till nightfall. This lulled all doubts of their bona fides. The Portuguese, still very weary, lay down again to sleep, this time not bothering to mount a guard.

When the two Indians reached the village, they spoke openly of the Portuguese. The news came to the ears of the Headman. 'Your first impression was correct,' said he to the boatmen. 'They are raiders, not merchants.' Immediately collecting a force of sixty villagers armed with swords and bows, he set out for the lac workers' camp. After reconnoitring the hut and finding the Portuguese asleep, he ordered his men to creep in and first seize the muskets.

'We awoke with a start in great consternation,' says Manrique. The Indians rushed them and bound their hands, though not before Trigueros, who had a concealed dagger, had wounded two of them. This resistance to arrest confirmed the Headman's suspicions. It also infuriated the villagers. They began beating the Portuguese in the face with their heavy shoes, spitting on them and cursing obscenely. The Headman now took his seat on a rug outside. The Portuguese were dragged before him and he proceeded to examine them judicially. Who were they? What were they doing? They told him the same story they had told the others. It appears that he had heard of the patrol's seizure of a vessel from Dianga, and so was convinced their explanation was false. They must have belonged to that vessel and certainly were kidnappers. Refusing to hear more, he ordered them fifty lashes each with whips of buffalo hide. This was carried out at once. 'They flogged us so unmercifully that all our shoulders were raw and streaming with blood,' says Manrique.

Then the Indians rowed them to the village, to the sound of drums, pipes, and flutes, for they were excited and very pleased to have taken some of the inhuman ruffians, who for so many years had made life a misery to them. Loud shouts greeted their arrival. Three Moslem priests came forward, saluted the Headman, and blessed him in the Prophet's name for his valour in capturing the accursed infidels. One of then harangued the crowd, saying in a wild screeching voice: 'You should know that these unbelievers are enemies of heaven and earth. They are enemies of heaven because their evil creed has always been to destroy the true faith. They are enemies of earth because of their foul deeds. Robbing, slaying, bathing themselves in blood, they seek to deprive us of life and liberty. Hardly a day but we wet our cheeks because of them, the tears gushing from our very souls at the loss of fathers, wives, of sons, and brothers, losses never ending and which can never be retrieved.'

As the priest screamed these words, he was overcome with emotion, put his hands to eyes and howled with grief. To Manrique he seemed 'a mean dog and a follower of the Devil.' But, in fact, his indictment was very understandable.

The villagers were now in such a state of frenzy that they rushed at the Portuguese with sticks and knives. The Headman had to use his armed following to drive them back. 'We must not take the law into our own hands,' he said. 'These men will be sent to the proper authorities for trial. You may rest content that on conviction they will suffer the penalty of their crimes by death.'

Satisfied with this assurance the crowd desisted. The Headman then gave orders to take the prisoners to his compound. They were a pitiable sight, with their bleeding shoulders, faces black and blue from the blows of the shoes, covered with spittle, their hands bound behind them. Yet, some villagers could not resist pricking them with arrows and striking them as they passed; and the women and children hung on their heels, plastering them with dung and mire and sewage. On reaching the compound they were put into an open stable with two elephants and seven horses, where they remained under guard, the butt of the crowd, their hands always bound, their wounds unwashed, and given but one meal in the twenty-four hours.

Four days of pain and wretchedness passed thus. On the fifth some well-armed police arrived. These men put iron collars on them and, unbinding their hands, linked them together by a chain attached to the collars. It was in this identical way that the Hindu and Moslem captives, whom Manrique had marched with into Arakan, were chained.

The police formed two lines and, placing their four prisoners between, ordered them to start. Their instructions were to take them to Midnapur, a large town four days' march to the south-west, where they would be handed over to the authorities.

As they were leaving the village, one of the policemen, annoyed because the Portuguese in their weak state were walking too slowly for his taste, raised his stick with intent to strike them, uttering at the same time a frightful obscenity. But the officer in charge reprimanded him severely, 'thereby proving,' writes Manrique, 'that where many evil men are gathered together, one good man, or one less evil than the rest, is yet to be found'. This little episode is in perfect dramatic balance to Manrique's own intervention on behalf of the exhausted Moslem prisoner during the Arakan march. In that case he was 'one less evil than the rest'.

The officer's kindness did not stop at the prevention of active cruelty. After a while, moved, it seemed, by seeing them go so sadly and without hope, he came up and, speaking gently, told them not to be afraid, that no harm would befall them while under his charge. Encouraged by this, Manrique assured him there had been a miscarriage of justice and, repeating the fiction that they were peaceful merchants, carrying on their business under the law of the land, when they were wrongfully arrested and mishandled by the Headman, he created a doubt in his mind of their guilt. 'In taking you to Midnapur,' the officer now said, a note of excuse in his voice, 'I am acting under instructions from the Headman and am in no way responsible for your arrest. You will agree that the Headman had reason to suspect you of being slave-raiders. If at Midnapur the magistrates say you are not, no blame can attach to me.'

Manrique was quick to see that his personality, veiled though it was by his squalid appearance, had made an impression. This he strove in subsequent conversations to deepen. In the result, they were treated with reasonable leniency nor forced to march beyond their strength. That night at a little village where they camped, the officer sent for oil to dress their wounded backs. But Manrique refused to allow this to be done, partly because he thought the oil might do the wounds more harm than good, and partly because he saw that the refusal could be used to create still further doubts in the officer's mind. Therefore he said: 'The magistrates must see how unjustly and cruelly the Headman has treated us. We shall appear before them in the exact state to which he has reduced us.'

The resolution here displayed and the hint of menace had exactly the effect which Manrique calculated. It convinced the police of their prisoners' innocence and made them the more apprehensive of being blamed. 'From this time on they began to address us two Portuguese as Sahib, and when we lay down to sleep that night, they brought us two mats and a cotton quilt.'

Though suffering severely from their wounded backs, the journey to Midnapur was otherwise tolerable. 'No-one was allowed to come near us as we passed through villages and thus we escaped much maltreatment.' As the marches were cut down to ease them, it was not till the sixth day that they reached the town. Yet, in spite of the mildness of their guards, they presented a most bedraggled appearance as they staggered up the street under the burning midday sun. 'As each man looked into the other's face, he perceived his own misery depicted as in a glass. We all wept bitterly to see how we had suffered—our faces bruised, filthy and pouring with sweat, our bodies a mass of wounds that were choked with dirt.'

Midnapur had a population of 33,000 and it seemed that most of it turned out to watch the chain-gang pass. Rumour had gone ahead of them and they were hailed as slavers, pirates, kidnappers, infidels, criminals beyond the pale of mercy. This universal execration shook them, it seems, more profoundly than any sufferings hitherto. Moreover, they would shortly be brought to trial. What hope had they of an acquittal? Where would they find witnesses? The fact was they *had* come from Dianga. How could they prove their business was unconnected with the slave raids? So overwhelmed by distress and foreboding did his companions appear, that Manrique felt he must give them spiritual comfort. After obtaining the officer's permission to retire for a moment into the courtyard of a half-ruined house, he addressed them in soothing words, quoting as was his wont from the writings of St. Augustine, and telling them that their tribulations were necessary if the gates of Heaven were surely to be opened for them.

When the officer saw that they were not relieving nature, which he had supposed was their intention, he called out to them to come on, as he must take them to the City Magistrate. After a further trying walk, a disorderly mob howling at their heels, they arrived at the court-house. There they found the Magistrate seated on a carpet with a purple cushion under his elbow. Business seemed to be very slack, for on the same carpet were two officials playing chess. The officer handed over a report from the Headman, which the Magistrate immediately read with attention. When he had done so, he caused it to be re-read to the prisoners. Its purport was that they were raiders from Dianga.

'What have you got to say in your defence?' he asked.

At this, Trigueros, who spoke Hindustani with great fluency, repeated the story which had been given to the Headman and the police officer, but added that Manrique was actually a priest, a missionary friar of the Augustinian Order. 'We have suffered grave injustices,' he concluded, 'and if necessary will take the matter to the highest authorities, even appealing to the Emperor himself.'

It may here be noted that Shah Jehan, after his sack of Hugli in 1632, had changed his policy of enmity to the Portuguese, perhaps because he thought it impolitic to throw them into the arms of the King of Arakan, and had permitted them to settle again at Hugli.

On hearing Trigueros's plea, the Magistrate asked them to be seated and with a sympathetic face declared they should have justice. Two clerks took down their names and the particulars of their defence.

'Have you any acquaintances in the city,' now asked the Magistrate, 'people who can testify to your identity and bona fides?'

Trigueros replied regretfully that they had not.

'Yet, perhaps,' said the other, 'I can find you witnesses. There are merchants here who trade with Hugli and Banja. Maybe, they will be able to throw light on the matter.'

A messenger was sent and presently three Mohammedan merchants of standing arrived. After a little conversation with the Magistrate one of them came up to Manrique and spoke to him in Portuguese. Naming some of the leading Portuguese at Hugli and testing Manrique's knowledge of them, he explained that the vicar of Banja—there was an Augustinian house there—was a particular friend of his. He had even sent his son to him to be taught Portuguese. If Manrique would now write to him, and if he replied that he knew him to be a friar of his Order, that would probably suffice to ensure an acquittal.

This was wonderful news, wonderful luck. Manrique wrote the letter at once and Trigueros was also enabled to write for references. Till these came, said the Magistrate, they would have to go to gaol. The merchant offered bail, but the Magistrate replied that the alleged offence was non-bailable and that he had no alternative but to commit them to prison.

'We are so worn out,' pleaded Manrique, 'that if we are left chained in the common dungeon, we can hardly hope to survive until our references have been taken up.'

The merchant here intervened, saying that he would undertake to see they were well treated in the gaol. When they had been duly committed, he accompanied them and on arrival took the gaoler aside and, no doubt, tipped him. Their chains were struck off, beds were procured, a doctor was summoned and their wounds treated.

It took nine days for the answers to come from Banja. There were two letters, one from the vicar and the other from the captain of the resident Portuguese traders. They were both entirely satisfactory. The City Magistrate immediately allowed bail, and Manrique and his companions were accommodated in the merchant's house. Their formal acquittal followed after a few more formalities. The Headman was ordered to pay two hundred rupees in damages. This he immediately did and Manrique made himself very popular by declining to take the money, declaring that all was forgiven and the episode at an end. This so impressed the City Magistrate that he invited both the Portuguese to dinner, and on their departure soon after for Banja, he presented them with valuable cashmir shawls.

Their kind merchant friend accompanied them on the first stage of the journey. He had sent ahead his servants to a halting-place under great banyan trees beside a little lake. When the travellers arrived, they found breakfast already spread. It was a lavish meal, eaten in the grateful shade, a pleasant breeze blowing over the water. The two Portuguese felt their hearts brimming over with gratitude towards this man, Moslem though he was.

At last it was time to say farewell. Manrique, being a Latin, showed his emotion in a dramatic way and fell on his knees before the merchant 'and with my hands raised to Heaven prayed God that He should not bestow more favours upon me than upon him.' In short, he asked that somehow or other the Moor be excused Hell and rewarded with Heaven. No Augustinian is likely to have addressed to God such a request before. Carried away by the merchant's extraordinarily good heart, the scales of bigotry fell from his eyes and he saw clearly that he was a good man, regardless of his creed, and in spite of it worthy of every reward which God could bestow upon him. Convinced, though only for the instant, that the Moslems were as deserving of the divine pity and salvation as the Christians, he embraced his friend with the tears running down his cheeks.

But his emotion was only momentary and the revelation it brought went with it. Nor did he see that his misfortunes had been a just retribution, a most apt turning of the tables. He was not a changed man. There is not a word in his book to suggest that he modified his views. He had a great opportunity, but he did not take it. His mind remained as closed as it had ever been. He did not grow an inch in spiritual stature. Under the violent promptings of his heart he had seen for a moment. Then bigotry shrouded his vision again.

To conclude this chapter. He reached Banja without incident; dispatched his business there as directed by the Provincial of the Order; went on to Hijli and carried through the little political mission with which the Viceroy had entrusted him; and took ship thereafter to the Augustinian monastery at Cochin, which he reached in March 1636, almost exactly eight years after he had left it on his travels.

XXX

The Strange Murder of King Thiri-thu-dhamma

Manrique gives no account of what happened in Mrauk-u after his departure. The sources for this chapter are some Arakanese palm-leaf manuscripts, the contents of which were translated for the author and explained to him in 1924 by Mr. San Shwe Bu of Akyab, in whose possession they were. Strange though the story is they tell, it will be found to fit with remarkable exactitude into the narrative already constructed from the *Travels*.

Let us take a look at King Thiri-thu-dhamma's position after the coronation. In the world of reality he was strongly placed from the defensive point of view. The homeland of Arakan was in little danger from Burmaor the Mughal. The approach to it through mountains, jungles, and over rivers was too difficult for either at that date, in face of the resistance which its navy and army of mercenaries could offer. The province of Chittagong was more open to attack, but the strong fleet stationed there, the number of rivers which it dominated, and the superior arms of the Portuguese, were adequate for its defence. From the offensive point of view, however, Arakan was in no position to do more than make naval raids on Bengal and Burma. It was without allies on the failure of the negotiations with Goa. A realist policy would have been the steady development of the rice trade, the maintenance of the fleet at full strength, and an administration which contented the people.

But Thiri-thu-dhamma had abandoned the normal for the abnormal. First he had fallen under the influence of a Buddhistic myth and saw himself as a potential world conqueror and saviour. Floundering deeper into the subliminal mire, he had proceeded to supply himself, in default of real means, with superreal accoutrements for his fantastic projects. The elixir made him strong enough to do what otherwise was impossible. His coronation had set the seal on his power. Not only was he now Keeper of the Mahamuni and Master of the White Elephant, with the knowledge of how to become invulnerable and invisible, but he was a crowned king and had received the blessing of the Order.

Yet in the process of rising to this lofty position, he had alienated a section of his people by the drastic means he had employed. They did not doubt his magical power, but they regarded it, not, like him, as the source of future glory, but as a thing which had injured them in the making. Though this popular dissatisfaction is mentioned by Manrique, he does not particularize, and it is to the palm-leaf manuscripts that we must turn for the full picture.

Here we find detailed information about the two ministers, Lat Rone and Kuthala, and the Queen, Nat Shin Mé, the Mistress of Paradise.

Lat Rone was the Chief Minister, a man whose father had been chief minister in the preceding reign, and whose family for generations had held important offices under the crown. He was a conservative statesman of the old type, a staunch upholder of the dynasty and of the Order, devout, faithful, elderly, and a scholar.

Kuthala was a very different type. Besides being a member of the council, he was Captain-General of the Household troops, and held or had held one of the governorships. His birth was higher than Lat Rone's, for he was of the blood royal, in the direct descent from Min Bin's brother. He was young, ambitious, handsome, and unscrupulous.

Nat Shin Mé was one of those formidable women who are commoner in the history of Asia than is generally supposed. Though her influence over Thiri-thu-dhamma was strong, she was not satisfied with her position, her desire being to become ruler of Arakan. Knowing Kuthala's character, and that he was reckless and impulsive, she proposed to him a palace revolution. With her assistance and the help of his soldiers, he could depose Thiri-thu-dhamma and take his place, both on the throne and in her affections. The proposal dazzled him. He was already enamoured of her. He gladly entered into the conspiracy. As for her, she regarded him merely as an instrument. When she had made him king and was his queen, he would be wholly in her power and obliged to obey her. Her character, she felt, was far stronger than his. She would know how to keep him her slave and dominate his every action.

The prophecy that Thiri-thu-dhamma would die after his coronation may well have been what suggested to her originally the ambition to supplant him. The assurance that he would die became in her mind an assurance that if she designed to cause him to die, she would be successful. His postponement of the ceremony must have been a continuing exasperation and perhaps he fixed the date at last partly because of pressure from her.

The compounding of the elixir had a double bearing on her plans. The anger it aroused and the threats of rebellion to which it gave rise were favourable factors. She could now count upon the sympathy of some part of the population. The King's murder would not arouse such universal detestation. But there was another side. How was she to succeed if he were now invulnerable? Poison might not act. It could not act if the elixir had been well and truly made. To suppose she did not believe in such elixirs would be to take her out of her period. That she had no doubt whatever of its power to shield him from corporal harm is proved by the very means she took to overcome it. Inasmuch as he was now protected by magic, only magic could destroy him. To sweep him away she must use an art against which the elixir could not prevail.

Such a method was ready to her hand. There existed a system of state magic which the crown had made use of from time immemorial. It has already been mentioned in these pages. In describing the so-called Yattara bell which hangs to-day in the empty shrine of the Mahamuni and which is a copy of the bell which was there in the seventeenth century, we alluded to the diagrams with which it is covered and to the belief that when the bell was struck, in accordance with the mathematical calculations composing the diagrams, a force was generated sufficient, should the realm be invaded, to roll back the enemy. This Yattara science came, no doubt, from Hindu India, whence all things occult have always come, but at this date it seems to have been more seen in Arakan than elsewhere. So frequently did the crown resort to it that even Manrique, during his second stay at the capital, was a witness on one occasion when it was being put into operation. 'I was standing', he says, 'at the altar of our church about nine in the morning and pronouncing the Introit of the Mass, when I heard shouts and cries of: "Fire!" Stopping the Office I at once sent to ask where the fire was. They came and told me it was close by in our quarter and that elephants were already breaking down the houses next to those which were burning. On hearing this I immediately began to remove the vestments, and several Christians running in helped me to get the vessels and altar cloths out of the building.' He goes on to say that the fire was extinguished after five houses had been destroyed. Now comes the curious part of the story. Some women had seen two men start the blaze. It was they who had called out 'fire!' and at their cries a crowd rushed to the spot and the men were caught. They were not, however, ordinary incendiaries, but employees of the Board of Astrology. On inquiry, Manrique learnt that they had been ordered to set fire to this particular spot at that particular hour and minute. He did not understand precisely why the Board of Astrology should have issued so extraordinary an order, but gathered that it had something to do with magic. A calculated place and time were essentials of the rite, which was an occult practice calculated to protect the crown from supposed dangers coming from that quarter. In fact, just as the note of the Yattara bell, struck on a deduced bearing and at a certain instant, had a power far transcending a note casually struck, a power which existed in an astrological field and so upset the astrological field against which it was directed, so did the burning of houses at a calculated place and time generate an occult force. The agents engaged on this arson were unable to plead that they were acting for the crown. Manrique saw the two men who started this particular fire taken immediately off to execution. He further states this fire to have been by no means the only one of the kind which occurred during his stay.

It was this art which the Queen decided to use against Thiri-thu-dhamma. Kuthala was either versed in it himself or he had men in his pay who were adepts. It may even be that the specialists or some of them on the Board of Astrology were suborned by bribes and consented to give their services. The palm-leaf manuscripts detail the procedure followed by Kuthala. He began work by having a calculation made showing the astrological relationship between his horoscope and the King's. This showed him in what, astrologically, he fell short of the King in power. Yattara supplied the means of correcting the adverse measurements in his favour. Accordingly he had inscribed on stone squares the calculation required to alter his chart into one superior to the King's. The burying of these squares at a certain instant on a determined spot would give him mastery over the ciphers which were the astrological expression of Thiri-thu-dhamma. The correct spots were shown to be in a circle surrounding the palace-city. The squares were secretly placed there with the ritual prescribed.

That to us Yattara sounds nonsensical is beside the point. Everyone in Mrauk-u believed in the potency of the art. And to have it used against you was as alarming as it would have been at that date in Europe for a man to learn that a witch was occultly attacking him. Manrique himself did not disbelieve. He ascribes the practice to the Devil and was quite as convinced of its evil efficacy as was the Archbishop of Goa that a devil dwelt in the supposed Kandy tooth.

In addition to burying the squares, Kuthala composed certain incantatory poems, written in such a rhythm and consisting of such an arrangement of symbolical letters that when uttered at the correct time and angle, they would increase the malefic influence of the squares. These poems were called *Nga-swe* and an example of one of them is to be found in the manuscripts. On translation it appears now to have no meaning at all and no doubt its virtue did not lie in meaning but in sound, sound coming like the bell's note from a certain direction. Boys were engaged to sing these poems at stated points outside the palace-city.

News that sorcery was being sung was reported to Lat Rone, the Chief Minister. He caused inquiries to be made and came to the conclusion that a magical crime was being committed, the intended victim being the King. His suspicions fell on the Queen and Kuthala. The reader will remember that the two persons burnt by the Inquisition at the *auto-da-fé* which Dellon attended were convicted of committing magical crimes. The belief that such crimes had reality was universal. Nor can it be said that the belief had no substance. We use a different terminology now, but when we speak of the power which suggestion has, particularly over primitive people, we are admitting that a mind may be vulnerable to the sort of fears which the witch-doctor is able to arouse in his victim.

After some hesitation Lat Rone communicated his suspicions to the King. We may think that he would have done better to have said nothing. As long as the King did not know what was being done, there was no danger. It would be the shock, we should say, arising from the knowledge that a magical assault was being made which would hurt him, not the magic itself. But Kuthala believed that Yattara could kill his master by its own force, whether he knew that he was its victim or not.

The manuscripts state that he was unable to convince the King of his danger. Thiri-thu-dhamma brushed aside his allegations. He refused to believe that the Queen whom he loved could harbour such designs. Her stronger character had always dominated him. Lat Rone's story seemed wholly incredible. Like other abnormal and deluded men, moreover, he felt very strong. The elixir, and those other indications of power and glory which he possessed, had given him an inflated feeling of security.

Lat Rone being unable to bring any concrete proofs now suggested that the truth of what he had said might be tested by omens. At the court of Mrauk-u omens were taken in various manners, but the method selected in the present case was that called 'hearing *taran*'. According to the theory of *taran*, if an important event were approaching, its reverberation would first reach the minds of those least ruled by reason. Such persons would become aware of it before its arrival into the upper consciousness and would inadvertently say something to indicate its existence and nature. To listen for such chance remarks, a man used to be sent to stroll through the streets. Experience showed that the most likely to make them were children, women, and artists, such as actors or poets.

The King agreed to this test and a confidential agent was sent out. On his return he reported to Lat Rone that he had heard observations which appeared to him significant. One of them was: 'King Hari has made stupid errors. He will die and ruin will overtake the kingdom.' Another declared: 'If an iguana becomes a crocodile, rivers cannot bear it; if an underling becomes an overman, the country cannot prosper.'

When these *taran* were repeated to Lat Rone, he was profoundly shaken. His suspicions became certainties. Thiri-thu-dhamma's life was in mortal danger. He hastened to tell him what he had heard. 'Your Majesty in infancy had the name Hari,' he reminded him. 'Who can doubt that the underling is Kuthala? Not only is Your Majesty's own life threatened but the kingdom itself is menaced with destruction.'

On this occasion Thiri-thu-dhamma listened with more patience and attention, but he was not yet sufficiently convinced to give orders for the seizure of the conspirators. He preferred to send for the Queen and confront her with the allegations which had been made. But Nat Shin Mé had no difficulty in setting his mind at rest. She knew well how to play on his belief in his own invulnerability. He had never been a match for her face to face. There is reason to suspect that she had begun to undermine his will by doses of datura, the narcotic drug by using which the Portuguese women in Goa had learnt how to blind and enslave their husbands. This might suggest she was sceptical of the elixir. But women of her kind believe and disbelieve from one moment to another. The Dowager-Empress Tzu Hsi declared, and then would deny, that the Boxers had an elixir which rendered them invulnerable.

When Lat Rone perceived that the Queen's position was unshaken, his nerve failed him and he decided to ensure his own safety before the catastrophe he foresaw destroyed both him and the King. In a last audience he asked permission to take the yellow robe and retire into a monastery. The permission was granted, and with sorrowful respect he bade his master farewell.

The palm-leaf manuscripts state that some months later the King was killed by the action of the Yattara squares.

If we are to take it that in fact he died bewitched, as Philip IV of Spain and Portugal was to die the following year when he discovered that malignantly charmed images had got among the relics which he wore round his neck, we must assume that at a certain point definite evidence convinced him that Yattara was being used against him. As he believed in that art, having practised it himself, the shock will have been terrible, and may well have sufficed to kill him. If it did not kill him, it will have reduced him to a state bordering upon idiocy. A fatal dose of datura or some other poison may then have been administered as a *coup de grâce*.

That he should have died drugged, frantic, hallucinated, ensorcelled, was fitting. A Buddhist king who, forgetting the compassion and sanity of the Eightfold Path, opened his mind to the evil suggestions of a wizard and murdered his subjects to obtain occult powers, had lain down with monsters, and because he had looked into the abyss, the abyss looked into him.

XXXI
The Murder of Friar Manrique

Manrique survived by thirty years the king whose extraordinary murder has just been described and was then himself murdered though in circumstances which were as drab as the other's were fantastic.

Except for this brutal and unexpected end, which links him in death with the man who in life was also curiously linked to him, his career after he left the Bay has little of the unusual and nothing of the astonishing. Not that he returned to the quiet of a monastic close. On the contrary, six months after reaching Cochin he went to Goa, where he obtained permission to go preaching to Japan, though Catholic priests were then forbidden to enter that country, and if they managed to do so were arrested and executed on account of former political intrigues by the Jesuits.

Leaving Goa in April 1637, he travelled by ship first to Malacca and then to the Philippines, entering Cavite Bay and staying at Manila. Thence he went to Indo-China, and on to Macao in China, where he hoped to find a ship to carry him to Japan. Failing in this, he turned back and by way of Macassar, Batavia, and Malacca reached the east coast of India in August 1640. But his narrative of these immense voyages is bald, and does no more than touch the surface of what he saw. There is no form or drama in his adventures. Reading him you have no feeling, as you have had before, that you are peeping deep into the oriental scene.

After landing in India he does not revisit any Portuguese centre, but travels to Lahore and sees Shah Jehan and the Mughal court. But he never got to close quarters as with the court of Arakan and his account of what he saw is so dull as to be scarcely readable. From Lahore he sets out overland for Rome, passing through Afghanistan, Persia, Iraq, and Syria, and comes at last to the Eternal City on the 1st of July 1643.

In the Augustinian monastery there he wrote his *Travels* which were published in 1649, licence and copyright for ten years being granted him by Pope Innocent X. The title-page shows that at the time of publication he had the rank of Maestro and the appointment at the Roman Curia of Procurator-General for the Augustinian properties and estates in Portugal, an administrative post for which his wide experience and practical mind well fitted him.

Twenty years pass and nothing is known of his activities, except that he continued in Rome attached to the Curia. If you look him up in the two great *Who's Who* of the Augustinian Order, Ossinger's *Bibliotheca Augustiniana et Chronologica* (1768), and Vela's *Ensayo de una Biblioteca Ibero-Americana de la Order de San Augustin* (1913) you will find his name and an outline of his career to 1649, but no further details of his work at the Curia. These two publications appear to be largely founded upon the earlier *Biblioteca Lusitana* of Machado (1741), and there too nothing is said about his years at Rome. But all three of these tomes end their biographical sketch with the same startling note: they state that in 1669, when he was a very old man—how old is uncertain because the date of his birth is not given anywhere, though he must have been over seventy and may have been nearly eighty —he was sent on a secret mission to London, perhaps to explore the possibility of bringing the Church of England back to Rome, for Charles II was whispered at the moment to be fingering this project. The aged Frate Maestro arrived safely in London. He had with him a personal servant, and a chest containing a considerable sum of money, no doubt for paying informers and otherwise advancing his business. He took lodgings beside the Thames and got into touch with Catholic agents. But the gold pieces in the chest proved too great a temptation for his servant, who forced the lid one day when his master was out. Then he lay in wait, resolved to cover the crime with another. Manrique, returning after dark, was done to death, his body put into the chest, and pitched into the river. At low tide the chest was stranded on a bank further down. A couple of sailors passing in a rowboat and seeing it on the mud thought, the way sailors do, it might contain treasure. After some difficulty they got it on to their boat and, all eagerness, broke it open. They were grievously disappointed to find only a corpse. Their nerve held, however, and they examined the body. As it was clearly, from the clothes, that of an ecclesiastic of rank, they took it ashore and reported to the police. The police had no difficulty in identifying it after inquiry. The servant was arrested, confessed, and was hanged.

That after surviving atrocious dangers from man and beast on land and sea in distant corners of the Orient over a period of fifteen years' active missionary and diplomatic labours Manrique should have fallen by the hand of his confidential man in a London lodging, is one of those twists of fate which make life on this planet so wholly incalculable. Somewhere in London they put him in the ground. It may be, we walk over his very grave. His bones may still be mouldering in it. If he had died, confessed and absolved, in his bed at the Augustinian monastery in Rome, his story would have seemed far more remote. That he died amongst us brings it home to us, brings the Land of the Great Image closer, makes Thiri-thu-dhamma less of a fable.

XXXII

Concluding Observations

The murder of King Thiri-thu-dhamma in 1638 is held by the Arakanese to mark the beginning of the ruin of their country. He left a son, one of the two to whom Manrique gave presents, the other having died in the interval. This child was proclaimed as a matter of course, but Nat Shin Mé's plans allowed for that. Circumstances enabled the Empress-Dowager Tzu Hsi to select children for the throne and keep the Regency for herself. But Nat Shin Mé's case was quite different. To overthrow the régime she had been obliged to conspire with Kuthala. Kuthala's price was the throne and her hand. However much it might have suited her to become Regent, she knew that course to be out of the question. She had no option but to make Kuthala king and marry him. In such a situation there was no room for Thiri-thu-dhamma's son. Within a month of his father's death he died of what was officially diagnosed as smallpox.

The council was summoned to consider his successor. There being no direct heir, the head of a collateral branch had to be selected. Kuthala, as the direct descendant of Min Bin's brother, though only by a concubine, was a possible candidate, but other princes had better claims. The Queen adopted the expedient of surrounding the council chamber with Kuthala's troops. The council swallowed its scruples and registered her wish. Kuthala was crowned and took the reign-title of Narapadigri. The manuscripts are emphatic that the Buddhist Order was shocked. The Shitthaung Arch-Abbot refused his blessing.

The ruin of the kingdom followed slowly but surely. Narapadigri reigned only for seven years. He became suspicious of Nat Shin Mé who, it appears, dissatisfied because her authority was not as absolute as she had anticipated, schemed to get rid of him. This may, indeed, have been always her intention. After a trial of strength he succeeded in expelling her from the palace. Yet the fear of death continued to haunt him. He believed that she, or some person ill disposed towards him, had undermined his astrological position with Yattara squares, precisely as he had undermined Thiri-thu-dhamma's. In desperation he built two pagodas, the Thet-daw-Shé and the Thet-daw-Saung, close to the palace. These pagodas still stand and the Yattara ciphers with which their walls are covered may be examined. Experts assured him that their position and the time of their building were such that the inscriptions they bore would be liberated on the psycho-astrological air and serve to neutralize the adverse vibrations which he feared were in operation. But it was no good. When he fell ill he knew his own counter-measures must be ill drawn. Like Thiri-thu-dhamma he died bewitched by the terror in his own heart.

Nat Shin Mé was unable to take advantage of his demise and passes out of history. Women of her type have always brought misfortune upon oriental states. They are feminine beyond what is understood by that word in the Occident. They embody what the Orient has always held to be the essence of femininity, qualities the opposite of the masculine. The Chinese have made a study from the earliest times of these opposites and much of their philosophical thinking is founded upon them. For them the pure feminine has the power of the earth and its characteristics; it is dark, negative, unintellectual; it is the abyss or like water or like the moon. These hints at definition suggest well enough what is meant. The character of most men and women is a compound of opposites. But when a woman has only the feminine qualities, a phenomenon which the East seems to provide more often than the West, she possesses a horrifying force, unreasonable, violent, intuitive, a force much feared by men, for it cannot be opposed by reason. A woman of the kind, should she enter and dominate a domain of the masculine such as an autocratic government, inevitably brings ruin because she represents its opposite. She has, to continue to use oriental synonyms, the quality of the ghost, of wind, of mist, and of the witch; she is like a madness and she makes mad; but she also has the force of archetypal form, and can give form, a form like an exhalation from the depths of the unconscious, but which is not animated by light or idea. All oriental women—and they have been many—who have dominated states, great or small, have belonged to this category, and the more essentially feminine they were, the greater the harm they did. As examples we may cite Nur Jehan, Jehangir's Empress, Supaya Lat, Queen of the last King of Burma, and the greatest or most terrible of all, Tzu Hsi, Empress-Dowager of China. There were others also, such as the Empress Wu of the Great T'ang, and the enchantress, Ta Chi, who ruined the House of Shang.

The items in Arakan's ruin may be shortly noted. In 1665 the Mughal Emperor, Auranzebe, succeeded in winning over the Portuguese mercenaries of Dianga by threats and bribes. Their defection, the possibility of which had so disturbed Thiri-thu-dhamma in 1630, was fatal. The Mughal invaded Chittagong the next year and occupied the province.

The loss of Chittagong was followed by a series of civil disturbances inside Arakan proper. Constant rebellions, usurpations and assassinations marked the seventeenth and eighteenth centuries. Between 1666 and 1710 were ten kings, their reigns averaging two and a half years each. Between 1710 and 1742 the average reign was under two years, and the last seven reigns, up to 1784, each lasted about three years. So insecure an administration was little removed from anarchy. The state could not have maintained its independence had not its decline synchronized with the decline of the Mughal, the eclipse of Goa, and the fact that the new power, the British, turned the Dutch out of the Bay and themselves remained fully occupied in India. The Burmese, too, were weak and distracted, but in 1760 their unification under the vigorous Alaung-paya dynasty sealed Arakan's fate. In 1784 they invaded and annexed the country. It is interesting to note that before their king, Bodaw-paya, did so, though he had secured his victory in advance by inducing the most influential of the Arakanese parties to support him, he took the precaution of tampering with the Yattara ciphers on the Mahamuni bell by sending ahead experts who knew how to deflect them. The Great Image itself he carried away to Mandalay, where it now is. For the Arakanese its loss was the end of the end. It was their head, their lifeblood, their very soul.

After 1638 Goa, and the vast Catholic dreams for which it stood, also withered away. In that year her possessions were practically intact. She had Muscat on the Persian Gulf, Bandal and Diu on the road to India. Between Diu and Goa were twelve fortresses. Below Goa she had many more, Cochin, Quilon, with Colombo, Galle, and Jafna in Ceylon; in the Far East, Malacca, Macao, and Timor.

Concluding Observations

In 1640 Portugal broke away from Spain, but it was too late. She was no longer capable of supplying her eastern possessions with sufficient men, munitions, and ships. A truce was made with the Dutch, but it did not last. Her great eastern fortresses began to fall to them one by one; in 1641 Malacca, in 1648 Muscat, the eastern and western doors of her trade route; in 1656 Colombo; in 1661 Quilon; in 1662 Cochin. Goa became a city of paupers. The vision seen by its founders and which throughout the sixteenth century had given the life of its inhabitants a higher meaning, the ideal which was spreading over the vast paganism of Asia love and happiness, the certainty of salvation, under a Holy Father uniting the world, had not been realized and was remembered no longer.

So ended for the time the Buddhist and the Catholic vision of a world state. The Dutch who had stepped in were without fancies of the sort. They were business people, though they made a business blunder. The cost of reducing the Portuguese fortresses was enormous and it had to be debited against the profits of their trade. To leave Goa alone would have been sounder and, by developing their own conquests in the great islands, to have broken her by breaking her monopoly. Meanwhile the British, business people like them but more careful, had been quietly and discreetly developing their trade with India, having come to an arrangement with the Portuguese and the Mughal. Then came the Anglo-Dutch wars in Europe and the defeat there of the Dutch fleet. This victory over the Dutch at home, together with the disintegration of the Mughal Empire, left Britain and France (for France had now come on the scene) a free hand in India. France's defeat followed and Britain became master of India and lord of the Bay.

Unlike the Portuguese, the British had only one ideal, trade. In the interests of trade, and not because of any dream to bring peace, happiness, and salvation to a distracted world, they governed their possessions justly, and only felt obliged to extend them when trade was refused by states on their borders. By the nineteenth century Asia and Africa began to be seen as vast areas to be carved up, so that their resources could be developed for the benefit of investors. The other nations of Europe, according to their resources, followed England's lead and demanded their share, the size of which depended upon their power in Europe, Asia no longer could raise a finger of protest. It lay there like a dead ox, awaiting dismemberment. All pointed to the world being divided among the white nations, Africa and Asia becoming their colonial possessions, trade preserves whose inhabitants were asked to stay their dreams by reflecting on the benefits of peace, protection, and a fraction of the profits. Apart from the fact that this ideal was essentially material, it was not a sound world system, because the peace and the profits, depending as they did upon a tricky political balance in Europe and the smooth adjustment of all sorts of difficult economic differences, were extremely unstable. If the nations of Europe fell out, the whole world was liable to be thrown into confusion. A poor man in Pegu or Batavia would have his house burnt and his children massacred because Berlin had a quarrel with London, a quarrel about which the man knew nothing and had no means whatever of composing.

Arakan passed into this system in 1825. Its overlords, the Burmese, annoyed us and we took it from them in that year. In 1885 we acquired all Burma in turn, and along with it the Mahamuni, a mere curiosity as far as we were concerned. To the Burmese it was still a very sacred object, though the idea that its possession protected the country or encouraged the hope of a new world saviour, had receded so far from any possibility of realization that it no longer caused anyone even to dream.

These latter days have shown us as curious a sequel to this long story as could well be imagined. An Asiatic nation, whose religion was a Buddhism modified by pagan beliefs of great antiquity, conceived that upon it was laid the task of rescuing Asia from its precarious fate of being in part, and likely to become wholly, divided into trade preserves among the militant nations of the extreme West. When all intruders had been driven out, Asia united under Japan could dream again, and with more reason than ever before, its old dream of a saviour who was Lord of the World and in whose time, and for a thousand years, there would be peace and universal salvation.

But how to usher in this golden age? That could only be done by acting at first in a manner opposite to the Eightfold Path. Compassion, honesty, charity, right conduct would have to be discarded for the moment. Thiri-thu-dhamma came to the same conclusion and to obtain the necessary power descended to magic, murder, and devilment. The Japanese took an analagous course, though to make themselves invulnerable and invincible they did not look for the secret of an elixir but the secret of weapons of miraculous power. They acquired the secret and choosing a moment when the rival business nations of Europe were about to fall upon each other, invaded China which had refused to join the grand emprise, and, when those nations did fall upon each other, extended the crusade to their Asian trade preserves. At the time of writing, May 1942, they have acquired all the French and Dutch possessions and have prosecuted their assault upon those of the British with such success that Malaya and Burma are theirs, as well as great islands belonging to Britain's collateral, America. This very month they entered Mandalay and the ownership of the Mahamuni has passed to them. But as they have taken a path opposite to the true Buddhist path, that symbol has no meaning.

And here is the paradox. Europe at the back of its mind has always had the same vision as the true Buddhists of a universal state founded upon charity and compassion, and of a universal Saviour. After the Portuguese had tried and failed to realize it, it was overlaid with temporal ambitions. Adam Smith's *Wealth of Nations* became a more important book than the New Testament, more exciting than the vision of the saints. But the appalling situation in which England was placed in the summer of 1940 shocked her to the foundations of her being. She began to dream again the ancient European dream, and other states followed her example. This deep change was brought about, not only by her own peril but by her confrontation with the opposite world-dream in Europe. Hitler's dream was to create a world polity, but that polity to be founded on ruthlessness, not compassion; on inequality, not fairness; on selfishness, not charity; on madness, not reason. So horrific an apparition could only be laid by its beatific opposite. To have sought to banish it by talk of dividends and a business paradise would have been as useless as for Christian to have tried to brush past Apollyon by wishing him good day.

So the stage is set, the old Christian vision against its opposite; and the old Buddhist vision degraded and harnessed to the opposite of the Christian, and so to its own opposite. With the fall of the opposite of the one, falls the opposite of the other. With the destruction of the protagonists of the opposites, the German and the Japanese, both the visions triumph and, as they are identical, they coalesce in a world system which, partaking of both, is stronger than either, better founded, more enduring, more reasonable, more free.

List of Principal Authorities

It is not proposed to set out here a long list of authorities for the period covered. The student who desires such a list cannot do better than refer to that given at the end of Volume II of the Hakluyt Society's edition of Manrique's *Travels*. He will find there over two hundred and fifty books, a number which is not by any means exhaustive. The author has consulted such of them as he thought would assist him and has had the help of the notes under the text of the *Travels*, though these are not always as correct or as well chosen as they might be. The main sources from which he has derived his information will generally be found cited in the body of his narrative. To repeat them, they are the text of Manrique's *Travels*; Forchhammer's *Papers on Subjects relating to the Archaeology of Burma* (1891); J. N. da Fonseca's *An Historical and Archaeological Sketch of the City of Goa* (1878); Dr. Dellon's *Relation de l'Inquisition de Goa* (1687); Pierre Dahmen's *Un Jésuite brahme* (1925) for the section on de Nobili; *The Voyage of François Pyrard of Laval* in the Hakluyt edition of 1888; *The Voyage of John Huyghen van Linschoten* in the Hakluyt edition of 1884, the illustrations being taken from the Paris edition of 1638; *The Voyage of Gautier Schouten to the East Indies* in the Amsterdam edition of 1676, from which the illustrations are taken; Mr. G. E. Harvey's *History of Burma* (1925). The above books were indispensable. Mention of others of smaller importance will also be found in the text. But the author is obliged to insist that the most careful perusal of these works would not have enabled him to write *The Land of the Great Image* without a personal acquaintance with Further India extending over two decades, an exploration of the sites in Arakan during two years, and an acquaintance with Mr. San Shwe Bu for a like period.

Index

Index

Index